The Role of the World Trade Organization
in Global Governance

The Role of the World Trade Organization in Global Governance reflects the core mission of the United Nations University Institute of Advanced Studies (UNU/IAS). In April 1996, the UN Secretary-General inaugurated the UNU/IAS as an in-house community of scholars established vigorously to pursue knowledge at the intersection between societal and natural systems. The programmatic theme of the IAS was created to be dynamic and flexible, focusing on finding creative solutions to the pressing global issues arising at this nexus. As a first overarching theme, the IAS adopted the concept of *eco-restructuring,* an approach to sustainable development that envisions shifting technological and societal systems towards a greater equity between developing and developed countries, between humankind and the environment, and between current and future generations. An integral component of the UNU/IAS *eco-restructuring* dynamic involves the examination of global institutions, regimes, values, and policies relating to sustainable development. These issues are dealt with under the programmatic sub-theme of *Multilateralism and Sustainable Development* (MSD). Within this programme, in-depth theoretical research is combined with relevant policy studies and the formulation of practical policy options. A strong capacity-building component that seeks to enhance the participation of policy actors in global environmental negotiations has also been built into the programme.

This book has been the result of collaboration between the *Multilateralism and Sustainable Development* programme and the Ford Foundation. The IAS has strategically focused upon trade, sustainable development, and related issues because it believes that this will constitute a crucial aspect of global governance policy at the start of the new millennium. Other books coming out of the research of MSD include *Trade, Environment, and the Millennium* (UNU Press, 1999) and *Trade, Environment, and Sustainable Development: Views from Sub-Saharan Africa and Latin America* (Environment and Multilateral Diplomacy Series, No. 1).

The Role of the
World Trade Organization
in Global Governance

Edited by
GARY P. SAMPSON

**United Nations
University Press**

TOKYO • NEW YORK • PARIS

United Nations University Press
The United Nations University, 53-70, Jingumae 5-chome,
Shibuya-ku, Tokyo 150-8925, Japan
Tel: +81-3-3499-2811   Fax: +81-3-3406-7345
E-mail: sales@hq.unu.edu
http://www.unu.edu

United Nations University Office in North America
2 United Nations Plaza, Room DC2-1462-70,
New York, NY 10017, USA
Tel: +1-212-963-6387   Fax: +1-212-371-9454
E-mail: unuona@igc.apc.org

United Nations University Press is the publishing division of the United Nations University.

Cover design by Joyce C. Weston
Cover photography by Pacific Press Service

Printed in Hong Kong

UNUP-1055

ISBN 92-808-1055-3

Library of Congress Cataloging-in-Publication Data

The role of the World Trade Organization in global governance / edited by Gary P. Sampson.
    p.   cm.
    Includes bibliographical references and index.
    ISBN 92-808-1055-3
    1. World Trade Organization.   2. World Trade Organization—
Developing countries.   3. Foreign trade regulation.   4. Commercial policy.   5. Free trade—Environmental aspects.   6. Free trade—
Social aspects.   7. International economic relations.
    8. Globalization.   I. Sampson, Gary P.
HF1385.R65   2001
382'.92—dc21   00-012453

Contents

Preface

There are many views as to the sources and characteristics of globalization and the actors responsible for the shape it takes. Differing views over its merits and de-merits have led to many passionate debates in recent years. However, one common element permeates these debates: it is agreed that the process of globalization is characterized by a greater degree of interdependence between nations. Equally well accepted is that international trade is an important feature of this interdependence. As trade in goods and services has been progressively liberalized over the past half-century, international trade has increased dramatically and so has the interdependence of nations and the process of globalization. The rules that govern trade, and therefore the role of the World Trade Organization in global governance, have proliferated accordingly.

The world spotlight was on the WTO at its third meeting of trade ministers in Seattle in December 1999. Many had hoped a new round of multilateral trade negotiations—the Millennium Round—would be launched at this meeting. Not only were the new negotiations not launched, but the meeting ended in disarray, with the WTO facing criticism from many quarters.

Conducting world trade according to multilaterally agreed rules has been a major contributor not only to the enormous expansion of the world economy over the half-century, but also to the avoidance of international conflict. Thus, if there is to be reform of the current trading system, it should be done with care in order to preserve the many strengths of the system while responding to legitimate concerns. Carefully guiding the process of globalization-with-a-human-face is a challenging task. This, indeed, is one of the most important challenges facing policy makers at the international level today.

In the aftermath of Seattle, it became increasingly apparent that many varying views were held by prominent personalities regarding the current and future role of the WTO in international affairs. A number of these personalities represent bodies of the United Nations and other intergovernmental organizations, government ministries, and non-governmental organizations. Some present the views of private corporations, think tanks, and the press.

It is timely to bring together the views of a number of these prominent people in one volume. The intention is to provide an opportunity for contributors to state clearly their interests in a well-functioning WTO trading system and to offer suggestions about what the WTO can do to meet the challenges it faces in areas of particular interest to them. A clear statement of these concerns and proposed solutions should assist the debate to proceed in a positive manner.

This volume has been prepared in conjunction with the Ford Foundation with the aim of assisting this debate. I thank the Ford Foundation for its support and all the authors for their thoughtful contributions. I sincerely hope that the ideas developed, and the insights and views proffered, may help us to move forward towards a better and safer life for all.

Hans van Ginkel

Abbreviations

APEC	Asia-Pacific Economic Cooperation
ASEAN	Association of South East Asian Nations
CFCs	chlorofluorocarbons
CICC	Coalition for an International Criminal Court
CITES	Convention on International Trade in Endangered Species of Wild Fauna and Flora
CSD	Commission on Sustainable Development
CTE	Committee on Trade and Environment
DSU	Dispute Settlement Understanding
ECJ	European Court of Justice
ERT	European Roundtable of Industrialists
EU	European Union
FDI	foreign direct investment
GATS	General Agreement on Trade in Services
GATT	General Agreement on Tariffs and Trade
GAVI	Global Alliance for Vaccines and Immunization
GDP	gross domestic product
GPA	Government Procurement Agreement
ICBL	International Campaign to Ban Landmines
ICC	International Chamber of Commerce; International Criminal Court
ICFTU	International Confederation of Free Trade Unions
ICJ	International Court of Justice
IISD	International Institute for Sustainable Development
ILO	International Labour Organization
IMF	International Monetary Fund
ITO	International Trade Organization
IUCN	World Conservation Union
LDCs	least developed countries
MAI	Multilateral Agreement on Investment
MDRTB	multi-drug-resistant tuberculosis
MEA	multilateral environmental agreement
MFA	Multifibre Arrangement
MNC	multinational company

MSF	Médecins sans Frontières
MTA	multilateral trade agreement
NAFTA	North American Free Trade Agreement
NGO	non-governmental organization
NPR-PPMs	non-product-related process and production methods
OECD	Organisation for Economic Co-operation and Development
PPMs	process and production methods
R&D	research and development
RBPs	restrictive business practices
SA	sustainability assessment
S&D	special and differential (treatment)
SMEs	small and medium enterprises
SPS	Sanitary and Phytosanitary measures
TB	tuberculosis
TBT	technical barriers to trade
TNC	transnational corporation
TPRM	Trade Policy Review Mechanism
TRIMs	Trade-Related Investment Measures
TRIPS	Trade-Related Aspects of Intellectual Property Rights
UNCTAD	United Nations Conference on Trade and Development
UNDP	United Nations Development Programme
UNEP	United Nations Environment Programme
UNICEF	United Nations Children's Fund
WHO	World Health Organization
WTO	World Trade Organization
WWF	World Wide Fund for Nature

Overview

Gary P. Sampson
Professor of International Economic Governance,
Institute of Advanced Studies,
United Nations University

In January 1995, the World Trade Organization (WTO) became the successor to the General Agreement on Tariffs and Trade (GATT). Seven years of intensive negotiations in the Uruguay Round gave birth to an organization with vastly expanded responsibilities for international economic affairs. The WTO is undeniably a major player in the field of global governance, and its rules and processes will profoundly affect the future economic and political orientation of its 139 member countries[1] as well as of the 30 countries in the process of joining.

By many objective criteria the WTO—and the GATT before it—have been remarkably successful at doing what they were mandated to do: liberalize trade and conduct international trade according to multilaterally agreed rules. Nevertheless, questions of a very fundamental nature are being raised about the role of the WTO in international affairs by a wide spectrum of interest groups. The manner in which these questions are addressed in the coming months and years will determine the role of the WTO in global governance.[2] It is not the intention of this Overview to summarize the contents of the following chapters or to draw conclusions. Rather I want to flag some of the principal policy issues that emerge when a selection of prominent people with different perspectives consider the role of the WTO in global governance.

The first two chapters, by Kofi Annan and Supachai Panitch-pakdi, respectively, set the stage for later chapters by posing the fundamental questions of what the objectives of the world trading system are, how they can best be met, and how competing interests can be balanced. Rubens Ricupero and Clare Short then address these questions by examining the legitimacy of the rules-based trading system and the need for developing countries to have appropriate representation in the decision-making processes in order effectively to promote a positive approach to a new "development" round of trade negotiations.

The chapters by Peter Sutherland et al. and Frank Loy also confront the critical issue of representation and governance. Frank Loy reasons that the credibility of the system depends on dealing satisfactorily with civil society's sense of exclusion from WTO governance. He advances a number of proposals in this respect. Peter Sutherland et al. consider the governance role of the WTO vis-à-vis other international organisations and look to improved representation in intergovernmental negotiations at the global level.

Many of the governance issues of a systemic nature that are raised in the first six chapters find expression in the contentious debate in the WTO on trade and environment. Claude Martin and José María Figueres Olsen et al. analyse in some detail the most important concerns that have emerged in this debate and offer important insights from a practical policy perspective. They provide a potent case study of the more general concerns surrounding the role of the WTO in global governance.

Martin Wolf forcefully addresses the fundamental question of what it is that the world needs from the multilateral trading system. The next four chapters respond in a very specific manner and from very different perspectives. Mary Robinson outlines what is needed from the trading system for the global economy to operate more effectively in respecting human rights. James Orbinski addresses the shortcomings in global governance—and particularly the responsibilities of the WTO—when it comes to ethical considerations such as access to essential medicines and health care more generally. Bill Jordan presents the view of labour on how the WTO could be more effective in contributing to worldwide economic and social development. Finally,

Maria Livanos Cattaui outlines the importance from a business perspective of a predictable and stable world trading system.

Increased importance of trade rules

The importance of trade rules in both domestic and global affairs has increased dramatically since the creation of GATT. So has the controversy surrounding a number of WTO agreements and dispute settlement rulings. There are a number of reasons for this.

Both the volume of international trade and the number of GATT/WTO member countries have increased greatly over the past half-century.[3] WTO rules now apply not only to the one-fifth of world production that is traded but also to goods and services that may never enter into trade. These rules extend well beyond border measures and reach deep into domestic regulatory structures. Domestic regulations relating to patents, financial services, subsidies, and support measures for agriculture are all subject to WTO disciplines. Some WTO agreements raise ethical questions about the patenting of life forms, the role of precaution in the absence of scientific evidence, compulsory licensing to provide access to essential medicines, and the rewarding of indigenous peoples for pharmaceutical discoveries. Recent disputes have also raised fundamental questions about the appropriateness of standards to protect health, the role of science in risk management, and the conservation of endangered species.

Unlike in the GATT, the WTO dispute settlement process moves forward automatically, with panel and Appellate Body reports adopted unless there is a consensus against them. The rule of negative consensus, backed up by a mechanism providing for compensation and sanctions in the case of non-compliance, has greatly increased the effectiveness of the process and made it very different from the compliance mechanisms of other international agreements. As a consequence, public interest has heightened, particularly in the light of recent high-profile disputes extending into sensitive areas of the environment, corporate tax measures, and public health. The fact that the dispute proceedings are closed to the public has exacerbated the sense of exclusion and the resentment of those outside the process and concerned with the outcome.

The rulings of the WTO Appellate Body have led some to the view that it has extended its authority beyond that granted to it by member governments. The Dispute Settlement Understanding limited the Appellate Body's jurisdiction to issues of law covered in panel reports and to legal interpretations developed by panels. It was prohibited from adding to or diminishing the rights and obligations provided in WTO agreements. Some recent Appellate Body reports, however, seem to indicate a new concept of evolutionary policy formulation through litigation; this is very different from consensus decision-taking after a debate by all members in the WTO General Council. Appellate Body rulings—such as the acceptability of *amicus* briefs submitted by non-governmental organizations—have caused considerable controversy among members while raising expectations among those hoping to achieve greater access to the process.

Two-thirds of WTO members are now developing countries, and many of the most successful of them have adopted outward-oriented development strategies. The importance of the WTO, as well as their interest and weight within it, has thus increased considerably. They have, for example, locked in domestic policy reforms through adopting legally binding WTO obligations. They also look to assured market access through bound tariffs and commitments in the services sectors to continue their export-led growth strategies. Their legitimate expectation is that the WTO will provide a forum where their views can be effectively expressed and their concerns adequately dealt with. They are therefore far more active in the WTO than in earlier times and have higher expectations about what the institution can and should do for them.

Another reason for the heightened interest in the WTO is that it came into being against the backdrop of an incredible revolution in the cost and speed of communications. Non-governmental organizations are now linked to one another through broad networks and coalitions that render them more effective and sophisticated than their earlier counterparts. The public image of the WTO is greatly influenced by the information conveyed through these electronic means. While many of these groups are not against trade per se, others are unabatedly protectionist, putting them on an ideological collision course with supporters of an open and liberal trading system. The events at the third Ministerial Meeting in Seattle in 1999, fuelled by coalitions of non-governmental organizations built on the World Wide Web, placed the public for the first time at the centre of a vital public policy discussion traditionally dominated by governmental representatives in closed meetings.

Five years of experience with the WTO and the heightened public interest it has generated have already led to many calls for reform. Reform will not come easily, however, if it means unravelling existing trade agreements or introducing new restrictions on international trade. From a systemic perspective, the pursuit of free trade has been a powerful driving force behind many policy decisions, ranging from the removal of the Corn Laws in England in the early part of the nineteenth century to the adoption of outward-oriented development strategies in developing countries over the past few decades. Those who constructed the WTO are proud of having created what has been described as the greatest ever achievement in institutionalized global economic cooperation. The current trade rules permit world trade in goods and services to be successfully conducted at the rate of close to US$1 billion per hour every hour of the day. This system will not be given up lightly.

In addition, seasoned trade negotiators place less weight on the Seattle demonstrations and the failure to conclude the meeting satisfactorily than do the press and others. Failed meetings are certainly not a new phenomenon at the GATT and the WTO, even at the ministerial level. The Mid Term Ministerial Review of the Uruguay Round in 1988 in Montreal ended in a stalemate, and the 1990 Ministerial Meeting in Brussels, which was to conclude the Uruguay Round, collapsed amidst large-scale violent protests largely led by European farmers. Nevertheless, the Uruguay Round was successfully completed, with all participating countries ratifying the results.

Thus, the central question that needs to be addressed is what wise policy makers ought to do to preserve the strengths of the rules-based trading regime while responding to the pressures on it.

The WTO: A target of criticism

It is sometimes overlooked that the WTO is an intergovernmental organization comprising almost 140 sovereign governments acting on behalf of their constituents in accordance with multilaterally agreed rules that have been adopted by consensus. If the WTO is accused of acting against public interests, it is this collectivity of governments that is doing so. As far as the WTO's own processes are concerned, it can be argued that it is a very democratic institution. Once negotiators have agreed to new rules or changes to existing ones, it is up to domestic parliaments to ratify what has been negotiated. Many parliaments have already been active in monitoring WTO negotiations, and others will certainly become more active as public interest in the WTO continues to rise.

Against the backdrop of the diverse criticism levelled at the WTO, an important question is why sovereign states would spend years negotiating agreements that have the sorts of negative effects on their citizens that is claimed. If the answer is that nation states unwittingly erred in joining or creating the WTO, then why do they not leave? No country has ever expressed an interest in leaving either the GATT or the WTO. If WTO agreements mean a loss of national sovereignty, why would 30 sovereign nations be so intent on joining the WTO?

A principal reason for the support by both large and small governments for the WTO is that they see adherence to multilateral rules—rather than political or commercial power—to be in their national interests. Rules bring predictability and stability to the world trading system and, although rule-governed trade may not guarantee peace, it does remove a potent source of conflict. It offers an alternative to unbridled force in the trading relations among states. And, although sovereignty is forgone by being a member of the WTO (as with any significant international agreement), what is gained is the possibility to participate through cooperation in the global economy.

Developing countries

Many developing countries voiced their dissatisfaction with their lack of involvement in the decision-making processes in Seattle, but this is a long-standing criticism. In addressing this concern, a number of important considerations have to be taken into account before drawing general conclusions.

First, it is important to distinguish between lack of involvement in meetings and exclusion from them. Small informal groups of countries meet frequently in the WTO because this is the most efficient way to proceed—particularly when drafting texts. Agreement between the most concerned countries can later be extended to those that are less directly concerned. Few would take issue with this process. Problems arise, however, when not all interests are represented in such meetings and the results are not widely and rapidly communicated. In many instances, this has been as much a problem for transition economies and small developed countries as for developing ones. Representation in meetings and the communication of outcomes have been far from perfect in the past and this process needs to be improved.

Secondly, it would be wrong to draw the overall conclusion that there has been a lack of presence of all developing countries in negotiations and that they have had little influence in GATT and WTO negotiations. Latin American countries were major contributors both to the stalemate at the Montreal Ministerial Meeting (because of the treatment of agriculture) and to the relaunching of the Uruguay Round some months later. Brazil, India, Argentina, Egypt, Colombia, and other developing countries all played a big role in their own way in the creation of the General Agreement on Trade in Services. There are numerous such examples. In reality, a considerable number of developing countries are always present when their national interests are involved and have been very effective at shaping agreements to take their interests into account. Many of these countries have invested a great deal in building a national capacity to service the WTO negotiations and their representatives expect to be present at all key meetings. It was perhaps the lack of involvement of officials from some of these countries that created the strongest reactions in Seattle.

Nevertheless, there is certainly a problem relating to the systematic absence of many developing countries (particularly those that are small) from both informal and formal meetings in the WTO. Most small delegations from developing countries do not have the appropriate resources either in Geneva or at home to service the increasingly frequent, complex, and resource-intensive negotiation process at the WTO. Full participation can come about only with a strengthening of their human and institutional capacities. As many of them do not have the resources or expertise to build this capacity themselves, they have to turn to technical assistance programmes offered by others. There is a pressing need for a considerable increase in the inadequate resources currently available to them through the regular WTO channels.

However, knowledge and resources are not enough for all countries to be effective in WTO negotiations. An important reality is that the WTO rules do not entirely remove the inequality in the power of nations. It remains the case that countries with big markets have a greater ability than countries with small markets to secure market access and deter actions against their exporters. As noted, some developing countries have been effective in past negotiations, but this has not been the case for all. With their new weight of numbers in the WTO, although the diversity of their circumstances and commercial interests will not necessarily permit common negotiating positions to be adopted, developing countries now have it in their power to make common cause for their collective good by ensuring that development considerations are taken fully into account in WTO agreements.

In this respect, it is important for developing countries to make known their concerns with respect to their existing commitments and their priorities for future negotiations. Of the almost 250 proposals that were submitted to the WTO General Council in preparation for the Seattle meeting, over half were submitted by developing countries. Developing countries adopted the positive approach advocated by the Secretary-General of UNCTAD and focused on what they wanted instead of passively objecting to what they did not want. A large number of these proposals were characterized by the sentiment that the results of the Uruguay Round were asymmetrical, tilting the balance of multilateral rights and obligations against developing countries. On the part of least developed countries, new initiatives and improved market access were called for in order for them not just to halt the decline in their share of world trade, but to increase it.

The proposals were principally aimed at adjusting the anti-dumping disciplines and at modifying certain provisions of the Subsidies

Agreement and the Trade-Related Aspects of Intellectual Property Rights (TRIPS) Agreement. The proposals also called for a fundamental reassessment of special and differential treatment provisions in a number of agreements and for making "best endeavour" provisions for technical assistance and the transfer of technology mandatory in nature. In addition, they looked to the reduction of tariffs and tariff peaks in developed country markets; improved market access in agriculture; the simplification of rules of origin; and an acceleration in the opening up of textile and clothing markets in developed countries.

In this context, it is relevant to ask whether or not these proposals would be best advanced in a new round of negotiations. The débâcle in Seattle was the result not of the unwillingness of developing countries to negotiate or of the protests in the streets, but of the failure of developed countries to agree on the conditions and substance of a new round of negotiations. In the event of a new round, developing countries would certainly benefit from the wider opening of markets and from the clarification and development of trade rules. To engage them in a new round, however, they must first be convinced that their development concerns will be taken fully into account.

There are those who would argue that, in any new round of negotiations, there should be greater emphasis on the goal of sustainable development, as acknowledged in the Agreement Establishing the WTO.[4] Many consider it to be important for the WTO to have a broader criterion against which the success of the multilateral trading system can be evaluated. For those actively concerned with human rights, for example, this would involve a realization that a truly rules-based international system would recognize that human rights are inextricably linked with the international economic system and provide the common moral and legal underpinnings for the global economy. Integrating human rights standards into all aspects of economic policy-making would help to ensure that markets are not only open and efficient, but also fair and just.

Desirable as this goal may be, the important question that has to be confronted is what mechanism would enable the integration of human rights and other social norms into the WTO. It is clear that writing social standards into WTO rules would greatly change the nature of the organization and would be strongly resisted by many WTO members. Although all members agreed to the Preamble of the Agreement Establishing the WTO, and thus the importance of sustainable development, the concept receives no further recognition in any of the legally binding agreements. Nevertheless, respect for social standards must be a priority at the global level. One potential solution lies in a strengthening of the enforcement mechanisms of institutions dealing with the environment, labour standards, and human rights rather than a broadening of the responsibilities—and therefore influence—of the WTO.

It is also argued that, because large global companies are beneficiaries of economic liberalization, they should share in the responsibility for dealing with its social and environmental consequences. With the aim of encouraging the private sector to act in accordance with internationally accepted principles in the areas of human rights, labour standards, and the environment, the Secretary-General of the United Nations has proposed a Global Compact between business and the United Nations. The vision of the Global Compact is that, by advocating effective global governance mechanisms, corporations will be doing their part to ensure that the global economic system meets the needs of all people.

Representation in the process

Why is it that some interest groups have such a different perception of the value of the WTO from that of their democratically elected governments? The answer is not simple. Much of the criticism is due to a lack of understanding of the WTO and how it operates. This is not surprising. The WTO agreements and processes are complex and the GATT was far from transparent in its activities. For more than 50 years, access to information on trade negotiations has been difficult for all those outside the process. If it is hard to find out what the WTO is doing, the critics say, the organization must have something to hide. The WTO inherited GATT traditions and, notwithstanding considerable effort on the part of the Secretariat to increase the public awareness of the WTO, it is still paying the price in the form of a misunderstanding of its functions and criticism of its lack of transparency.

What will not be removed through a better understanding of the WTO is the resentment on the part of well-informed groups whose narrow preferences have been passed over by governments acting in what they perceive to be their overall national interests. This raises fundamental questions about representation, advocacy, and the legitimacy of a state acting on behalf of its citizens. Unlike a number of other international organizations, the WTO permits only representatives of governments and selected intergovernmental organizations to participate in or observe the processes of its regular activities. This has led to claims that the WTO is not accountable or responsive to public concerns, and to proposals for comprehensive agendas for increased transparency and public participation in the WTO and its dispute settlement process.

Overall support for these proposals has been marginal at best and in certain instances hostile. WTO members justify their reluctance on the grounds that the WTO is both a legally binding instrument and a forum for negotiations, which makes it very different from other multilateral organizations that provide for public participation. The argument continues that national representatives must on occasion subordinate certain national interests in order to achieve marginally acceptable or sub-optimal compromises that, by definition, require trade-offs. Doubt is expressed whether such a system could continue to work effectively if these trade-offs were open to scrutiny by precisely those special interest groups that would have opposed them. It is also argued that, even in intergovernmental organizations that provide for public participation, final decisions are taken in closed meetings with the real trade-offs frequently never known outside the closed sessions.

Further, developing countries do not consider developed country non-governmental organizations to be natural allies for many of their causes (see below). They view the demands for opening the WTO as leaving themselves grossly under-resourced, to face both powerful governments of developed countries and their non-governmental organizations, and as tilting the negotiating balance further to their disadvantage. Some would also question whether many non-governmental organizations can rightfully claim a presence when they themselves are not necessarily democratic, accountable, or on occasions even broadly representative of the interests they claim to represent.

Notwithstanding the difficulties with respect to increasing transparency and participation, there remain a number of practical ways of meeting many of the concerns without upsetting the established rights and obligations of members or otherwise negatively influencing the negotiating processes. In the run-up to the Seattle meeting, all negotiating proposals were posted on the WTO website with no apparent ill effects. This would have been considered unthinkable to many delegations even in the recent past. Similarly, symposia organized by the WTO Secretariat where groups and individuals outside the negotiating process can make their views known to government officials have met with success. So too have regional seminars organized by the WTO Secretariat in developing countries on contentious issues such as trade and the environment. Imaginative proposals have also been made with respect to access to dispute settlement proceedings. One such proposal is that a mechanism should be established where disputes of particular concern to environmentalists could be dealt with outside the WTO through a consultative process in which relevant facts could be put on the table by all interested parties, from governments, non-governmental organizations, industry, academia, and local communities.

Standards: Labour, environment, and health

To minimize unwanted encroachment on national sovereignty, non-discrimination is generally interpreted in the WTO to mean that products that are physically the same (i.e. like products) cannot be discriminated against in world trade solely on the grounds of how they were produced. Thus, goods produced in an environmentally unfriendly manner are like environmentally friendly ones, just as imported goods produced without respecting core labour standards are no different from others. In short, preferred standards for production processes in the importing country cannot be imposed on exporting countries through trade restrictions.

Denying the possibility to discriminate in trade in this manner, and thus preventing powerful governments from riding roughshod over less powerful ones, holds a special attraction for many developing countries. They consider any discussion of minimum environmental and labour standards to be an assault on their national sovereignty. Even if such standards reflect the priorities of well-meaning groups in wealthy countries, they may well be inappropriate for developing countries' levels of development. Of equal importance is the view that the desire to impose standards is nothing more than a thin disguise for protectionist forces representing producer interests unable to compete with developing country exports. For this reason, developing countries frequently find themselves in opposition to non-governmental organizations and governments in developed countries when it comes to discussing environment and labour standards. The enforcement of preferred standards through trade restrictions appeals to environmental groups or those wishing to enforce core labour standards. That this option is denied them by the WTO is a clear source of friction.

Within their own borders, however, governments have a sovereign right to adopt whatever standards they consider "appropriate" to enforce labour standards or to protect the local environment and the health of their citizens. With growing awareness and concerns over health, coupled with more sophisticated products and production processes, the complexity of regulations has increased, as has the opportunity for these measures to be used for protectionist purposes. When standards differ between countries, they have the potential seriously to impede trade. Thus, a particularly important consideration for the maintenance of an open trading system is determining when national standards affecting trade are responding to "legitimate" concerns and when are they unnecessary barriers to trade. From a policy perspective, the important question is who has the responsibility for dealing with the issues of appropriateness and legitimacy.

One issue is determining the minimum degree of scientific validation that is necessary for an exporter to be obliged to accept a standard in an importing country as being legitimate rather than an unnecessary barrier to trade. This then begs the question of the role of "precaution" when there is insufficient scientific evidence to establish the existence of a serious risk, but there are substantial potential negative consequences. Who has the burden of proof in demonstrating that there is—or is not—a real risk? What if there is agreement in both the importing and the exporting countries on the scientific evidence, but there are different preferences about how the risk should be managed?

Although the WTO should avoid being the arbiter in controversies over the legitimacy of trade measures based on societal preferences rather than scientific evidence, this appears inevitable. It will be most surprising if matters relating to risk assessment and risk management do not become increasingly important in WTO legal proceedings and, as a consequence, in the agreements that deal with them. There have already been serious trade disagreements, for example, over appropriate standards for meat treated with hormones or antibiotics. The trade in genetically modified organisms and products derived from them involves even greater commercial, health, social, and ethical considerations. Regulatory differences between countries in Europe and North America with respect to these products largely reflect societal preferences about risk management—not disagreement over scientific evidence.

Future directions

The WTO is too important an institution for anyone to ignore, but there is also no consensus on where it should go. Its fiercest critics want it closed down. Others want its powers curtailed. On the other hand, there are those who seek to strengthen the WTO and extend its reach to new areas. If the WTO were to have responsibility for new and significant multilateral agreements on investment and competition policy, its importance in global affairs would increase massively, as was the case with the negotiation of the General Agreement on Trade in Services in the Uruguay Round. This diversity of views means there are very different policy prescriptions for the future direction of the WTO and its role in global governance.

There does seem to be agreement, however, that the WTO is only one part of a system of global governance that now requires refurbishment. The functions of the existing multilateral institutions need to be clearly defined, and policy-making at both the national and the international levels calls for greater coherence. There is less agreement on the respective roles of the various institutions.[5]

One view is that the multilateral trading system should not be called upon to deal with such non-trade issues as human rights, labour standards, and environmental protection. To do so would expose it to even greater strain at a time when it is already overburdened. In any event, this is not where its mandate or expertise lies. This school of thought sees merit in addressing these issues in existing institutions. Given that the United Nations and its specialized agencies are charged with advancing the causes of development, the environment, human rights, and labour, they should be strengthened and provided with the necessary resources to carry out their tasks successfully. The WTO could then go ahead and deal with a narrower agenda than it now seems to be acquiring.

An opposing view is that the vacuum in global governance could be at least partially filled by the WTO taking on even more responsibilities. The argument at its most fundamental level is that the strong multilateral rules-based trade regime, attained through the WTO, is essential to developing a system of governance of the global market. The trading system cannot act in isolation when there exists a wide variety of issues—including environmental protection, access to essential medicines, and respect of core labour standards and human rights—that belong on the international agenda and that are directly affected by trade itself or the rules that govern it. Proponents of this school of thought argue that the WTO must be given a mandate to take development goals and social and environmental issues fully into account in future trade-liberalizing negotiations as well as in existing or future trade rules.

The fact of the matter is that there is no world government to determine the appropriate division of labour among existing multilateral institutions or to decide when new organizations need to be created or existing ones closed down. Without such a supranational body, it has been suggested that there is a need for a global process with concerted, broad, and high-level political leadership. Thus, a summit meeting of heads of state—a Globalization Summit—has also been proposed to address the global problems that require global solutions.

Given these very different views of the role of the WTO in global governance, a modest but potentially important proposal is that a group of eminent persons with a practical understanding of the multilateral trading system and the issues it now confronts be established to explore—outside the context of negotiations—what trade policies are required for a better future and to advance proposals for action. In more than half a century of experience with the rules-based multilateral trading system, there has been only one such group—the Leutwiler Group. This group addressed a number of systemic issues (within the context of GATT) prior to the launching of the Uruguay Round and issued an influential report entitled *Trade Policies for a Better Future; Proposals for Action.*[6] Few would deny the important contribution of this report to the Uruguay Round negotiations in terms of new policy orientations. It may well be timely to consider the convening of such a group today.

Conclusion

The WTO has extended its reach far beyond that of GATT, and its importance in international economic and political affairs has increased dramatically. As the chapters in this volume indicate, there is broad support for maintaining the rules-based trading system and the benefits it bestows. However, there are very different perceptions of the responsibilities of the WTO in the realm of global governance and what they should be in the future.

Current criticisms of the WTO are in large measure linked to these different perceptions. Some say it is not living up to its responsibilities, while others say it is meddling in their affairs. Achieving a common understanding of the role of the WTO is an absolute priority for the international community if the enormous contribution that the multilateral rules-based trading system has made to world economic growth and stability over the past 50 years is to continue for the next half-century and beyond.

The failure to launch a new round of negotiations in Seattle has provided a breathing space for reflection, which should be used constructively. A number of proposals are advanced in this book that provide a basis for discussion and eventual policy action. The coming months and years will test whether there is the requisite political will to address and resolve some of the key systemic issues now facing the international community in terms of global governance.

Notes

1. In what follows, these 139 member governments will be referred to as the WTO members. While the 15 countries of the European Union are individual members, they are represented at WTO meetings (with the exception of the WTO Budget Committee) by the European Commission, which speaks on their behalf.
2. This chapter does not enter into the question of what constitutes governance, but for present purposes it can be described as the sum of the many ways that individuals and institutions—public and private—manage their common affairs. There are many actors on the stage of governance at the global level; these certainly include international institutions such as the WTO. See Commission on Global Governance, *Our Global Neighbourhood: The Report of the Commission on Global Governance,* Oxford: Oxford University Press, 1995, p. 2.
3. GATT had an original membership of 23 countries. The volume of world merchandise trade increased 18-fold between 1948 and 1998 and 43-fold for manufactured goods.
4. Unlike the Preamble to the GATT, the Preamble to the *Agreement Establishing the World Trade Organization* acknowledges the importance of sustainable development. Members recognize "that their relations in the field of trade and economic endeavour should be conducted with a view to raising standards of living while allowing for the optimal use of the world's resources in accordance with the objective of sustainable development." The texts of all the WTO agreements can be found in WTO, *The Results of the Uruguay Round Negotiations: The Legal Texts,* Geneva, 1995.
5. A similar conclusion was drawn during the Uruguay Round with respect to policies and institutions relating to trade, money, and finance. A negotiating group was created to examine ways to bring greater coherence to global economic policy-making. The Functioning of the GATT System Group produced a "Ministerial Declaration on the Contribution of the World Trade

Organization to Achieving Greater Coherence in Global Economic Policy-making." Ministers recognized that "difficulties, the origins of which lie outside the trade field can not be redressed through measures taken in the trade field alone."

6. See the Leutwiler Report, *Trade Policies for a Better Future; Proposals for Action,* Geneva: GATT Secretariat, 1985.

1

Laying the foundations of a fair and free world trade system

Kofi Annan
Secretary-General, United Nations

According to popular myth, the trade negotiations in Seattle in November 1999 were blocked by the peoples of the world joining together in the streets to defend their right to be different, against a group of faceless international bureaucrats. In other words, there was a kind of global grass-roots uprising against globalization—however paradoxical that may seem.

The truth is more prosaic. Those of us who had hoped to see the launch of a "development round" that would at last deliver to the developing countries the benefits they have so often been promised from free trade, instead saw governments—particularly those of the world's leading economic powers—unable to agree on their priorities. As a result, no round was launched at all, development or otherwise. The developing countries played a more active and united role than in previous conferences, but the industrialized countries remained locked in arguments among themselves. Their governments all favour free trade in principle, but too often they lack the political strength to confront those within their own countries who have come to rely on protectionist arrangements. They have not yet succeeded in putting across to their peoples the wider interest that we all share in having a global market from which everyone, not just the lucky few, can benefit.

The protests in the streets were important in their way. They highlighted the fact that globalization has casualties, as any historic change in human society is bound to have. And the protesters were justified in insisting that those who do best from globalization have both an obligation to do more to look after those casualties and a strong interest in doing so—since, otherwise, they risk a global backlash that could wipe out all their gains.

But globalization is not an enemy of development. The main losers in today's very unequal world are not those who are too much exposed to globalization, but rather those who have been left out. As a commentator in the *Financial Times* put it, "The world's poorest societies and peoples have been not so much exploited by the modern economic system as almost entirely outside it."[1] This exclusion is something that should trouble all of us. How and why is it that such large parts of the world are excluded from the benefits of globalization?

Towards a multilateral trading system

It is worth recalling that the United Nations—the major source of legitimacy in the international system—was the political and legal framework within which the world community first sought to lay the foundations of a fair and free world trade system. The General Agreement on Tariffs and Trade (GATT) was drafted and negotiated within a United Nations Committee and concluded as an annex to the International Trade Organization (ITO), which was approved in 1947 at the United Nations Conference on Trade and Employment in Havana. Even though the ITO never came into being, it was the United Nations that later provided the staff who went on to form the first GATT Secretariat. The GATT became the cornerstone around which the multilateral trading system was built.

It was also at Havana that the Latin American countries first insisted on the link between trade and development. Later, when the developing countries of Africa and Asia achieved independence, they joined in a global initiative to create an international trading system consistent with the promotion of economic and social development throughout the world. The UN Conference on Trade and Development (UNCTAD) was established in 1964 with the mandate to pursue this objective.

As the successor to GATT, the World Trade Organization (WTO) represents a new order in multilateral trade. It intensifies multilateral trade disciplines and extends them into new areas; and it provides the improved, and more secure, access to markets that is a prerequisite for successful export-oriented development strategies. On the other hand, it also imposes tighter constraints on the range of policy options open to developing countries in pursuing their development strategies.

The WTO has become a forum for continuous multilateral negotiations. Indeed, many countries find themselves engaged in trade negotiations simultaneously at the regional and subregional levels. Developing countries need to be able to exploit the export opportunities that this opens up for them, but also to defend their acquired rights and interests and to formulate development-oriented trade policies. No less important is the need to establish the universality of the WTO itself.

Towards a trading system that works for the poor

In the past, developing countries have been told time and again that they stand to benefit from trade liberalization and that they must open up their economies. They have done so, often at great cost. For the poorest countries the cost of implementing trade commitments can be more than a whole year's budget. But, time and again, they have found the results disappointing—not because free trade is bad for them, but because they are still not getting enough of it.

In the last great round of liberalization—the Uruguay Round— the developing countries cut their tariffs, as they were told to do. In absolute terms, however, many of them still maintain high tariff barriers, thereby not only restricting competition but also denying crucial imports to their own producers, and thus slowing down economic growth. Even so, they found that rich countries had cut their tariffs less than poor ones had. Not surprisingly, many of them feel they were taken for a ride.

Industrialized countries, it seems, are happy enough to export manufactured goods to each other, but from developing countries they still want only raw materials, not finished products. As a result, their average tariffs on the manufactured products they import from developing countries are now four times higher than the ones they impose on products that come mainly from other industrialized countries.

Ever more elaborate ways have been found to exclude third world imports; and these protectionist measures bite deepest in areas where developing countries are most competitive, such as textiles, footwear, and agriculture. In some industrialized countries, it is almost as though emerging economies are assumed to be incapable of competing honestly, so that whenever they do produce something at a competitive price they are accused of dumping, and are subjected to anti-dumping duties. In reality, it is the industrialized countries that are dumping their surplus food on world markets—a surplus generated by subsidies worth US$250 billion every year—and thereby threatening the livelihood of millions of poor farmers in the developing world, who cannot compete with subsidized imports.

It is hardly surprising, therefore, if developing countries suspect that arguments for using trade policy to advance various good causes are really yet another form of disguised protectionism. In most cases, that is not the intention; those who advance such arguments are usually voicing genuine fears and anxieties about the effects of globalization, which do need to be answered. They are right to be concerned—about jobs, about human rights, about child labour, about the environment, about the commercialization of scientific and medical research. They are right, above all, to be concerned about the desperate poverty in which so many people in developing countries are condemned to live.

But globalization must not be used as a scapegoat for domestic policy failures. The industrialized world must not try to solve its own problems at the expense of the poor. It seldom makes sense to use trade restrictions to tackle problems whose origins lie not in trade but in other areas of national and international policy. By aggravating poverty and obstructing development, such restrictions often make the problems they are trying to solve even worse.

Practical experience has shown that trade and investment not only bring economic development but often bring higher standards of human rights and environmental protection as well. All these things come together when countries adopt appropriate policies and institutions. Indeed, a developing civil society will generally insist on higher standards as soon as it is given the chance to do so.

What is needed is not new shackles for world trade, but greater determination by governments to tackle social and political issues directly—and to give the institutions that exist for that purpose the funds and the authority they need. The United Nations and its specialized agencies are charged with advancing the causes of development, the environment, human rights, and labour. We can be part of the solution.

The private sector, too, can be part of the solution. Transnational companies, which are the prime beneficiaries of economic liberalization, must share some of the responsibility for dealing with its social and environmental consequences. Economic rights and social responsibilities are two sides of the same coin. It was with this in mind that, in January 1999, I proposed a Global Compact between business and the United Nations, under which we will help the private sector to act in accordance with internationally accepted principles in the areas of human rights, labour standards, and the environment. The response so far has been encouraging, and I believe we can achieve a great deal by working together more closely.

But the World Trade Organization, for its part, must not be distracted from its vital task, which is to make sure that a new round of trade negotiations really does extend the benefits of free trade to the developing world. Unless we convince developing countries that globalization does indeed benefit them, the backlash against it will become irresistible. That would be a tragedy for the developing world, and indeed for the world as a whole.

Trade is better than aid. If industrialized countries did more to open their markets, developing countries could increase their exports by many billions of dollars per year—far more than they now receive in aid. For many millions of poor people this could make the difference between their present misery and a decent life. Yet the cost for the rich countries would be minuscule. In fact, industrialized countries might even be doing themselves a favour. It has been calculated that some of them are currently spending as much as 6 or 7 per cent of their gross domestic product on various kinds of trade protection measures. No doubt some of their citizens are benefiting from this, but there must surely be a cheaper and less harmful way to help them. In addition, tariffs and other restrictions on developing countries' exports must be substantially reduced. For the least developed countries, duties and quotas should be scrapped altogether. Developing countries should also receive technical assistance, both in the negotiations themselves and in implementing and benefiting from the agreements once reached. At present, some of them do not even have missions in Geneva.

Towards a trading system that spreads its benefits fairly and widely

In the wake of Seattle and the UNCTAD X meeting held shortly thereafter in Bangkok in February 2000, some of the key questions we face are as follows:

- How can we ensure that all developing countries, especially poor people within them, benefit from the growth of private investment and can borrow at affordable rates? We know that some of the obstacles to private capital flows, such as the prevalence of conflict in neighbouring countries, are hard, if not impossible, for states to overcome. Might it be the role of overseas development assistance to subsidize the risk premium that investors pay in such cases?
- How can we make new technologies more widely available and ensure that they are better used? From Bangalore to São Paulo, we see extraordinary examples of new skills bringing about dramatic changes. Not only is Microsoft investing billions of dollars in India, but Indian software companies are buying up firms in the United States. Yet half the world's population have never made or received a telephone call, let alone seen a computer. What are the conditions that make the difference? Which of them can states provide, as opposed to those that are more a matter of the state keeping out of the way? And how can we enable developing coun-

tries to benefit from advances in technology and medicine (which patents currently place beyond their reach), without reducing the incentive to those in industrialized countries who achieve such advances?

- Is there a role for external assistance in helping small-scale entrepreneurs in developing countries to find their way around in the international markets? Can we build on the experience of the Grameen Bank, thanks to which women in rural Bangladesh now have mobile phones and can check world prices for their products, instead of being at the mercy of middle men?

- How can we develop new partnerships, reaching beyond old-fashioned intergovernmental cooperation, to advance the cause of development? One such example is Netaid, a partnership between the United Nations Development Programme, Cisco Systems, and the entertainment community to raise consciousness about extreme poverty in the world and to raise the money to fight it. Another is GAVI, the Global Alliance for Vaccines and Immunization. In the Millennium Report entitled "We the Peoples" that I submitted to the Member States in April 2000, I announced several new initiatives that also rely heavily on expanding the range of UN partnerships. One is supported by the Web MD Foundation and is intended to create a "Health InterNetwork" to provide access to medical information. Another is led by Ericsson Communications and involves providing mobile and satellite telephones and microwave links for humanitarian workers in order to improve deliveries of relief aid. A third initiative is to establish a volunteer corps, called the United Nations Information Technology Service (UNITeS), to train groups in developing countries in the uses and opportunities of the Internet and information technology. I am sure that many other kinds of cooperation are still waiting to be imagined.

- What can we do to ensure that the voice of developing countries is not only heard, but listened to, in future discussions on international trade rules? UNCTAD, the World Bank, the World Trade Organization, and donor governments acting bilaterally are all seeking to help developing countries to prepare better for international negotiations and to implement agreements once reached. (This can cost more than the entire annual budget of some of the smallest and poorest countries.) Here too, perhaps, there could be a bigger role for civil society and business.

Towards a global market embedded in universal values

The first half of the twentieth century saw the world almost destroyed by war, partly as a result of its division into rival trade blocs. The second half, by contrast, saw an unprecedented expansion of global trade, which also brought unprecedented economic growth and development, even if as yet very unequally distributed. That expansion did not happen by accident. After the carnage and devastation of the Second World War, far-sighted statesmen deliberately constructed a post-war economic and political order governed by rules that would make free trade possible and thereby, they believed, make future wars less likely. Broadly speaking, they were right.

Several factors combined, at that time, to make such a liberal world order possible. One of them was a broad consensus on the role of the state in ensuring full employment, price stability, and social safety nets. Another was that most big firms were still organized within a single country—so that international economic relations could be negotiated between states, each of which corresponded to a distinct national economy, and could be controlled by raising or lowering barriers at national frontiers. And that in turn made it relatively easy to put in place a set of international organizations that were based on, and in their turn supported, the economic order: the World Bank, the International Monetary Fund, GATT, and the United Nations.

Today's world is very different. Today, networks of production and finance have broken free from national borders and become truly global. But they have left the rest of the system far behind. Nation states, and the institutions in which they are represented, can set the rules within which international exchanges take place, but they can no longer dictate the terms of such exchanges exclusively among themselves. And the new global economy is not embedded, as the old national economies were, in a broad framework of shared values and institutionalized practices.

The result is that, on top of the gross imbalance of power and wealth between industrialized countries and developing ones, there is now a second imbalance: the gap between the integration of the world economy and the continued parochialism of political and social institutions. Whereas economics is global, politics remains obstinately local. It is for this reason that so many people, even in the industrialized world, feel vulnerable and helpless.

That is why humankind has arrived at such a historic juncture. We have the power to decide whether the twenty-first century will be like the first half of the twentieth, only worse—or like the second half, only better. We cannot take the onward march of free trade and the rule of law for granted. Instead, we must resolve to underpin the free global market with genuinely global values and secure it with effective institutions. We must show the same firm leadership in defence of human rights, labour standards, and the environment as we already do in defence of intellectual property.

In short, we must emulate the wisdom, and the will-power, of those who laid the foundations of the liberal world order after the Second World War. They made change work for the people—and we must do the same.

Note

1. Martin Wolf, "The Curse of Global Inequality," *Financial Times* (London), 26 January 2000, p. 23.

2

Balancing competing interests: The future role of the WTO

Supachai Panitchpakdi
Deputy Prime Minister and Minister of Commerce, Thailand

The world economy has become more and more integrated and interdependent through increasing trade and capital mobility. Global trade and financial liberalization are believed to be the driving forces of world economic growth. The world's total output is now about 8 times what it was in 1948, but the value of world merchandise trade is 18 times as large. The problem is how to distribute the gains from increased global trade among countries in order to convince them of the benefits from further liberalization.

To many countries, greater trade flows have apparently brought gains, including greater per capita income and higher export earnings. However, obstacles and barriers to trade still exist, especially against the poorer countries. These must receive closer and greater attention in the global trade talks to ensure that open trade can concretely—and not just potentially or ideally—benefit all economies in the direction of free trade and efficient production.

If the future trade agenda of the World Trade Organization (WTO) is to be sustainable and is to command the support of the whole international community, then the WTO's members, both great and small, must be equal partners in its formulation and must be able collectively to claim ownership of it.

In particular, to sustain the primacy of the multilateral trading system for developing countries, which account for two-thirds of

WTO member countries, work has to be embarked upon in order to achieve a more equitable distribution of gains from international free trade, which will have a positive impact on these countries. The WTO must be able to prove to the world that the rule-based multilateral trading system can contribute to reducing income inequality and yielding sustainable development. To achieve our objective of making the system work for all members on a more equitable basis, we may need to look at the working mechanisms of the WTO to see whether or not there is some room for improvement.

Balancing interests

For the benefits of trade liberalization to be distributed as evenly as possible between developed and developing countries, a forum is needed in which all interests can be balanced. This requires, first and foremost, that the markets of the developed and developing countries be open to each other.

Although trade liberalization has stimulated growth and employment, not all countries have felt the benefits, nor have all restrictions to trade been eliminated. In addition, many countries believe that important trade concessions granted by developing countries under the Uruguay Round agreements have not been matched by sufficiently improved access to the markets of industrialized countries. The benefits of trade liberalization have been unevenly distributed among individual countries as a result of distorting policy measures, such as the use of contingent protection measures that limit access to markets. Many countries feel increasingly marginalized from the mainstream of the globalizing world economy.

One of the reasons cited for this apparent shortcoming was the lack of effective participation by many developing countries in the Uruguay Round. This resulted in many developing country members, particularly the least developed countries (LDCs), signing up to commitments whose consequences and implications were not assessed in terms of their applicability to the LDCs' level of economic development. Furthermore, the clash of fundamental interests with regard to issues of priority between developed and developing countries has resulted in an impasse, with many countries now refusing to embark on further trade liberalization.

The WTO was created as a forum in which every member has an equal voice. Compromises therefore have to be sought. Before any further liberalization is possible, members have to perceive the WTO as an arena where competing interests can be balanced so as to be able to forge coherent multilateral trade policies.

Effective participation in negotiations

To attain this balance of interest, it is necessary for all members to be able to project their concerns and views in such a manner that positive action can be taken. The WTO is after all a negotiating forum for legally binding commitments. To be in a position to take advantage of this, all members need to participate effectively in the process. To date, however, most issues have been steered by a handful of members and this at times has resulted in a slanted view of the issue at hand. To achieve a more coherent view, the WTO must ensure the full and effective participation of the developing countries and LDCs—which constitute the majority of WTO members—in its trade agenda through the process of institution- and capacity-building.

For example, in the ongoing mandated negotiations on agriculture, improved market access, and reduced competition from richer countries, subsidies are crucial for most developing countries, both to develop their present structure of trade and to diversify into products for new development. Increasing participation in these negotiations could work in favour of the developing countries by giving them a greater voice. Ideally, developing countries need to put forward their own positive negotiating agenda, instead of adopting the negative approach of merely blocking any proposal, as in the past. In order to do this, they must know what they want and what they can offer in the negotiations. They should also be able to make use of the dispute settlement system to enforce their rights.

To benefit from being part of the global trading regime, some reforms and institution-building in these countries will be needed.

At a basic level, this should include the training of administrators and policy makers, as well as legal reform, ranging from intellectual property and bankruptcy laws to financial law. Capacity-building for developing countries should focus not only on meeting obligations under the WTO but also on the capacity to produce, which encompasses infrastructure, financial resources, appropriate trade policies, and other supply-side capacities. Supply-side constraints will have to be eliminated through domestic restructuring policies that are predictable and transparent to foreign direct investment. Technical assistance needs to be more focused and efficient and include such important areas as negotiating capacities. In this regard, there is a clear need for strong coordination and coherence between the activities of international institutions.

Many of the developing countries and LDCs cannot afford to have representation in Geneva, so financial assistance may be given, either in cash or in kind, so that they can be present at important meetings on a temporary or a permanent basis. No doubt, new technology such as video conferencing and information technology could be used to keep non-resident representatives abreast of the issues.

In addition, to enable developing countries and LDCs to benefit fully from the dispute settlement procedures, a group of developed and developing countries have together established the Advisory Centre on WTO Law. The aim was to reduce the cost of participating in a dispute, which often entails legal fees that are prohibitive for most developing countries. This would allow developing countries to make use of the dispute settlement procedures to protect and enforce their rights garnered under the Uruguay Round agreements. This is a form of investment in technical assistance that is very welcome because the users of the Advisory Centre are able to develop their own capacity-building in terms of enhanced WTO knowledge at the same time.

Improved transparency

An effective consensus-based decision-making process could be achieved by increasing the transparency with which decisions are taken. It is often said that the consensus principle is at the heart of the WTO system, and is a fundamental democratic guarantee that is not negotiable. Recently, criticism has been levelled at the WTO for the secretiveness of its decision-making, which results in the exclusion of most developing countries and LDCs from its key decision-making processes.

Although the WTO needs to address these concerns and should strive to make the process as transparent and as inclusive as possible, the problem is perhaps not as terrible as it is made out to be. The membership has agreed that consultations should be held in which all would be able to express their views. From these consultations, it appears that radical reform might not be necessary. Rather, the practice of decision-making by consensus should prevail and be maintained with simply some fine-tuning. In short, what is required is a system by which the state of play of any ongoing negotiation in any group is immediately communicated to all member countries for information sharing and ultimate decision-taking.

The problem regarding the external transparency of the WTO is not as acute as that of its internal transparency, but there may be room for improvement. Today, the public near and far would like to see the WTO more open and more accountable. Because the success of the WTO will partly depend on public support, greater efforts should be spent on making information readily available to all interested parties. In this regard, the WTO should expedite the derestriction of its documents and most information should be available online. All of these steps will make the public better informed about WTO negotiations and operations.

Representation in the WTO

The WTO membership has increased from the original 125 to 139, and in the foreseeable future is expected to expand to 160–170, with a greater role and more participation by developing countries. Improvements to the management structure of the WTO may be necessary in the future to allow the WTO to be more responsive to the needs of members. Although the idea of an executive board has not found favour with members in the past, the time may come when such a concept, with appropriate modifications, will be the most effective way of managing the WTO. Even though an arrangement along the lines of the World Bank's Development Committee or the IMF's Interim Committee may not be acceptable to the WTO membership, several ideas have been floated in this respect. Prime Minister Tony Blair has already suggested the appointment of a group of eminent persons to advise the General Council on the future path of the WTO. Back in 1983, Director-General Arthur Dunkel established a panel of seven distinguished persons to report on problems affecting the international trading system. The panel, representing industrialized and developing countries, made 15 specific recommendations to support a more open multilateral system as a counter-measure to the crisis prevailing in the trading system at the time. We should not preclude the possibility of resorting to such a panel to help us resolve some of the threatened divisions over the pending trade and non-trade issues facing the WTO at present.

Involvement of the private sector and NGOs

The active participation of private sectors and NGOs is a welcome development and we may have to take their legitimate concerns into consideration in our future deliberations. The NGOs could provide valuable inputs and share their thoughts and main concerns to improve the working of the WTO process.

There are, however, many stages at which interest groups and stakeholders can participate effectively in the formation of their government's trade policies. In addition, the WTO has held a number of symposia with NGOs. At Seattle in 1999, for instance, immediately before the opening of the third Ministerial Conference a symposium was held in which 672 accredited NGOs participated. The strong dynamism of NGOs makes them increasingly influential in all areas and they should be given an appropriate role to play in the constructive formation of our New World Economic Order.

Coordinating with the IMF and the World Bank

The very close linkage between trade and finance in the unstoppable process of globalization makes it essential that the WTO coordinate more closely with the IMF and the World Bank to ensure that their policies are cohesive and mutually supportive.

In the new global electronic economy, it is easy for fund managers and international investors to move vast amounts of capital instantaneously, sometimes affecting even seemingly strong and sturdy economies. Financial dislocation can therefore impinge upon the flow of trade. Liberalization of the financial sector should be done gradually and only when sound macroeconomic policies, a healthy banking system, the right timing, and adequate supervision and regulation are all present. However, a sufficiently open trading regime and efficient product markets can help prevent the adverse impacts of excessively volatile financial flows.

Globalization affects not just one particular country that has to restructure itself in time to reap the benefits of the process, but all the international bodies. The IMF, the World Bank, and the WTO all have to devise every possible means to share in the monumental task of making trade and finance work for development.

In conclusion, to ensure that faith in the rules-based multilateral trading system is maintained, members need to work together to make it strong and equitable. A new development paradigm must be gradually evolved so that the WTO can take account of the differing interests of its members. Members can do this not by imposing an ideological agenda but rather by balancing competing interests and both increasing transparency in the decision-making process and attaining effective participation of all members.

3

Rebuilding confidence in the multilateral trading system: Closing the "legitimacy gap"

Rubens Ricupero
Secretary-General, UNCTAD

Introduction

I am a firm believer in the multilateral trading system. It is the most effective way of defending the interests of the weaker members of the trading community. However, this does not mean that we should passively accept the system as it is, in terms of the decision-making process and particularly in terms of the imbalances and asymmetries that have accumulated over the years As stated in the Bangkok Plan of Action negotiated by the member states of the United Nations Conference on Trade and Development (UNCTAD), what is needed is a "commitment to a multilateral trading system that is fair, equitable and rules-based and that operates in a non-discriminatory and transparent manner and in a way that provides benefits for all countries, especially developing countries."[1]

Recent events, particularly those related to the third Ministerial Conference of the World Trade Organization (WTO) at Seattle and the uncertainties concerning its follow-up, pose serious challenges to the international community. One of the challenges is that the legitimacy of the multilateral trading system in which we all believe is being increasingly questioned. There is therefore an urgent need to analyse the factors that led to the inability to forge a consensus on a new agenda for multilateral negotiations, so that steps to close the "legitimacy gap" can be taken. In my statement at Seattle, I observed that, for any international organization, "legitimacy" depends on three main interrelated factors: universal membership and accession mechanisms; participatory and effective decision-making; and fair sharing in the benefits of the system.[2] This chapter deals with these questions and other related matters.

The road to Seattle

Seattle was not an isolated event in the evolution of the multilateral trading system. Without delving too far back in history, the 1990 Brussels Ministerial Session of the Trade Negotiations Committee of the General Agreement on Tariffs and Trade (GATT), in which I participated in my capacity as Ambassador of Brazil to GATT, also broke up in disarray—this time as a result of an impasse caused by the refusal of a small number of Latin American countries, members of the Cairns Group, to continue the negotiations when it became evident that the European Community was not prepared at that stage to envisage anything more than a minimal outcome to the negotiations on the reform of agricultural trade. For those Latin American countries, the negotiation process would have lost any real meaning had the Brussels Conference resulted in such an outcome, because it would have precluded the possibility of their deriving a fair share of the benefits from the eventual results.[3]

At Marrakesh in 1994, some countries pressed for the introduction of a future work programme for the new proposed organization, containing new issues that had not been dealt with in the Uruguay Round, as a component of the final package. A compromise was reached in the form of a statement by the Chairman of the Trade Negotiations Committee listing possible issues for inclusion in the work programme. This included items proposed by developed countries, such as labour standards, investment, and competition policy, as well as some of interest to developing countries, including compensation for the erosion of preferences, commodities, and immigration. In the period between the official establishment of the World Trade Organization and its first Ministerial Conference, developed countries pursued these issues.

The idea of negotiating multilateral rules for investment within the WTO attained a particularly high profile, owing to the parallel negotiations of the Multilateral Agreement on Investment (MAI) in the Organisation for Economic Co-operation and Development (OECD). Developing countries had differing views on the advisability of bringing the negotiations to the WTO, where they would have some influence over the outcome, or leaving them in the OECD, where it would not bind them. Many developing countries opposed the inclusion of investment in any WTO work programme, and even more firmly opposed any mention of labour rights; there was also significant resistance to further work on environment and even competition policy. During the period of negotiation of what was to become the Singapore Declaration, those developing countries focused attention on keeping these issues off the agenda.

When I attended the WTO Ministerial Conference in Singapore in December 1996, it was the first time I had participated in a meeting of the GATT/WTO since leaving my post as Ambassador and Permanent Representative of Brazil to the GATT shortly before the completion of the Uruguay Round. I was struck by the extent to which the WTO had evolved beyond the GATT, and in particular by the new and intensified challenges, complexities, and opportunities facing developing countries in the multilateral trading system. One manifestation of this evolution was the adoption of the Information Technology Product Agreement and the rapid completion of the negotiations on financial services and basic telecommunications. Together these were seen, particularly by developed countries, as enhancing the legal foundation of the globalization process, which was presented as bringing benefits to all. The developing countries, by contrast, had not formulated initiatives to obtain action in their favour, nor had they fully recognized the extent to which the WTO had become a forum for a continuous negotiating process.

After my participation in the Singapore Conference, and drawing upon my experiences from the Uruguay Round negotiations, I came to the conclusion that developing countries needed to draw up a "positive agenda" in which they would systematically identify their interests and set realistic objectives with respect to all issues, not only those where they were *demandeurs,* and would pursue these objectives by formulating explicit and technically sound proposals in alliance with other like-minded countries. This would be a concrete way of both strengthening the multilateral trading system and enhancing the participation of developing countries in the decision-making process. It has also been my experience that negotiating proposals carry much more "weight" when they are in consonance with the culture of an organization founded on the belief that free trade should be pursued as far as possible.[4] On the basis of a fresh and ambitious mandate that UNCTAD had just received at its Ninth Conference, in South Africa (1996), I decided to launch the "positive agenda" programme within UNCTAD, with a view to assisting developing countries in building their capacity to identify their interests, formulate trade objectives, and pursue those objectives in international trade negotiations.

In the light of the results of the second WTO Ministerial Conference in 1998—on the occasion of the fiftieth anniversary of the GATT system—it was considered likely that the third Conference would launch a major trade initiative. The second Conference established a preparatory process for the third Conference, where it was evident that a decision on future negotiations would have to be taken because of the time limits set in the WTO multilateral trade agreements (MTAs) themselves, both for the review of certain agreements and for the initiation of negotiations on agriculture and services. Pressure was also mounting for a much more comprehensive "Millennium Round" (a term coined by Sir Leon Brittan). This preparatory process would be "proposal driven," thus placing every WTO member under pressure to submit proposals to ensure that trade issues of specific interest to each of them would not be omitted in future negotiations. This impetus quickened the pace and sense of urgency of UNCTAD's work on the "positive agenda."

Almost 250 proposals were submitted to the WTO General Council in the preparatory process for the Seattle Conference. Developing countries assumed an active role by submitting over half of these proposals. They concentrated largely on two aspects: (a) how to ensure that the built-in agenda for negotiations on services and agriculture would focus on their particular interests, and (b) specific actions related to the MTAs, including the mandated reviews, grouped together under the broad title of "implementation." Within the category of implementation issues, proposals addressed the question of special and differential treatment for developing countries (S&D) with the objective of elaborating more contractual language for undertakings of the "best endeavour" type. Implementation proposals were also aimed at agreed interpretations of the MTAs to deal with specific problems that had arisen in practice, particularly those that did not take account of the special characteristics of developing country economies, administrations, and enterprises (e.g. high interest rates and difficulties in identifying inputs). The obstacles they faced in meeting the administrative and procedural obligations were also the subject of proposals, especially for the extension of the transitional periods for the agreements on Trade-Related Aspects of Intellectual Property Rights (TRIPS), Trade-Related Investment Measures (TRIMs), and Customs Valuation. An important element in the proposals was the concept of "imbalance" in rights and obligations. The TRIPS Agreement was the object of particular attention by a number of developing countries, partly in response to the pressure to forgo the flexibility and transitional provisions that had been built into the Agreement. Some developing countries raised specific issues concerning the transfer of technology in connection with several MTAs.

The preparatory exercise in the WTO was led by the Chairman of the General Council, Ambassador Ali Mchumo of Tanzania, who had assumed an inordinate burden owing to the prolonged vacancy of the post of WTO Director-General. Mr. Mike Moore took office only on 1 September 1999, and it was almost another two months before the Deputy Directors-General assumed their posts. The drafting process got off to a bad start: a text circulated on 6 October had to be quickly withdrawn because it was seen as omitting the majority of proposals submitted by the developing countries, and the hastily assembled 8 October text simply annexed the missing proposals. A comprehensive draft was circulated on 19 October that incorporated all the proposals into a structured comprehensive text, but without any further drafting. Only on 17 November was the Chairman in a position to circulate, under his own responsibility, a partial text, which reflected a certain degree of agreement (albeit with square brackets) and alternative wordings; however, it omitted the key issues of agriculture and implementation. Thus, the major players clearly demonstrated their unwillingness to compromise on what they considered to be politically sensitive issues before the Ministerial Conference.

The fact that ministers arrived in Seattle to face an incoherent text laden with square brackets might seem to have doomed the third Ministerial Conference right from the start. The situation was reminiscent of the ill-fated 1990 Brussels Ministerial Conference, with one major difference: the Brussels Conference was intended to conclude a negotiation with the acceptance of a series of binding agreements; the Seattle Conference, in contrast, was only attempting to agree on an agenda to commence negotiations, including the "built-in" agenda where no formal decision was required. It should have been feasible to arrive at a compromise that would have (a) satisfied the immediate political objectives of the major players; (b) left open the possibility of entering into the comprehensive negotiations sought by the European Union at a future date, i.e. at the fourth Ministerial Conference; and (c) assured developing countries that all their proposals would be addressed in the negotiations. The reason this did not happen is another story. It can be told only by those who were in the "Green Room" in Seattle (a process in which a group of up to 40 member countries, including many developing countries, tries to reach preliminary agreements on matters under negotiation, and then present them to the rest of the delegations). However, the collapse did come as something of a surprise. A non-paper dated 3 December and issued at 5.00 a.m. seemed to have incorporated most of the interests of developing countries, and it was understood that a compromise had been reached on agriculture. Obviously, these did not "fly" in the Green Room, where it was reported that one major delegation had been unable to take any decision and time had simply run out because the conference facilities were no longer available.

The healing process:
The Bangkok Conference

The tenth session of UNCTAD (UNCTAD X) took place shortly after the Seattle Conference, in February 2000. It was, as I have previously stated on several occasions, the first major economic conference of the new millennium. Owing to a combination of factors, some of them unforeseen, the conference proved to be unique, in that it did not resemble previous UNCTAD conferences. It provided, among other things, an opportunity to initiate a "healing process" after Seattle and give the multilateral trading system a new impetus.

UNCTAD X constituted a major effort at international consensus-building. The traditional negotiation of a consensus text, the "Plan of Action,"[5] took place in parallel with a series of debates involving the major actors in the world "political economy." These included the Secretary-General of the United Nations, heads of state and government, ministers and senior officials from the member states, leaders of international financial institutions, representatives of parliament and of non-governmental organizations, entrepreneurs from small and medium enterprises (SMEs) and transnational corporations (TNCs), heads of agencies and regional commissions of the United Nations system, the Director-General of the WTO, and academic experts. Their dialogue focused on the options for a new development paradigm compatible with the rapidly evolving global system. The general consensus was that a new inclusive global order to correct the effects of market failures and minimize the dangers of marginalization was required to manage globalization better in the future. Consensus on the way in which the global system should function could be reached only by balancing competing interests, not by imposing an ideological agenda.

UNCTAD's new Plan of Action was drawn up against the background of these discussions and the overall "ambience" they provided to the Bangkok Conference. The Plan urges UNCTAD to continue with the "positive agenda" work, improve the developing countries' understanding of the multilateral trading system, and support them so that they progressively become effective players in the system. It reflects the perception that the system is not providing equitable shares of the benefits among countries and between various groups within countries. One achievement of UNCTAD X was to reach a consensus that the international community should address the current imbalances and asymmetries, including those caused by human, institutional, and financial constraints.

In outlining the measures to integrate developing countries successfully into the world economy, the Plan of Action highlighted the range of measures affecting their trade that should be addressed, and agreed that the conditions necessary for the effective implementation of the WTO agreements had not always been met. Any new agreement should contain adequate provisions for assistance to developing countries to enable them to establish the infrastructure and other conditions necessary for the effective implementation of the agreements and to ensure that these countries benefit from the opportunities offered by them. The Bangkok Plan of Action essentially set out the core elements of an agenda for the "development round," which I discuss below.

Although the potential impact in the WTO of the deliberations at Bangkok should not be overstated, the outcome of UNCTAD X will undoubtedly be seen as exerting a favourable influence on the current efforts to build new confidence in the multilateral trading system.

The way forward: Closing the "legitimacy gap"

Is there a "legitimacy gap"? Since the collapse of the Seattle Conference, there has been much debate over the "crisis" in the multilateral trading system. A wide spectrum of views has emerged. At one end are those who would give the impression that the system is on its last legs. These include the most militant NGOs, which have taken credit for blocking the launching of a new round of multilateral trade negotiations, thereby, in their view, protecting the world from the evils of globalization. On the same side of this spectrum, one finds many members of the academic community who are analysing the "crisis" in the system, which is now the subject of a large number of seminars in North America and Europe. At the other end of the spectrum lie the practitioners—those most involved in trade matters in general and in the daily work of the WTO in particular, who avoid being drawn into discussing any "crisis" and assure us that it is business as usual.

As noted above, the multilateral trading system has experienced crisis and difficulties in the past. They are not new. At the same time, the system has continued to grow and will probably experience new difficulties in the light of the complexity of the issues at hand. In my view, the task ahead is to find ways to realize the commitment to the multilateral trading system made at UNCTAD X. One task consists of closing what I have termed the "legitimacy gap." What needs to be done, and the role of UNCTAD, are discussed below.

Membership and accession mechanisms

Over 40 countries have been in the process of accession since 1997, ranging from the fifth-largest trading entity—China—to tiny island countries. Technical assistance to the majority of these countries has become an important activity for UNCTAD, and one in which we receive considerable support from developed country donors. It is becoming more evident that the process of accession to the multilateral trading system is cumbersome and painful. Ten countries have acceded to the WTO, six of which fall into the category of economies in transition (including four ex-Soviet republics). One of the major complaints has been that acceding countries are being obliged to accept higher levels of obligation than the present WTO members, and that developing countries are not being permitted to enjoy the S&D treatment incorporated in the MTAs. Many of the countries in transition to a market economy are not adequately prepared to negotiate commitments on trade measures that affect the operation of market mechanisms.

The agreement between China and the United States, followed by that with the European Union, set the stage for the accession of China to the WTO after 14 years of negotiation. China's membership will greatly strengthen the organization and change the traditional debate. However, certain aspects of the agreements enable countries to continue to maintain discriminatory measures against China for an extended but fixed period, and could be the source of tensions in the future if restraint is not exercised by China's trading partners.

The least developed countries (LDCs) face special difficulties. Of the 19 LDCs that are not yet members of the WTO, 10 are in the process of accession, but Vanuatu is the only one at an advanced stage. One country, however, which has virtually no trade interests with Vanuatu (its bilateral trade is valued at less than US$1 million, while Vanuatu has reportedly spent around US$400,000 in the process of accession), has blocked Vanuatu's accession, insisting that it make much more drastic tariff concessions. Vanuatu is considering its future course of action, which includes the possibility of withdrawing its application.[6] A proposal by the European Union for the "fast-track" accession of LDCs could be a useful step towards simplifying and speeding up the process for them. In the same context, it seems difficult on any grounds to deny to the acceding LDCs the S&D treatment accorded to those LDCs that are already signatories of the MTAs.

The integration of the LDCs into the multilateral trading system requires much more than their accepting the WTO obligations; it also calls for actions by their trading partners. But their limited supply capacity, poor infrastructure, and low level of skills pose a major challenge. Enhancing that supply capacity and ensuring that their export bases not only grow and diversify to include higher-value products, but also achieve sustainable development, will require specific international support measures, including the granting of duty-free access for all LDC exports. More generally, an enormous capacity-building effort has to be initiated to provide LDCs with the institutional and educational tools needed to evaluate the impact of trade policies and to put into place the corresponding measures to meet social demands. The support of the international community in this process is essential. It is for this purpose that in May 2001 the third United Nations conference on the LDCs will take place in Brussels, hosted by the European Union. We have to make sure that this time the opportunity is not missed and that the initiative culminates in a practical, results-oriented conference.

Participatory and effective decision-making process

The challenge facing the international community in effectively integrating the LDCs into the multilateral trading system leads me to consideration of the second component of the "legitimacy gap" problem mentioned above, namely, participatory and effective decision-making. Much has been said of the inequity of the Green Room process. As Ambassador of Brazil, I was one of the "habitués" of the Green Room during the Uruguay Round. It should be admitted that for the sake of efficiency it is normal for small groups to gather to discuss specific, often very technical, issues. The problem arises when the deals made within such groups are imposed on those not present. It is no longer possible to assume that agreements can be negotiated among a small group of countries in a non-transparent manner and then imposed on the other members. This was clearly articulated in the strong statements circulated in Seattle by the Latin American and Caribbean and African groups, to the effect that they would not be able to join a consensus on agreements in whose negotiation they were not fully involved.

An important development in the new system, and one closely connected with the issue of effective participation, is that all countries have accepted roughly the same level of obligation. Unlike in the past, when countries could pick and choose at leisure which agreements to join after detailed examination in their capitals, the WTO is based on the notion of the single undertaking conceived during the Uruguay Round, which requires all countries to accept all agreements at the same time. Thus, delegations are aware that decisions arrived at informally in the WTO could eventually lead to the acceptance of new obligations, implying new legislation, expensive adjustments in administration, and greater competition. It is thus not acceptable for them to be left out of the decision-making process. No government can afford to have to explain to its legislature that its officials were not involved in the decisions that will have to be incorporated into national law. Moreover, the strengthening of accountability in developing countries has made them tougher trade negotiators, as they have different interest groups watching for any indication that governments have not adequately defended national interests. As the United States Trade Representative pointed out at the end of the Seattle Conference, more imaginative techniques of negotiation and decision-making have to be devised.

There is ample evidence that this sense of being excluded from the decision-making process is being felt very acutely. The idea of a limited consultative group is, therefore, a non-starter. However, a number of developments under way could streamline the process. One is the strengthening of subregional integration among developing countries, which is leading to more intensive coordination and sharing of tasks and to the possibility that, although there may be a large number of delegates present, only a limited number will actually be taking part in the debate.

The Seattle process demonstrated the ability of developing countries to assume a proactive role in setting the agenda for future multilateral trade negotiations. UNCTAD made its contribution to their efforts in the context of its "positive agenda" exercise explained above, which provided them with the indispensable research, analytical, and conceptual inputs in the formulation of their negotiating positions in the light of their own trade interests. Following the new emphasis formulated at Bangkok, this assistance is also now focused at the subregional level, to assist developing countries in integrating their economies and coordinating their positions in order to interact better with their negotiating partners in multilateral negotiations. UNCTAD's Commercial Diplomacy Programme aims at assisting developing country officials to acquire negotiating skills, and supports the efforts of institutions in developing countries to incorporate such training into their regular curricula.

However, all the efforts in developing negotiating skills and defining clear negotiating objectives cannot by themselves overcome large disparities in economic and political power. Coalition-building and subregional coordination could contribute to enhancing this power, but ultimately the main leverage available to countries would be to deny legitimacy to agreements reached without their participation.

As Joseph Stiglitz pointed out in an article prepared just before the Seattle Conference, international organizations are directly accountable not to the citizenry but rather to national governments, and particularly to agencies within these governments. They lack the democratic legitimacy that derives from the electoral process and thus must derive legitimacy from the manner in which they conduct their business. He argues that "if policies are forged on the basis of widespread international discussions, a process of global consensus building, then their legitimacy is enhanced. If, by contrast, policies seem to reflect the power of a few large countries (the G-7, the G-3 or the G-1), then the legitimacy is reduced. If the policies seem to reflect special interests, legitimacy is reduced."[7] Viewed in this context, Seattle seems to have taken place at a time when just such unfavourable aspects prevailed.

In an interesting paper presented to a Harvard conference held in June 2000 in honour of the late Raymond Vernon, Professors Keohane and Nye note that the legitimacy of institutions flows not only from "inputs" in the form of procedures and accountability, but also from "outputs," that is, their capacity to deliver results.[8] They observe that the WTO has delivered on trade liberalization, which "may have conferred some legitimacy on the WTO even in the absence of procedures assuring transparency and participation." It has thus satisfied one powerful constituency—"multinational corporations that seek to expand their own exports and investment abroad." The analysis of Stiglitz in juxtaposition with that of Keohane and Nye points to the conclusion that, in the view of a number of observers, there is a "legitimacy gap" that needs to be addressed.

Fair sharing of the benefits

The third important component of the "legitimacy gap" problem is that of ensuring a fair sharing of the benefits of the system. The imbalances recognized at UNCTAD X consist of the imbalances in the WTO rules and obligations themselves, which particularly affect the developing countries, and imbalances in the ability of countries to derive economic benefits from these rules and obligations and from the trade liberalization achieved within the negotiating framework they provide.

Examples of the first set of imbalances have been clearly documented in various studies, including that by UNCTAD in the context of its positive agenda exercise.[9] They have been reflected in the proposals submitted by developing countries in the process leading up to Seattle. A large number of those proposals are characterized by the sentiment that the results of the Uruguay Round were asymmetrical, tilting the balance of multilateral rights and obligations against them, and that the primary purpose of any new multilateral trade initiative should be to correct these imbalances. This is reflected in the position that implementation should take priority and that new initiatives should await the effective implementation of the commitments in favour of developing countries.

These commitments relate to such areas as agricultural subsidies, anti-dumping duties, tariff peaks directed to products exported by developing countries, the absence of meaningful commitments on the movement of natural persons, the slow removal of quotas on textiles and clothing, and the promotion of the transfer of technology. The commitments contrast sharply with the strict disciplines that the developing countries were required to accept in the Uruguay Round and the short transitional periods for their implementation. The developing countries also perceive an imbalance in their ability to assert their rights in the WTO, particularly in a context where the decisions of the Dispute Settlement Body and the Appellate Body appear to be in some contradiction with the exclusive authority of the Ministerial Conference and the General Council to adopt interpretations.

Developing countries frequently refer to their perception that it is the developed countries that actually benefit from special treatment, because they are permitted to use measures unavailable to developing countries for technical reasons, relating to notifications or situations extant at the establishment of the WTO, or measures unavailable for financial reasons. In their view, this is most flagrant in the case of agriculture, where the major trading countries have reserved the right massively to subsidize exports, displacing the exports and domestic production of developing countries; to subsidize domestic production; to maintain tariffs at rates well exceeding 100 per cent; and to apply a special safeguard mechanism under which restrictions can be applied on the basis of international prices or import volumes with no injury criterion. Furthermore, the "peace clause" on agriculture does not expire until 2003 and could be extended, and the transition period for the phase-out of restrictions on textiles and clothing runs until the beginning of 2005, with little liberalization until the final deadline (to be contrasted with the shorter periods for TRIPS and TRIMs). In addition, anti-dumping duties enjoy partial protection from the dispute settlement mechanism. Finally, the post-Uruguay Round negotiations resulted in considerable liberalization of financial and telecommunications services and information technology products, but very little liberalization of goods or services of export interest to developing countries, such as the movement of persons.

In addition, developing countries find their obligations onerous. The transitional periods for developing countries to implement the agreements have proved to be insufficient in light of the inadequacy of their administrative resources and access to financing. I have pointed out in several statements that the major developed countries have enjoyed "transitional periods" approaching half a century to implement their GATT obligations in the agriculture and textiles sectors; by contrast, developing countries are being asked to implement the whole set of intellectual property instruments, on which many have no prior legislation, within a mere five years. The extension of transitional periods (particularly in the TRIPS, TRIMs, and Customs Valuation agreements) has become a central element in developing countries' proposals. Developing countries have advocated a "peace clause," under which developed countries could exercise due restraint in invoking the dispute settlement mechanism against those developing countries that were not able to comply fully with their obligations before the expiry of the transitional periods, similar to the one that they have agreed to maintain until 2003 on agriculture. Unfortunately, some such disputes have already been initiated against developing countries' alleged non-compliance with the TRIPS and TRIMs agreements.

The cost of implementation has been amply studied and documented. As early as 1994, UNCTAD estimated that the first year of implementation of the TRIPS Agreement could cost a least developed country almost US\$20 million.[10] More recent studies by the World Bank have produced much more dramatic figures, estimating that the implementation costs of three MTAs (i.e. those on Sanitary and Phytosanitary Regulations, TRIPS, and Customs Valuation) could equal a year's development assistance for a developing country.[11]

An additional cause of frustration has been the fact that, in many agreements, S&D provisions have been phrased in terms of best-endeavour clauses, and it is difficult to establish whether they have been effectively implemented. In these cases, calls have been made for "concretizing" the provisions in such key areas as anti-dumping, sanitary and phytosanitary regulations, and TRIPS, all of crucial interest to developing countries. In this context, there has been a "resurrection" of the principle of differential and more favourable treatment for developing countries. Developing countries no longer equate S&D with general exceptions to the rules, but seek to interpret the rules so that they take account of the real problems they face in the administration of the agreements, and which their exporters face as a result of the implementation of the MTAs by their trading partners. The proposals relating to anti-dumping and subsidies and countervailing measures are intended to introduce provisions that would reflect the realities of the situation faced by developing countries in competing for world trade in a globalizing world.

The second type of imbalance mentioned above concerns the inability of developing countries to extract benefits from the system. To exercise their rights in ensuring that their more powerful trading partners respect the rules requires considerable training and strengthening of the capacity of their administrations to engage effectively in the daily debate in the WTO on issues of vital interest to their countries. In order to take advantage of the market access opportunities offered, most developing countries will have to overcome a supply constraint and will need to broaden and diversify their productive base through investment, technology, and managerial skills.

An important number of developing countries have encountered difficulties in attracting foreign direct investment and obtaining access to technology to build up a competitive supply capacity. The creation of a favourable investment climate in developing countries is essential, but aspects of this "supply-side" problem can also be addressed within the system. Secure access to markets is crucial to attract export-oriented investment. This is why UNCTAD has stressed the need for the preservation of the Generalized System of Preferences and other preferential arrangements for developing countries, for tighter rules on anti-dumping and countervailing measures, and most importantly, as stated above, for ensuring that any arrangement to provide duty-free access in favour of the least developed countries is "bound."

Developing countries cannot create a more competitive supply capacity without greater access to technology. What is worrisome is that, as technology advances, the gap between developed and developing countries is widening rather than narrowing, as had been envisaged some decades ago. At the June 2000 Harvard University conference mentioned above, Jeffrey Sachs presented a map of the world that identified the 23 countries that provided most of the world's technological innovations (defined as producing at least 10 US patents per million citizens) in 1997. Whereas some countries are capable of incorporating new technologies into their production and consumption structures, others are "technologically disconnected."[12]

Article 7 of the TRIPS Agreement states that the protection and enforcement of intellectual property rights should contribute to the promotion of technological innovation and to the transfer and dissemination of technology. In UNCTAD's first assessment of the Uruguay Round results, it was considered that, although the TRIPS Agreement would lead to higher prices for imported technologies for developing countries, stronger protection of intellectual property could lead to greater opportunities for the transfer of technology, particularly new technologies. The former would seem to have materialized, but the latter continues to be no more than an aspiration for many developing countries.[13] Furthermore, Article IV of the General Agreement on Trade in Services (GATS) provides for the negotiation of specific commitments by developing countries relating to their "access to technology on a commercial basis."

What is at stake is the distribution of the benefits of globalization. The rules set during the Uruguay Round have provided what is becoming an effective legal framework to enable those possessing the technology and the capital—the TNCs—to exploit their potential. In fact, "the WTO has been described as a constitution for a single global economy."[14] This was inevitable: the multilateral trading system would have become irrelevant had it not adapted to the trade and investment opportunities presented by the new technologies. However, adequate rules and "safety nets" have not been provided to protect and further the interests of those as yet unable to benefit from, or even to avoid being harmed by, globalization. In this perspective, the system provides a "fast lane" that enables some to move ahead more quickly, leaving the others behind. Thus, rebuilding confidence in the system and closing the "legitimacy gap" demand some type of "affirmative action" programme to provide those unable to compete with special opportunities to assist them to produce and trade competitively. One concrete action relates to the "development round."

Towards a "development round"

The current phase of "confidence-building" in the WTO has included a decision on initiating a process to address implementation-related issues. It establishes a mechanism for reviewing the outstanding implementation issues and concerns, particularly those raised during the preparations for the third Ministerial Conference, including by a number of developing countries. Particularly noteworthy is its specific reference to paragraphs 21 and 22 of the draft Ministerial Text of 19 October 1999, which reflects the proposals of developing countries submitted during the preparatory process for Seattle. The General Council, meeting in special sessions that started on 22 June 2000, will address these issues; the process should be completed no later than the fourth session of the Ministerial Conference, but some concrete results could be achieved as early as October 2000. This work could constitute at least a first step towards a "development round." The negotiations under the built-in agenda on agriculture and services provide the core of such a development round, because they offer a framework within which to address particularly glaring imbalances in the rules and benefits of the existing multilateral trading system. In fact, if not *de jure,* the new round has already started.

Calling a multilateral negotiation a "development round" will not make it one. In my statement to the third Ministerial Meeting in Seattle on 30 November 1999, I emphasized the need to convert rhetoric into action, to close the "legitimacy gap" by demonstrating the ability to deliver fair benefits to all members. The fact that the Millennium Round was not launched at Seattle should not be a deterrent to continued pursuit of the objectives, and in so doing enhancing and strengthening the system. It is the results that count, not the name. A "development round" would have to produce certain minimum results, which could include:

- *On agriculture:* a dramatic reduction in the massive export subsidies provided by developed countries, with a programme for their total elimination; a significant increase in tariff quotas, combined with improvements in their administration; a framework for effectively negotiating reductions in domestic subsidies; greater assistance to developing countries to enable them to comply with sanitary and phytosanitary regulations; and translating the needs of the net food importing developing countries and the LDCs into meaningful provisions that extend beyond food aid. Additional provisions for inclusion in a "development box" treatment should take account of the needs of developing countries with large populations of primarily subsistence farmers employed in the agricultural sector, and those of small, vulnerable island economies.
- *On services:* improvement of the commitments relating to the movement of natural persons, including measures to reduce the scope and improve the transparency and predictability of economic needs tests and to promote the recognition of professional qualifications; addressing anti-competitive practices where they particularly disadvantage developing countries, such as in the

tourism sector. This could be complemented by arrangements to make Article IV of GATS more operational, particularly its provisions on access to technology and information networks.

- *On implementation issues:* a "peace clause" to give developing countries more time to implement the obligations of key agreements; further interpretations of the MTAs to deal with aspects that frustrate developing countries' access to markets, most specifically in the agreements on anti-dumping, subsidies, and countervailing measures; acceleration of the phase-out of textile quotas; and conversion into binding obligations of the best-endeavour provisions to provide special and differential treatment.

- *On TRIPS:* the creation of confidence among all members by finding ways effectively to promote the transfer of technology and to provide financial and other incentives to enhance the flexible implementation of the agreement.

- *On tariff negotiations:* a reduction in tariff peaks and tariff escalation, and a standstill on (or "grandfathering" of) GSP preferences to enable developing countries to retain their current conditions for access to markets.

- *On accession to the WTO:* facilitation through more streamlined arrangements, particularly for LDCs, and arrangements to ensure that all acceding developing countries, including LDCs, benefit from the relevant S&D provisions of the MTAs.

- *On measures in favour of LDCs:* conversion of existing measures into a single coherent system to provide duty-free and quota-free treatment to their exports, which would be "bound" in the sense that any imposition of such measures would be subject to the general disciplines of the WTO, such as the Agreement on Safeguards and the Understanding on Dispute Settlement.

In order to progress in this direction, the multilateral trading system will have to become less impermeable to the emerging consensus in the international community, as reflected in the ideas expressed at UNCTAD X and the prevailing spirit there. In my closing statement of 19 February 2000 to that conference, I stressed that it would be overly adventurous to announce that we now have a "Bangkok" consensus to replace the "Washington" consensus of the 1980s.[15] What we did achieve was to capture the dynamic currents arising from opposite ends and gradually draw them towards some common ground. I also expressed the view that the building of an international community should rest on the fundamental idea of generalized reciprocity. However, the reciprocity of international economic relations must be real. It cannot be merely conventional; it cannot be founded on only a nominal equality of countries that is belied in all the practices of negotiation, decision-making, and dispute settlement. Precisely because, thus far, global integration has affected only a dozen developing countries, the economic world is still divided. In such a world, real reciprocity means taking account of the underlying asymmetry of economic structures. Real reciprocity has still to be constructed.

Closing the "legitimacy gap" will require serious efforts to build real reciprocity and create the conditions for a new "development round." These are important components of renewed impetus and commitment to the multilateral trading system.

Notes

1. UNCTAD, tenth session, Bangkok, 12–19 February 2000, *Plan of Action,* Doc. TD/386; online at http://www.unctad-10.ch/pdfs/ux_td386.en.pdf.

2. Reproduced in UNCTAD, *A Positive Agenda for Developing Countries: Issues for Future Trade Negotiations,* UNCTAD/ITCD/TSB/10, Geneva and New York, 2000.

3. See Rubens Ricupero, "Los países en desarrollo y la Ronda Uruguay: desencuentros de un amor no correspondido?" in Patricio Leiva, ed., *La Ronda Uruguay y el Desarrollo de América Latina,* Santiago, Chile: Clepi, 1994.

4. Rubens Ricupero, "Integration of Developing Countries into the Multilateral Trading System," in J. Bhagwati and M. Hirsch, eds., *The Uruguay Round and Beyond: Essays in Honour of Arthur Dunkel,* Berlin: Springer, 1998.

5. UNCTAD X, *Plan of Action.*

6. Roman Greenberg, "The Pacific Island States and the WTO: Towards a Post-Seattle Agenda for the Small, Vulnerable States," Suva, 2000 (mimeo).

7. Joseph Stiglitz, "The Trading System at the Millennium," in Roger B. Porter and Pierre Sauvé, eds., *The WTO and the Future of the Multilateral Trading System,* Cambridge, MA: Harvard University Press, 2000, pp. 38–39.

8. Robert O. Keohane and Joseph S. Nye, Jrs, "The Club Model of Multilateral Cooperation and the World Trade Organization: Problems of Democratic Legitimacy," paper presented to a conference entitled "Efficiency, Equity

and Legitimacy: The Multilateral Trading System at the Millennium," 1–2 June 2000, Cambridge, MA.

9. UNCTAD, *A Positive Agenda for Developing Countries.*

10. See UNCTAD/TDR/14 (Supplement), Geneva, August 1994, p. 202. See also UNCTAD, *The TRIPS Agreement and Developing Countries* (commissioned by the World Intellectual Property Organization), UNCTAD/ITE/1, 1 March 1997.

11. J. M. Finger and P. Schuler, "Implementation of the Uruguay Round Commitments: The Development Challenge," paper presented to the Conference on the WTO Negotiations, Geneva, September 1999.

12. Jeffrey D. Sachs, "A New Framework for Globalization," paper presented to a conference entitled "Efficiency, Equity and Legitimacy: The Multilateral Trading System at the Millennium," 1–2 June 2000, Cambridge, MA.

13. See Carlos Correa, "Technology Transfer in the WTO Agreements," in UNCTAD, *A Positive Agenda for Developing Countries.*

14. Statement by Renato Ruggiero at the Trade and Development Board of UNCTAD, 8 October 1996.

15. Closing Statement by Rubens Ricupero, Secretary-General of UNCTAD, at UNCTAD X, Bangkok, 19 February 2000, "From the Washington Consensus to the Spirit of Bangkok: Is There a Bangkok Consensus or a Bangkok Convergence?"; online at http://www.unctad-10.ch/index_en.htm.

4

Making the development
round a reality

Clare Short
Secretary of State for International Development, UK

Developing countries continue to join the system of the World
Trade Organization (WTO) in large numbers. There were 57 in the
General Agreement on Tariffs and Trade (GATT) in 1979 at the end
of the Tokyo Round, 68 in 1988 at the start of the Uruguay Round,
and 98 in 1994 at the end of the Uruguay Round; today over 100 of
the total membership of 138 are developing countries. Some 30 or
so other developing and transition countries have applied for accession, including China.

Given this weight of numbers, developing countries have the
opportunity to press for multilateral trade rules that are fashioned to
their liking and to ensure that future trade negotiations in the WTO
yield agreements that are in the interest of development. Despite the
diversity of their circumstances and commercial interests, they have
it in their power to make common cause for their collective good.

This chapter looks first at why trade is important in development
and why trade policy needs to be high up in the order of decision
makers' priorities. Turning then to the multilateral trade system, it
looks at how developing countries have come to exercise an increasingly decisive influence in the WTO, and at some of the opportunities that this offers them as they adjust to the pace of change in the
global economy. The prospect of a new round of trade negotiations
makes decisions on how to seize these opportunities urgent. Some

parts of the agenda for a new round are not controversial; others are more so. The issue is where the advantages for development lie—whether in a narrow round or in a broader agenda.

Developing countries have drawn attention to the paradox of participation in WTO affairs—the fact that, though they need a rules-based system of trade, the rules are becoming too onerous for them to apply. Should this cause them to call a halt to the process of opening markets, agreeing new rules, and revising existing ones? Or are there better ways of dealing with the problem of implementation?

Trade in development

The broad sweep of history shows a close correlation between increased trade and increased prosperity. Profitable and income-raising exchange was practised some thousands of years before the theory of comparative advantage was propounded. The classical economists developed a rationale for open markets. Experience since their time among developing as well as developed countries bears out their intuition.

Developing countries in East and South-East Asia have steadily increased their trade over the past 40 years, sustaining high rates of economic growth and bringing dramatic declines in their rate of poverty. They could not have achieved this if they had not found growing markets for their exports and if they had not taken advantage of technological advances and foreign know-how available in an increasingly globalized world. Countries in sub-Saharan Africa, by contrast, have grown too slowly to raise per capita incomes or to reduce their rate of poverty. It is no coincidence that their trade has not prospered and that their share of world markets has fallen.

Developing countries have never been in any doubt about the importance to them of open markets for their exports. Since the 1960s they have pressed their case, with significant success, in the GATT and in the UN Conference on Trade and Development (UNCTAD) for lower tariffs, the elimination of non-tariff barriers and "voluntary" export restraints, and preferential market access.

They have been less unanimous about how far to reduce the protection of their own markets, and some have voiced concern about their marginalization in the global economy. There is a widely felt fear, in concerned public opinion in the North as well as in the South, that the growing integration of the world economy is increasing income disparities and is leaving the poor out of account.

These concerns have been examined closely by scholars on the basis of econometric assessment of the data. Some ambiguities remain, but the clear picture is that trade and economic growth are statistically closely associated and that income poverty is reduced when per capita incomes rise. Obviously policy in other areas also matters and will influence how much the poor benefit from growth. Other results show that trade policies of openness—including a competitive exchange rate and reasonably low tariffs—are more favourable to growth than are policies of protection. There is no support in the data for restrictive, protectionist trade policies by developing countries.

There are two caveats. The existence of open external markets and of open trade policies does not guarantee success in trade-based economic growth. Other factors are crucially important, such as human resources, investment, sound macroeconomic policy, and low corruption. The poor, too, have no guarantee of participation in the fruits of trade-based growth. Some are vulnerable to the changes brought by shifts in external market demand and by altered policies. No policy of trade reform is complete without an assessment of the costs of adjustment for the poor, and without anticipatory measures to facilitate the transition. The pace of reform should be such as to minimize the frictional costs without losing the gains from efficiency and growth.

These conclusions set the scene for today's debate. Developing countries are right to seek better access in foreign markets for their exports. They are right when they undertake judicious and well-planned reforms to open their markets and encourage investment. But to take full advantage of the opportunities that world markets offer them they also need to pay attention to the gamut of other factors—human resources, policies, laws, administration—that contribute to a successful enterprise economy.

The Uruguay Round—an unfinished agenda

Developing countries support the multilateral trade system and join the WTO because they are looking for better and more assured market access in other countries for their exports. Eight successive rounds of trade negotiations since the GATT was founded in 1948 have brought average developed country non-agricultural tariffs down from 40 per cent to a bound rate of below 4 per cent. The Uruguay Round began the process of reducing agricultural protection— though on this there remains a long road to travel. The Generalized System of Preferences, which developed countries put in place after Part IV of the GATT was agreed in 1965, and which provides unilateral preferences to most developing and all least developed countries, has been a further attraction for these countries to join the multilateral trade system.

The WTO system also offers a wide measure of protection from the uncertainties and unfair trade practices characteristic of barter and other forms of bilateral trade arrangement. Developing countries are not now obliged to part with their exports at below market price in order to buy imports, or to accept shoddy goods in return. The binding of tariffs by developed countries protects them from capricious tariff increases.

Until the Uruguay Round, however, developing countries, including those that had been long-standing members of the GATT, were not active participants in the construction of the multilateral trade system. Although they did commit themselves to apply its rules and they were content to take advantage of the disciplines adopted by the developed countries and of the step-by-step reduction of their tariffs, they also exercised little bargaining power in removing some major obstacles to the development of their trade. These included the quotas on their textile and clothing exports imposed outside the GATT under the Multifibre Arrangement, the high tariffs on textiles, clothing, leather goods, and fishery and agricultural produce, and the adverse consequences of the policies of agricultural protection and subsidy practised by many industrialized countries.

In the Uruguay Round some 70 developing countries participated actively for the first time, undertaking regulatory commitments and in some cases also committing themselves to market opening. They signed all the Uruguay Round agreements—on agriculture, tariffs, services, intellectual property, customs valuation, investment measures, etc. But they were not at the time fully prepared; they were reacting to an agenda set by the developed countries. In recognition of their "special and differential" status and of the implementation problems they were likely to face they were allowed to bind their tariffs higher than their applied tariffs, and they were given longish periods of time and promises of technical assistance to implement new agreements on rules. As it turns out this flexibility has been insufficient, and many countries have been unable to achieve full implementation by the deadlines set.

Developing countries have been disappointed with the Uruguay Round agreement on textiles and clothing. This provided for the reintegration into the rules of the WTO, over 10 years, of items covered by the Multifibre Arrangement. The agreement was backloaded, leaving over half the product categories to be brought back under WTO rules only in 2005. The earliest categories to be reintegrated were no longer subject to quota, so reintegration brought no tangible improvement in market access for the developing countries whose exports were (and continue to be) quota restricted. Even when quotas are finally abolished in 2005, textile and clothing imports into many developed countries will remain subject to high tariff barriers.

Another source of disappointment had been agriculture, especially for those countries with a comparative advantage in livestock, dairy, sugar, cereals, and temperate fruit and vegetables. The Uruguay Round covered agriculture for the first time in a trade round. It made progress in requiring that quotas be converted into (often very high) tariffs, in removing subsidies directly related to production, and in requiring some reduction in the overall level of agricultural supports including export subsidies. But the baseline set for calculating subsidy cuts was too high, given a fortuitous subsequent rise in market prices, so that the Agreement on Agriculture has in practice impinged little on policy. Developed countries, particularly the European Union and Japan, continue to make their markets inaccessible to competing imports and to subsidize their exports.

The regulatory reforms in the Uruguay Round have not helped the developing countries as much as they had hoped. There were agreements on product standards—the Technical Barriers to Trade agreement and the Sanitary and Phytosanitary Measures agreement—which gave guidelines for the setting of new standards, restraining their potential use as discriminatory and protectionist devices against imports. In practice they have not prevented the proliferation in developed countries of new quality, and even process, standards and labelling requirements, especially for food products. These may be costly and difficult for developing countries to comply with. Developing countries also experience difficulties in complying with the requirement that they report on the standards that they enforce on their own imports.

All has not been negative for developing countries after the Uruguay Round, however. They benefit from the 40 per cent reduction in developed countries' average tariffs (from 6.5 per cent to 3.8 per cent). Simulation studies mostly show that developing countries stand to gain as much from the Round relative to their gross domestic product (GDP) as developed countries do. Only countries in sub-Saharan Africa that enjoyed preferential access to developed markets and lost some margin of preference came out of the Round (slightly) net losers. Nevertheless, enough problems have arisen and have been experienced sufficiently widely for developing countries to feel pervasive dissatisfaction about the outcome of the Round.

This leaves the developing countries with a choice of objectives. They could focus primarily on repairing the unsatisfactory features of the Uruguay Round, or they could broaden the agenda to reach for a new order in trade relations that will give them not only the static benefits of more open markets but also the dynamic advantages of more open trade resulting from efficiency-promoting competition and stronger investment incentives.

The meaning of a "development" round

A new round of trade negotiations has been a prospect, though not yet an agreed one, since the second WTO Ministerial Meeting in

Geneva in 1998. It seemed appropriate to start a new round in 2000 because the Uruguay Round agreements on agriculture and services mandated a resumption of negotiations on these two issues in this year. In addition, the implementation of other agreements such as TRIPS (Trade-Related Aspects of Intellectual Property Rights) and TRIMs (Trade-Related Investment Measures) were also scheduled for 2000. Experienced trade negotiators advise that progress is unlikely to be achieved, especially in agriculture, on a purely sectoral basis in isolation from negotiations on the whole range of WTO issues. Hence the momentum that was building prior to the WTO's third Ministerial Conference in Seattle in November–December 1999 for a new trade round. The momentum has slackened since the débâcle of Seattle, but WTO members still expect a new round to begin in the near future, if not in 2000 perhaps after the Fourth Ministerial, which may occur in 2001.

Is it worth going to the trouble of a new round of complex negotiations at this time? The answer for development is an emphatic yes, because of the unfinished business of the Uruguay Round, and because of the significant benefits that developing countries can draw from the wider opening of markets and from the clarification and development of trade rules and the confidence that their adoption of these rules will inspire in investors, both local and foreign.

Wider market opening

First, as regards market opening, developing countries stand to gain substantially from a vigorous attack on agricultural protection in the North, from another decisive reduction of non-agricultural tariffs in the North, and from the further opening of their own markets to imports of goods and services from all countries, including other countries in the South.[1]

The lion's share of benefits from agricultural trade liberalization goes, admittedly, to the consumers in the North who will pay lower prices when cheaper imported supplies become available. Efficient exporters of agricultural produce at present subject to protection will, of course, benefit from wider external markets and perhaps higher prices. These include developing countries in the Cairns

Group of agricultural exporting countries such as Brazil, Argentina, Chile, South Africa, and Thailand. Vietnam should find bigger and more lucrative markets for its rice exports. African countries should find better markets for their cotton and groundnut exports to the protected US market and for their fruit and vegetable exports to the European Union, which now charges seasonally high tariffs.

To achieve their goals, developing countries will want to press for action on the three aspects of agricultural protection on which commitments were made in the Uruguay Round: market access, domestic supports, and export subsidies. They will particularly want to see that the high rates of duty now levied, following the tarification of quotas, are brought down, that there are tighter restraints on domestic subsidies, and that exports subsidies are made actionable under normal WTO rules.

In regard to non-agricultural tariffs, the advantages of further reduction are heavily weighted in favour of developing countries. Developed countries now have on average very low rates of protection, but they persist with high protection on certain items of particular interest to developing countries. In a new round, developing countries will have the opportunity to press the case for a significant reduction of the "peak" tariffs on their exports of textiles, clothing, leather goods, and fish.

A recent calculation shows that some 75 per cent of the income benefits of an across-the-board reduction in tariffs on manufactures would accrue to developing countries, with the major beneficiaries being in South and South-East Asia.[2] However, to achieve this, developing countries would have to participate in the cut in tariffs because some 40 per cent of their exports of manufactures already go to other developing countries. Many developing countries have reduced their tariffs considerably, usually autonomously of their WTO commitments. But their average tariffs are still high—13 per cent overall, compared with the less than 1 per cent that developed countries charge on imports from other developed countries. In some countries the average is much higher than this. In India it is still as much as 27 per cent. These barriers are an impediment to the growth of South–South trade, as well as being a hindrance to investment and innovation in the export-oriented sectors of the countries that erect them.

Opening markets to trade in services has the potential for a very high pay-off for developing countries because of the vital importance to their overall economic performance of their transport, communications, commercial, and financial sectors. They pay a high price for inefficiencies in these sectors, which can be drastically reduced by opening them to competition, including competition from foreign service providers. Where the market for telecommunications has been opened, tariffs have fallen steeply.

Liberalizing trade in services, however, often has to go hand in hand with an up-dating of domestic regulations for consumer protection, government procurement, and the promotion of competition. This is the main reason why there have been so few commitments by developing countries under the General Agreement on Trade in Services (GATS). It is in the interest of developing countries to prepare constructive offers to open those of their service sectors where they have managed to improve their regulatory frameworks.

There is still no agreement in the WTO on air transport and maritime services. The cost of transport to and from developing countries remains excessive, as it has been for a long time. Countries are reluctant to relinquish the monopolies of their domestic flag carriers, but they do so at great cost to their importers and exporters and to travellers. Countries such as Chile which have opened their maritime transport to competition have achieved significant cuts in their freight rates, and thus in their terms of trade. WTO members should make the effort to reach agreement on air and sea services in the new round.

Stronger regulations

Alongside market opening, developing countries have objectives on trade rules, for instance on the use of anti-dumping measures, on standards, and on trade facilitation.

Developing countries are concerned to see that anti-dumping and countervailing duties are not used unfairly against them—as has been the case recently when world prices for steel have been low and steel exporters have had to drop their prices to maintain their sales.

There are rules limiting the use of these defence instruments to cases where damage is caused to domestic industry that is attributable to competition from dumped or subsidized imports. These rules are interpreted too liberally, and duties levied too readily and maintained for too long. The result is that suppliers against whom duties are applied lose the confidence of their customers, and hard-earned market share is lost. Developing countries are not the only victims, but they are particularly affected as they seek to establish their credibility in foreign markets. They have an interest in the strict interpretation of the rules and a plugging of the loopholes.

On standards, developing countries have the dual objective of achieving greater transparency and conformity to internationally agreed norms on the part of developed countries while at the same time preserving the flexibility that they enjoy on their own reporting obligations. They will want to ensure that the authorities responsible for health, safety, and environmental protection in their principal markets are restrained in applying new product regulations and in taking precautionary action and principled in devising new standards. Standards should be both necessary and non-discriminatory in their effect on suppliers in developing countries.

Developing countries also have a strong interest in supporting new rules on the facilitation of trade—rules that reduce the bureaucracy and delay associated with customs clearance, that streamline procedures, and that standardize and simplify paperwork. The cost of compliance with customs procedures in foreign markets is relatively higher for their exporters than it is for exporters in developed countries for reasons of scale. Conversely, the dysfunctions of developing countries' own customs may have profoundly negative spillover effects in terms of reputation and business confidence.

A related concern is rules of origin. Developing country exporters benefit from tariff preferences accorded to them by developed countries under the Generalized System of Preferences and various bilateral preferential arangements. But only exports satisfying prescribed rules of origin can take advantage of these preferences. These rules vary from country to country and from arrangement to arrangement, and are sufficiently complex as to discourage the full use of concessional tariffs. Developing countries have a strong collective interest in pressing for greater uniformity, simplicity, and user-friendliness in rules of origin.

New agenda items

There has been great debate about the need for and timeliness of reaching agreement in the WTO about frameworks of rules governing investment, competition, and government procurement—the so-called "new agenda" introduced into the WTO's work programme at the first Ministerial Conference in Singapore in 1996.

The opponents of WTO agreements on these issues say that this will impair developing countries' sovereignty, place them at the mercy of rapacious multilateral corporations, and prevent developing countries from giving legitimate preference to indigenous suppliers through the exercise of discretionary powers over private investment decisions and in government purchasing. In reality there is a strong developmental case for multilateral agreement to make progress on these issues, even though the road to the universal application of tightly defined disciplines is bound to be long.

There is no rational case for opposing foreign direct investment in developing countries. There is overwhelming evidence that it fosters economic growth through the capital, technology, know-how, and access to markets that it brings. The great majority of developing countries welcome inward investment and seek to encourage more of it, for example by offering fiscal incentives. In some countries, foreign investment represents a high proportion of all private investment.

WTO members committed themselves in the GATS to respect the disciplines of transparency, non-discrimination and national treatment, market access, and judicial protection in respect of foreign direct investment in those service sectors on which they made offers. Service sectors account for some 40 per cent of foreign direct investment in developing countries. These countries have also committed themselves in varying degrees to the same disciplines in bilateral investment treaties—of which there are now some 1,700. These commitments help to reinforce the often hesitant confidence of investors, and they point the way to domestic legal and regulatory reforms needed to foster enterprise.

The case made by some developing countries against including investment in the new round is predicated on the thought that any agreement will be instantly binding and universally applicable, and will represent too profound a shock to current practice. However, their experience of the GATS belies this. It is possible to have a "bottom–up" style of agreement in which the parties have a wide latitude in deciding the sectors, pace, and depth of their commitments. It is also necessary to have a flexible agreement, because all countries in the world, and not just the developing countries, want to avoid commitment in some sectors. The challenge is to make a flexible agreement sufficiently strong to achieve credibility in the eyes of investors.

The objectors to rules on inward investment argue that, once foreign investors (which by definition are multinational) are established, they will become a law unto themselves, undermining the domestic social order, damaging the environment, and destroying domestic competitors. However, foreign investors are, and certainly should be, subject to domestic laws and regulation on the environment and conditions at work, just as they are subject to laws on companies, competition, and taxation. If these laws are not strong enough, they should be strengthened. It may be necessary to delay implementing multilateral disciplines on investment while this takes place. But this is no reason to deny the need for multilateral disciplines or continually to defer consideration of them.

The case for a multilateral framework on competition follows from the reality of increasing international investment and from the possibility that some multinational investors may abuse their market position yet be too large for individual developing countries to regulate without outside assistance. The principle of cooperation between national competition authorities has existed for many years, but cooperation in practice has been very limited. One reason for this is that such cooperation involves the exchange of commercially confidential information, which can be passed only to other parties that are thoroughly trusted. A multilateral agreement on principles is a valuable building block in constructing this confidence. It is also a spur to national competition authorities to improve their practices to the point at which other authorities agree readily to cooperate with them. It is an incentive to building a public institution that is an essential part of an efficient enterprise economy.

Efficient government procurement is also vital in an efficient and competitive economy. Wasteful public expenditure financed by excessive taxation or mounting public debt is demonstrably detrimental to development. Public expenditure on goods and non-labour services accounts for a significant share of final demand, typically ranging from 5 per cent to 15 per cent of GDP. The opening of markets to import competition is seriously incomplete if this market is reserved for protected domestic suppliers. It is in the interest of all, except rent-seeking suppliers and corrupt officials, to move to open and competitive procurement practices. The practical issue is one of pace and sequence. A rather complex plurilateral agreement on procurement already exists among some 40 countries. A flexible multilateral agreement could provide for flexible convergence on best practice by all WTO members.

Implementation: The paradox of a rules-based system

The rules-based, multilateral system of trade poses a serious conundrum to its developing country participants, one that is likely to deepen as the trade system extends to new areas and becomes more complex. The conundrum is how developing countries—some with limited administrative resources—are to implement trade rules and fulfil their WTO commitments.

The problem has arisen since the trade system started to tackle non-tariff barriers to trade and specifically regulatory and administrative barriers. As tariffs have been reduced, these barriers have become increasingly important. They are inherently less transparent than tariffs, so to reduce them countries are asked to codify and communicate their regulations and then to agree to timetables for eliminating practices inconsistent with WTO principles. Examples of this are:

- the Uruguay Round Agreement on Trade-Related Investment Measures (TRIMs), which proscribed certain practices such as requiring foreign investors to use domestic inputs in preference to imported ones or to export a minimum percentage of their output, because they violate the principle of national treatment in Article III of the GATT;

- the Agreement on Technical Barriers to Trade (TBT), which requires notification of domestically applied product standards;
- the Agreement on Trade-Related Aspects of Intellectual Property Rights (TRIPS), which requires WTO members to implement minimum standards of intellectual property protection, if necessary through new legislation;
- the Uruguay Round Agreement on Agriculture, which prescribes upper limits on the subsidies that governments can pay to their farm sectors; and
- the Customs Valuation Agreement, which requires WTO members to levy duties on the basis of the value of goods declared in bills of lading, thereby imposing on them the burden of verifying the accuracy of these values.

These agreements, unlike the Uruguay Round commitments on tariffs, require developing countries to take prescribed action by prescribed deadlines. Their deadlines have been more extended than those for developed countries, but, in the event, some countries have been unable to comply fully. The deadline for developing country compliance with the TRIPS and TRIMs agreements passed on 1 January 2000, leaving a number of countries in technical breach. Though it is hard to generalize, the agreements may also be costly to implement, especially for small poor countries. They may need to create new institutions or reform existing ones, to hire and train staff, and to upgrade their information technology. With the exception of intellectual property protection, where fees for filing patents may more than offset the cost of running a patent office, implementing the Uruguay Round increases budgetary outlays without offsetting receipts. Not surprisingly, developing countries have not complied in many areas.

Implementation and adjustment difficulties were anticipated in the Uruguay Round and were addressed by allowing developing countries (and *a fortiori* the least developed) longer deadlines for implementation and, in certain cases, exemptions. These elements of flexibility were provided for all countries in a class, irrespective of their particular circumstances. They were a new facet of the "special and differential" treatment accorded to developing countries first introduced into the GATT in the 1950s and then extended in the 1960s to cover also non-reciprocal preferential market access.

The question now facing the WTO is how to revise the extended deadline approach to implementation now that its deadlines have been passed. Should new extended deadlines be set for all countries, or should there be tailor-made implementation paths for each country, or should countries failing to implement now be exposed to dispute settlement action?

None of these options is wholly attractive. An across-the-board extension of timetables for all developing countries offers a further incentive for delay, strengthens the case of those who argue that there should be no new trade round because implementing the last one was too difficult, and could ultimately create a two-tier WTO. The multilateral trade system cannot be stable in the long run if many of its members, accounting for a quarter of world trade, feel unable to apply the rules. Exposing developing countries to trade disputes and possible sanctions at this juncture would be even more destructive to the system, and would be more immediately and seriously harmful to developing country economies.

The best solution to the present conundrum is for countries in difficulty to agree to tailored road maps in the WTO for completing their implementation. While countries are exercising their best endeavours to complete the course they should be immune from dispute action. This is the approach adopted by the Implementation Review Mechanism created by the WTO General Council in June 2000. It may be laborious because of the large number of individual implementation plans to be devised; and it will call for more effective trade-related assistance than has been provided to date.

A new trade round will provide the opportunity to revisit those WTO rules that cause the most implementation difficulty. When the rules come to be recast and when new rules are made in the new round they should be accompanied with specific commitments of assistance for those members requiring it. In past trade rounds there have been non-binding assurances that assistance would be provided. In the event this has not been adequate. In future, countries needing support could specify their needs, and their implementation of future agreements could proceed at a pace set by the receipt of specified assistance.

Capacity-building for trade

To find the way out of the conundrum—that the rules-based system of trade, which is in the interests of developing countries, also creates what many countries find are unmanageable implementation problems—all the signposts point in the direction of more and better trade-related assistance.

There is already a good deal of trade-related assistance on offer, both multilateral and bilateral. Many well-intentioned initiatives have been launched, and many donor institutions are involved. Assistance is currently being provided by the WTO itself to enable countries to know the rules and their rights and obligations and (for aspirant members) to prepare themselves for accession. There are a number of initiatives, including those of the Commonwealth and the South Foundation, to give guidance to groups of countries in defining their negotiating positions on issues. The World Bank and UNCTAD have numerous projects, both thematic and in-country, to unpack trade policy issues, to examine their implications, and to assist with implementing WTO disciplines and other reforms. A great many donors, bilateral and multilateral, are involved with supporting trade development, i.e. the ability of producers in developing countries to produce for export and to overcome problems in entering foreign markets. Many are also involved with the building of the national institutions, such as efficient customs services, institutes of trade policy research, and standards inspectorates, that they need in order to prosper in trade. Some countries, including the United Kingdom, both support the initiatives of established multilateral agencies and pursue awareness-raising, training, and institutional capacity-building initiatives of their own.

It is a symptom of the state of trade-related assistance, however, that there is no clear picture of the total effort of all agencies or of the resources devoted to each type of activity. There are currently initiatives to catalogue donors' activities, though these remain partial. There is general agreement that there should be greater coherence and coordination, but in practice this has proved difficult to achieve. The Integrated Framework, an initiative launched in 1997 following a decision at the first WTO Ministerial Meeting the previous year in Singapore, illustrates the point. The intention was to coordinate the trade-related support activities of six multilateral agencies in the least developed countries to help them participate more fully and effectively in the trade system. Their interventions were to be demand led and based on needs assessments. An evaluation of the Integrated Framework published in July 2000 expresses disappointment at its limited achievements and shows how difficult it can be to implement sustained, effective, and coordinated programmes of assistance on the ground.

Useful lessons have, however, been learned from experience. Some of these are drawn in the evaluation of the Integrated Framework. Other have been identified in the Development Assistance Committee of the Organisation for Economic Co-operation and Development, which has looked at best practice in trade-related assistance. The key lessons are:

- The country receiving assistance must be proactive in knowing its objectives, formulating its needs and requirements, and putting assistance received to early practical effect. Some supply-driven initiatives such as UNCTAD's Joint Integrated Technical Assistance Program (JITAP) have received inadequate attention on the part of some recipients and, where this has happened, have had little effect.
- Assistance is best provided as a contribution to implementing wider, high-profile programmes of reform that have strong political backing. If trade issues are perceived as being of low priority, the effect of capacity-building support may be ephemeral.
- Significant programmes of trade-related capacity-building support should be mainstreamed into country cooperation strategies, and should be the subject of high-level dialogue about objectives, means, and performance assessment as other priority elements in

country programmes. Donor agencies should not mount major programmes outside this framework.

- There should be close coordination on the ground between assistance-providing agencies to ensure consistency between their activities, to ensure that they adopt a common approach to the development of local institutions, and to simplify the interface with donors for recipient governments.
- There should be a concerted effort by donors to raise the profile of trade-related assistance—to explain what it is, what is on offer and from what source, and in what circumstances, and in what manner, developing countries might seek assistance.
- There should be a small number of referral agencies—recognized and well-informed sources of guidance and initial advice for developing countries about how their needs may best be formulated and to what donors they might turn for the capacity-building support that they require.

How might trade-related assistance work in practice to help with problems encountered in implementing WTO rules? The European Union has proposed a "milestone" approach to tailoring assistance to the differing needs of each country. Based on case-by-case assessments of implementation problems and requirements and of feasible timetables, this would give those countries requiring it an entitlement to the assistance they need to complete implementation. Timetables for implementation would no longer be uniform for all developing countries and based on guesswork about the time required, but would be adapted to circumstance. This proposal is to be piloted in countries wishing for assistance in implementing the Agreement on Customs Valuation.

The purposes of the milestone approach are to reinterpret special and differential treatment in a positive light and to create a WTO in which all countries eventually become rule-abiding members. The special and differential status of developing countries would be not a pretext for opting out, but rather the passport to customized programmes of support. A practical difficulty is that, if applied for on a large scale, it would become hugely complicated to administer and monitor, leading to delays and uncertainty about the status of countries' commitments. If each of 100 developing countries opted for assisted implementation programmes for each of five or six WTO agreements, there would be 500 or 600 such programmes to undertake. It would be necessary to focus the closest attention on the countries with the greatest need.

Technical solutions may be difficult to find, but the principle is clear enough. New WTO rules must be feasible for developing countries to implement and must in due course be implemented by all, subject to agreed flexibilities. Where assistance is required, this must be provided as part of the agreed package. Commitments to technical assistance in the new round should thus become specific and binding, unlike those in the Uruguay Round and in previous agreements where they were simply declarations of best endeavours.

However, even with this important change, the paradox of the rules-based system would remain. Small and poor countries would continue to experience unmanageable implementation problems, and would continuously run the risk of incurring dispute settlement action against them. Other, structural, solutions need to be considered. Working through regional bodies to implement WTO agreements is one such solution.

Regional cooperation in multilateral trade

Small and poor countries need to find economies of scale in order to be able to participate fully and effectively in the work of the WTO and to apply its rules. On their own they have the greatest difficulty in maintaining a sufficient representation in Geneva to cover the day-to-day meetings in the WTO and to participate effectively in complex negotiations on new rules. In their capitals, ministries often have insufficient resources to assess and decide policy issues and to devise clear instructions.

Small countries' problems go wider than this. Liberalizing trade in services often calls for regulatory change and mutual recognition of qualifications and standards. As seen already, properly implementing WTO agreements on technical barriers to trade and sanitary and phytosanitary measures, on customs valuation, and on trade-related intellectual property rights calls for sophisticated capacity.

There is considerable scope for countries to pool their resources and to establish common services to fulfil these functions. They can thereby achieve major economies of scale and an effective international presence. Examples of this are not hard to find. The practice of regional consultation and coordination between ambassadors in Geneva is already well established, for example among African and ASEAN countries. Countries in the Caribbean have a Regional Negotiating Machinery which performs major trade policy functions on their behalf. It does not replace national governments in the WTO but, using pooled expertise, it does vital prior staff work and is responsible for much routine trade diplomacy work.

Countries in customs unions are able to share the back-up information and data bases enabling them to implement the Customs Valuation Agreement. Countries that can agree on common codes of product standards can pool their reporting and inspectorate functions and make common cause in future trade negotiations. Regional cooperation is also practised in the protection of intellectual property rights—as in francophone Africa.

Where practical and politically feasible, regional cooperation on WTO matters should be vigorously pursued, and just as vigorously supported by donor agencies. It would be a great shame if groups of developing countries were unable to contribute properly and to pursue their interests in the next trade round because they have not deployed their resources collectively. It is for them to decide how to do this, but the international community should stand behind them when they have decided.

Conclusion: Preparing for a development round

There can be little doubt that the multilateral system of trade plays to the advantage of developing countries, opening markets and giving them assurance about the rules of the game and access to the WTO system of dispute settlement. It is also clear that the system is imperfect, and that developing countries stand to gain substantially from new agreements which are within their grasp to open markets further and to tighten regulations. New agreements could also powerfully serve their interest by sending positive signals to international investors and by linking with their agendas of domestic reform to improve the environment for enterprise and competitiveness.

One condition for achieving these ends in the near term is the start of a new round of trade negotiations in the WTO. Without a new round, significant progress is unlikely, even in agriculture and services on which the processes of negotiation have already started as mandated in Uruguay Round agreements. A second condition is that developing countries have the capacity to define their objectives and to pursue them with vigour in negotiations, pooling their resources if need be to achieve more effect. Thirdly, there has to be a desire on all sides for a successful outcome—one that will serve the multifaceted interests of the developing country majority in the WTO. The parties cannot approach the round with narrowly national agendas. A broad agenda, including new agenda items, that enables all countries to make gains is the most likely to achieve agreement. Finally, there have to be processes of preparation and confidence-building—to avoid another fiasco like Seattle. This event undermined the confidence of many members in WTO practices. Much has been done to restore confidence in decision-making processes and to banish feelings of exclusion. More needs to be done, and new solutions found, particularly in the connected fields of implementation and capacity-building support. With good will and understanding on all sides, solutions can be found and a basis of consensus established from which to take a new step forward towards a developmental order of world trade.

Notes

1. The static gains to GDP adjusted for terms of trade from a 50 per cent reduction in protection applied in agriculture, industrial products, and services are calculated to amount to 1.4 per cent for the world as a whole but to as much as 10.4 per cent for ASEAN countries, 4.9 per cent for Brazil, 4.4 per cent for India, and 6.3 per cent for the rest of Latin America and the Caribbean

(N. Nagarajan, "The Millennium Round: An Economic Appraisal," European Commission Economic Paper No. 139, November 1999).

2. W. Martin and T. Hertel, "Developing Country Interest in Liberalising Manufacturers' Trade," paper presented to the WTO/World Bank Conference on Developing Countries in the Millennium Round, Geneva, September 1999.

5

Challenges facing the WTO and policies to address global governance

Peter Sutherland, John Sewell, and David Weiner
Chairman, Goldman Sachs International;
President, Overseas Development Council;
Senior Fellow, Overseas Development Council

Origins of the WTO's new challenges

The multilateral trading system, with the World Trade Organization (WTO) at its centre, is the most important tool of global economic management and development we possess. Its record—under the old General Agreement on Tariffs and Trade (GATT) as well as its successor, the WTO—has been remarkable. Over the past 50 years, it has created wealth in its industrialized members, brought poor nations from backward, rural economies to super-competitive commercial giants, and opened up prospects for today's poorest countries to advance.

Yet, although the institution has already shown itself to be a success, and it has much more to offer in the future, the WTO today is under strong attack. Much of this criticism is a reflection of a perception, on the one hand, that the WTO has not—and will not—resolve every problem facing the global economy and social development and, on the other, that the machine is out of gear, idling, and failing to tackle the new challenges presented by the process of globalization.

Many governments appear to believe that they, and the institution, are best left to digest what has already been achieved. That has

left other key constituencies displeased with the WTO's performance and led some to be openly hostile. Some developing countries,
which now comprise the overwhelming majority of the organization's members, claim it is inherently biased against their interests
and produces asymmetrical agreements. They are also disappointed
by the level of trade-related technical support they have received
from donor countries and other multilateral institutions in order to
cope with the pressures of implementing WTO commitments.
Lacking either the courage of their own convictions or confidence in
their ability to prevail over domestic opposition, the chief financial
backers of the WTO have failed to provide adequate funding for a
WTO Secretariat (by far the smallest of all the major multilateral
institutions) that is already overburdened by technical assistance
demands as well as by dispute settlement cases and new accessions.

Industrial governments, sometimes acting as proxies for powerful
civil society interests, are frustrated by the stubbornness of developing
countries in opposing new measures or discussions on labour standards, environmental standards, and the transparency of WTO operations. Furthermore, there are growing indications that parts of the
business community are growing impatient with the slow pace of
WTO decision-making and are dissatisfied with negotiating results
that appear to them to be least-common-denominator solutions.

The organization is subject to a nearly unmanageable array of conflicting pressures. Some civil society groups are lobbying for its powers and mandate to be *expanded.* They want trade sanctions to be used
to enforce agreements on labour, environmental, or other standards.
Other civil society groups are pushing in the opposite direction.
They want the WTO's authority to be pared back in ways that they
believe will strengthen existing social and environmental standards
or protections.

At the same time, the WTO is suffering from an alarming lack of
leadership on the part of most of its largest members. The major
industrial countries, whose unity has traditionally been essential to
progress on substantive issues or institutional reforms, are divided.
These same countries have done an extremely poor job of making a
public case for more open trade and the continuation of economic
liberalization upon which much of their current wealth is based.

Several of them also have failed to provide adequate income and training support for those workers, primarily the lower skilled, who have been adversely affected by trade liberalization. The follow-up to the UK Labour Party's electoral motto "Education, Education, Education" can be summarized in most instances as far too little, far too late. As a result, public support for open trade has been further undermined.

The breakdown of the Seattle Ministerial Meeting was an indication of the disturbing state of affairs in the trading system. Not that the picture is wholly black. Important work is taking place now in Geneva on the two key sectors—agriculture and services—designated for further work at the end of the Uruguay Round. This work is progressing well, if quietly, and has the potential to provide a significant boost to global trade expansion. But the conclusion of these negotiations, in some eyes at least, is wholly dependent on the launching of a broader trade round. And that, as Seattle demonstrated only too vividly, is not going to be easy.

In seeking to drive the process of trade reform further forward, the WTO faces one set of problems that relate to national politics and should be transitory, and another that could be called structural. Here we focus on the structural issues. Solutions to some of the WTO's problems can be envisioned, and several promising ones have recently been proposed. But many of the more serious challenges the WTO faces are the consequence of much broader trends and developments. These challenges can ultimately be addressed only in the course of renovating the current system of global economic governance, of which the WTO is but a part. The WTO and the multilateral trade system it oversees are in trouble, in other words, less because of their own flaws than because of more fundamental failures of global economic leadership.

This chapter sets reform and strengthening of the WTO in the context of the emerging debate over global governance and proposes reforms in WTO structure and decision-making that respond to several of the organization's key problems. The final section shifts to the challenges of global governance, particularly international economic governance. It argues that the WTO's mandate must be adjusted simultaneously with the mandates of other international economic institutions, and that the issue of the coherence of the current multilateral system of institutions needs to be addressed in a systematic way at the highest political level.

Suffering from success

This is not the place to recite the history of post-war trade negotiations. Nor must one grasp all of that history to understand how the WTO arrived at its current predicament. It is important to underscore, however, that the WTO, in many ways, has been a victim of its own success.

The WTO and its predecessor, the GATT, have had remarkable success, particularly in bringing down traditional tariff and non-tariff barriers to trade during the eight post-war global trade rounds. In the five decades following the creation of the GATT, average tariff levels on manufactures in the industrial countries declined from around 40 per cent to less than 4 per cent. The value of world merchandise trade increased 18-fold during that same period, an average annual increase of 6 per cent, or three times the average annual growth rate of per capita GDP.[1]

The dismantling of border barriers during successive post-war trade rounds ultimately brought trade negotiators face-to-face with a variety of domestic regulatory, institutional, and structural influences on trade flows. Convinced that many of these trade-related factors impede the free flow of goods and services, trade negotiators began to tackle some of them in the Uruguay Round. Because they are closely linked to domestic business practices, cultural preferences, and political arrangements (some with deep historical roots), negotiations on these matters have tended to be more sensitive and complex than negotiations on traditional tariff and non-tariff barriers. Finally, the increasing ambition of multilateral trade negotiations in areas that had previously been regarded as the prerogatives of domestic policy-making has prompted a correspondingly wider range of civil society stakeholders to take an interest in what the WTO does.

The impressive record of the GATT and WTO in reducing trade barriers has profoundly influenced the calculations of developing country governments, trade negotiators, and civil society institutions. The drawing power of the GATT and WTO for developing and transitional economies is underscored by the existence of a 30-country accession queue throughout the 1990s. More than 100 of the WTO's 139 current members are developing countries. Moreover, as many observers have pointed out, the performance of the WTO's dispute settlement mechanism has attracted the attention of a wide range of social and political activists, who wish to see the WTO's enforcement authority put in the service of their favoured causes.

But the achievements of the GATT and WTO only partly explain what is happening to the WTO today. Three trends, each of which we have just briefly touched upon, go a significant way toward explaining the challenges now facing the WTO and the multilateral trading system: (1) the increasing participation of developing countries in the GATT and the WTO; (2) the growing attention of multilateral trade negotiators to barriers to trade *behind* national borders; and (3) the increasing influence both over the multilateral trade agenda and over the trade policies of key industrial countries of networks of civil society groups.

Developing countries and the WTO

If the key international economic story of the first two post-war decades was the astonishing transformation of Western Europe and Japan from devastated recipients of reconstruction aid into first-rank industrial powers and competitors of the United States, the story of the three succeeding decades has been the equally remarkable emergence of developing nations as significant players in the global economy. One measure of this trend is the share of developing nations in world exports of manufactures, which increased from 4 per cent to more than 24 per cent between 1963 and 1997.[2] Another measure is the massive increase since the 1980s in investment in developing countries by industrial country firms and portfolio investors, and increasingly by investors from emerging market countries. The ratio of the stock of foreign direct investment to GDP nearly tripled for developing countries, from 5.9 per cent to 16.6 per cent, between

1980 and 1997.[3] Aggressively seizing export and investment opportunities created by the expanding world economy, a number of poor
nations turned themselves into major industrial powers in just three
decades.

These aggregate figures hide a tremendous diversity in the developing world, however. It is now necessary to distinguish clearly
between the emerging economies and the middle-income developing countries, on the one hand, and the poorer countries, including
those classified as least developed by the United Nations. The latter
have their own unique set of concerns about the trade system and the
WTO, motivated by the fact that they are in effect isolated from the
global economy. Contrary to the overall developing country trend,
the share of international commerce of the world's four dozen poorest countries, whose population exceeds 1 billion, is shrinking. Since
1980, the exports of least developed countries (LDCs) have grown
only one-fourth as fast as the developing country average.[4] The participation of the poorest nations in world commerce is limited in
scope as well as in depth. Unprocessed raw materials account for 75
per cent of their exports. Most generate more than 70 per cent of
their export earnings from their three top exports.[5] This dependence
on a narrow range of exports makes poor countries more vulnerable
to external shocks, and primary commodities have lost half their
value relative to other products over the past two decades.

The growing stake of developing countries in the world economy has both strengthened their claim to a role in its management
and increased their confidence in asserting that claim. Historically,
the poorest developing countries have been slow to assert themselves in the GATT and the WTO. In both institutions every
member country formally enjoys an equal say in the development
of consensus decision-making—a feature that would appear to
offer less powerful countries some leverage to achieve their aims.
Until recently, the developing countries' strategy appears to have
been largely defensive. They have sought to ensure "special and
differential treatment" in trade agreements and a series of concessions and exceptions from certain internationally agreed disciplines
on the grounds they were at a lower level of development to other
WTO members.

The Seattle meeting of the WTO demonstrated that the politics of developing country participation in the WTO has changed. Although the media paid great attention to the protests in Seattle's streets, these were not the cause of the meeting's failure. Rather, it was the virtually total lack of consensus among the industrial countries, joined with the refusal of the developing countries to agree on the new round agenda and other issues, that led to the breakdown of the discussions. The unified front presented by developing countries was not a surprise to many close observers of the WTO: many of the concerns raised by developing nation delegations in Seattle had figured prominently in preparatory sessions for the Ministerial Meeting for more than a year prior to the event, and some have been staples of WTO discussions since the conclusion of the Uruguay Round. But the unprecedented unity of developing countries and their willingness to stand in the way of a consensus in favour of starting a new round were surprising to many Ministerial participants and observers.

Some developing countries in Seattle were also deeply dissatisfied by what they perceived as a selective, exclusionary system of decision-making in the WTO. The traditional so-called "Green Room" process, in which a group of up to 40 member countries, including many developing countries, tries to reach preliminary agreements on matters under negotiation, and then present them to the rest of the delegations, came in for sharp criticism in Seattle.

Ironically, in Seattle, WTO Director-General Mike Moore and US Trade Representative Charlene Barshefsky, the co-chairs of the Ministerial Meeting, made a concerted, good-faith effort to broaden the participation of delegations in the negotiations. They divided the Ministerial agenda into several sections, created working groups for each, and invited all delegations to participate in all the working groups. Their goal was to keep Green Rooms to a minimum. But developing country delegations, in particular, had difficulty covering all of the working groups, and as the Ministerial week proceeded and agreements remained elusive, the temptation to pull together smaller groups of countries for harder bargaining—Green Rooms, in other words—understandably grew. In communiqués released towards the end of the week, large groupings of African and Latin

American countries denounced what they described as the Ministerial's exclusive and non-democratic negotiating structure.

The governments of the so-called "Quad" countries (the United States, the European Union, Canada, and Japan) made considerable efforts in Seattle to build winning coalitions between themselves and like-minded developing nations. But the growing numbers of *active* developing countries had transformed not only the politics but the maths of bargaining in the WTO. Events in Seattle clearly suggest that the WTO is testing the limits of its consensus-based decision-making system, which would appear to be ideally suited for an organization of no more than several dozen *active* members.

Poorer developing countries have long complained that WTO discussions are dominated by a handful of powerful member countries. Many developing nations simply lack the Geneva-based staff and resources necessary to cover the WTO effectively; some have no representatives in Geneva at all. In addition to an extensive weekly schedule of formal meetings, WTO members come together in various groupings for a large number of informal gatherings, during which many of the organization's most important decisions are hammered out. A selection of influential developing countries are routinely invited to these meetings (e.g. Argentina, Brazil, Mexico, Egypt, India, South Africa, ASEAN members), but the majority do not participate. Even if they are aware that a meeting is taking place, some delegations argue, they are rarely invited to participate; even if they are invited, many lack the staff or expertise to participate effectively. According to some developing country representatives, they are frequently confronted with "take-it-or-leave-it" decisions which they had little role in shaping.

Before and during the Seattle Ministerial, developing countries also aggressively pressed concerns on the "implementation" of Uruguay Round agreements. They argued that industrial countries had failed to implement—in the spirit, if not the letter—some of their commitments faithfully, particularly in the crucial textile and agriculture sectors and in the anti-dumping agreement (with the United States singled out for special criticism). Dozens of countries also demanded additional time and technical assistance for their own implementation of the agreements on Trade-Related Aspects of

Intellectual Property Rights (TRIPS), Trade-Related Investment Measures (TRIMs), Sanitary and Phytosanitary Measures (SPS), and Customs Valuation. Many countries believe they should have been given "credit" for unilateral trade liberalization measures taken pursuant to structural adjustment and other economic reform programmes.

In order to avoid marginalization, the LDCs have sought two additional measures in recent years: technical assistance from the WTO and aid agencies that will enable them to participate more effectively in the WTO and in multilateral trade negotiations, and duty-free access to major export markets. Both matters were discussed at length prior to and during the Seattle Ministerial, and further negotiations have taken place since then. But a worthwhile package of technical assistance has yet to be approved by Quad countries, giving the poorer nations one more reason for being deeply disappointed in the WTO.

Reasonable people can disagree about the legitimacy of each of these developing country complaints about the WTO. Some of the criticisms are overstated, some are made for bargaining purposes, and developing countries can sometimes be faulted for failing to acknowledge the gains from the Uruguay Round and other trade liberalization initiatives. The important point here is to recognize that these concerns are sometimes strongly felt by developing countries, that developing countries have come to dominate the WTO numerically, and that they are increasingly willing to use their numbers to thwart the negotiating objectives of the WTO's more powerful members. The economic emergence of developing countries thus poses a significant—though, we would argue, healthy—challenge for the governance of the multilateral trading system.

The changing character of trade negotiations

The evolving character of multilateral trade negotiations poses the second major challenge confronting the WTO. Many observers have argued that the relatively "easy" work of multilateral trade liberalization had been completed by the end of the Tokyo Round in 1979. The Uruguay Round, together with many regional and bilateral liberalization initiatives, has since completed the elimination (in certain industrial sectors) or dramatically reduced most tariffs, quotas, and other border barriers to commerce. Outside the very high levels of protection maintained by industrial countries in sectors such as agriculture and textiles and the still generally high tariffs in many developing nations, the chief obstacles to increased international commerce and the rapidly expanding electronic delivery of goods and services are now said to lie elsewhere. The focus of attention is now domestic regulatory measures, business practices, structural impediments, competition policies, and other features of domestic economies whose purposes are often not directly related to the regulation of trade.

Two analysts have aptly described this change in the predominant focus of trade negotiations as a "paradigm shift."[6] This is not a theoretical proposition, however. A number of significant liberalization initiatives, and several more presently under discussion, have grappled with these new "trade-related" issues. Prominent examples include the Uruguay Round's agreements on services, TRIPS, TRIMs, and government procurement, as well as parts of the agricultural trade deal, the investment-related provisions of the North American Free Trade Agreement (NAFTA), and any number of the European Union's single market initiatives.

Not surprisingly, negotiations on these new paradigm issues have proven extraordinarily complex and contentious. The policies and practices targeted in these negotiations are often far less transparent than traditional border barriers. They sometimes have deep roots in national history, culture, government–business relationships, and institutions. As in most trade talks, trade ministries typically lead national delegations in these negotiations, and trade ministers are jealous of their turf, but expertise and authority over new paradigm issues often reside in other ministries and with other officials, with different agendas.

It is often the case with the new issues that a wide variety of domestic constituencies—constituencies with little or no direct connection to the trade sector—perceive themselves to have a stake in the policies and practices affected by these liberalization initiatives. But the challenge for trade negotiators does not, of course, only come from the *defensive* efforts of domestic stakeholders seeking to protect policies, practices, and values-linked trade. Increasingly in recent years, non-governmental organizations (NGOs) have taken the initiative in insisting that certain values (e.g. labour and human rights, environmental protection) are in fact linked to trade and should therefore be addressed in trade negotiations. And the stakeholder groups concerned about these linkages—both defensive and "offensive"—are often as interested in the implications of trade for policies and practices in other countries as they are about conditions in their home countries.

The trade/labour and trade/environment issues have proven especially contentious for at least two reasons. First, the stakeholders that take an offensive posture on these issues (mainly industrial country NGOs and trade unions) want environmental and labour standards to be enforced with trade sanctions. Those that take a defensive posture (developing country governments that view trade-linked standards as a disguised protectionist threat, but also industrial country environmental NGOs concerned that certain kinds of trade liberalization will undermine existing standards) tend to be equally highly motivated and do not want these issues discussed as part of trade negotiations. Secondly, as the first point implies, industrial country and developing country stakeholders tend to be on opposite sides of both sets of issues. To be precise, in the WTO, as elsewhere, the relationship between developing country governments and industrial country civil society groups is emerging as a key source of tension.

One must be careful about making excessive generalizations about the labour and environment issues, however. Multilateral discussions on the trade/environment link are much further along than are discussions on trade and labour issues. Several WTO agreements directly or indirectly address environmental matters, and the WTO's Committee on Trade and the Environment, although criticized by many for failing to find solutions to key outstanding issues, has served as a useful focal point for discussion and analysis—two prerequisites for consensus. On the labour standards issue, in contrast, there is nearly unanimous opposition to the creation of a trade and labour standards working group inside the WTO. It is worth noting that, in contrast to the WTO's discussions on trade and environment issues, which enjoy broad multilateral support, the case for a formal WTO programme of work on trade and labour standards has been made principally by one country, the United States.

Although the concerns that motivate them are extremely diverse, those who seek to address these new paradigm issues through trade negotiations often share a common aspiration: the harmonization of regulatory standards, laws, and business practices that vary from nation to nation. Collectively, their efforts raise fundamental questions about global governance: Should the harmonization of standards be a goal of international economic bargaining? Will it occur even without deliberate efforts by governments? Can the global economy achieve its full potential without significant further harmonization of standards across nations, just as successful national economies required the adoption of common standards by constituent political units (e.g. states or provinces)? Or can national differences be maintained without substantial losses of efficiency? Can and should a variety of national approaches to the regulation of the economy be maintained simultaneously, or will globalization inevitably lead to convergence between nations? To the extent that harmonization is pursued, how should nations decide which standards to apply? Does the political sustainability of global economic development require the adoption of common social and economic safeguards (e.g. protection for rights and the environment, social safety nets) analogous to the kinds of safeguards that have proven critical to the success of national economic systems?

It is clear from these preliminary questions that the WTO as an institution and the trade ministers principally responsible for guiding its work are not equipped to address such issues. This is not to suggest that the WTO should not take up new challenges. A plausible case can be made for discussion of many new issues in the WTO. The question that needs to be asked of each issue, though, is whether it is *ripe* for WTO treatment. Is there agreement on what part of a particular issue is affected by trade and is therefore a legitimate concern of trade negotiators? Is there something like consensus on the question of whether there ought to be a common international standard in a given area, against which national measures can be judged in violation? Introducing new issues into multilateral trade talks before they have fully ripened risks damage to open trade, to the values motivating the advocates of the new issues, and to other values.

In the absence of greater international consensus on the broader governance challenges noted above, most efforts to introduce new paradigm issues into the multilateral trade system have been highly contentious. The record in the WTO during the past several years confirms this, and the damage to world trade—so far mainly in the form of lost opportunities for further liberalization—has been sizeable.

The role of civil society in the multilateral trade system

Although many besieged trade officials in national governments and the WTO might not agree, the involvement of civil society groups in trade policy debates can be a positive development for the multilateral trade system. Some of the perspectives and concerns that these groups are bringing to bear on governments and on the WTO are a valuable counterweight to the industry perspectives that, in some countries, are still the dominant external input into official trade policy discussions. But the growing involvement of NGOs in trade policy often is not as constructive as it should be, and figuring out ways to make it so is the third major challenge facing the WTO and the multilateral trade system.

Several issues require addressing. First, there is a need to devise mutually acceptable mechanisms for coordinating the input of civil society groups in the WTO and in the preparation of multilateral trade negotiations. The principal burden of managing the contributions of civil society must continue to be shouldered by the government of the country in which a given NGO is located. However, some NGOs have become large global institutions and others have forged international alliances. This, together with the supranational character of many of their concerns, may argue for additional measures to be taken at the multilateral level.

Many WTO members will oppose steps that appear to give NGOs a formal role in an intergovernmental organization. For their part, some NGOs might regard any formalization of their contributions to multilateral trade discussions as a form of co-optation. Both sets of concerns can be overcome, as long as the role of NGOs remains an advisory one and national governments retain the sole right to negotiate within the contractual framework that the WTO represents.

If NGOs were to be given an enhanced advisory role in the multilateral trade system, though, they must accept additional responsibilities. In particular, NGOs must become more accountable to the public and to governments. Too often in recent years, NGOs involved in trade debates have made questionable claims about the scope of public support for their positions. Information on the sources of their financial support has also often been hard to come by. Ironically, corporate participants in trade debates tend to be more transparent in both respects, often because the laws of their home nations require them to be.

Without additional information on NGO membership and finances, it will be difficult for governments to make well-informed judgements about their work or, in cases when it is not possible to consider all relevant views, to make decisions about which groups should be given an opportunity to address a particular issue. In exchange for any role in trade policy debates—largely at the national level—NGOs should be required to accept new standards of disclosure for membership and financial data.

The long-term viability of the WTO, and of the multilateral trading system, requires action by governments on two levels: the first is within the WTO itself; the second concerns the governance of the multilateral system, of which the WTO is a part.

A more agile WTO

The first step is to address the problems and challenges described in the previous section in order to make the WTO a more agile organization. These include the knotty issue of trade and labour standards, increasing "transparency" within the WTO, and improving decision-making within the institution.[7]

Defusing the labour standards debate

The relationship between trade and labour standards has been a highly contentious issue in the WTO since the United States first proposed the establishment of a WTO working party. After some 15 years of unresolved debate, one may wonder whether time will ever be ripe for dealing with this issue in the *formal* part of the WTO's work. Now, as before, the question is not about the intrinsic importance of labour standards, about which there is no doubt; it is, rather, about the most relevant and effective way to promote the observance of internationally agreed labour standards.

The majority of developing country governments question the sincerity of the labour rights concerns expressed by advocates of a formal trade–labour link in the WTO. These governments believe that a desire to protect high-wage manufacturing jobs from lower-wage competition is the primary motivation for industrial country pressure on this issue. Developing countries are also convinced that any discussion of the trade–labour nexus inside the WTO is bound to evolve into formal negotiations that will, ultimately, culminate in the use of the WTO's enforcement authority to curb their exports. As a result, developing nations—the countries whose labour practices would, presumably, be subject to the most intense scrutiny—refuse to support the creation of a trade–labour working group within the WTO, let alone the incorporation of labour standards in the institution's legal provisions—the so-called "social clause." Indeed, developing country attitudes on the issue seem to have hardened over the past few years.

The campaign to make labour a formal part of the WTO's work programme has poisoned the negotiating environment for a variety of other important WTO issues, including some that matter a great deal to the United States. Before and during the Seattle Ministerial, a large number of developing countries appeared to support a negotiating strategy under which their agreement to support the launch of a new global round would ultimately be contingent upon agreement by the United States and others to drop the labour rights issue. Although there were, of course, other preoccupations on the part of poorer nations, no other single issue has acquired this "make or break" status in developing country calculations on a new trade round. From this point forward, unless it is taken off the WTO docket and moved to a different venue, the labour standards issue will pose a major obstacle to further trade liberalization, in which all WTO members have a stake.

In the near term, multilateral discussions of labour issues probably can be more productively and effectively addressed outside of the WTO. Even if differences in labour standards and practices are believed to confer certain unfair competitive advantages, those standards and practices will ultimately much more likely respond to *development* policy than to *trade* policy. Even if the WTO can enforce its agreements through a dispute settlement system that can authorize the imposition of compensatory trade sanctions, the system is likely to be more effective in changing trade policy than as a tool of economic and social reform.

There are only two reliable long-term ways to help developing countries improve wages, labour standards, and their enforcement. The first is to help them to achieve higher and more equitable growth, which will lift wages; and the second is to provide technical assistance and financing to trade unions to strengthen their organizing efforts, and to government labour authorities to bolster legal regimes and enforcement capabilities.

Labour rights do indeed belong on the international agenda, both in their own right and because it is not possible to argue that labour practices and labour standards do not impact trade, and vice versa. But they need to be handled by an institution with the competence and mandate to address them with the seriousness they deserve. The International Labour Organization (ILO) is the obvious candidate. It should be strengthened, and receive the support necessary to carry out this task.

Tackling the trade–labour issues would clearly benefit from a coordinated programme of research and multilateral dialogue among key stakeholders. Such a process need not take place in the WTO for it to be effective. During the Seattle Ministerial, the European Union had proposed the initiation of trade–labour discussions in a forum that would have been jointly supported by the secretariats of the WTO and the ILO but would not have a formal constitutional tie with either institution. Developing country governments had expressed some willingness to consider the EU proposal before the Ministerial collapsed. That proposal should be revived.

Discussion of trade and labour issues outside of the WTO would stand a better chance today of narrowing gaps in the understanding of key facts and building common ground on potential multilateral steps than would talks within the WTO, where developing countries remain in a defensive crouch. A discussion of trade–labour issues outside of the WTO appears to be all the multilateral traffic can bear at this point, in any case, and advocates of a WTO trade–labour discussion should be willing to settle for it. If their arguments have merit, they will make headway with their opponents. One can even imagine that, over time, the protagonists in this debate will be able to agree on the scope of a subset of trade–labour issues that would be appropriate for formal WTO negotiations.

Increasing "internal" and "external" transparency

Some developing country governments and non-governmental organizations are concerned about the "transparency"—the openness—of decision-making in the WTO. Their dissatisfaction has become a point of controversy within the organization.

It must be said that a considerable number of developing countries—large and small—have long been at the heart of GATT and WTO decision-making. In many cases, involvement has been a simple reflection of the skills and engagement of their Geneva representatives. Nevertheless, too many developing countries see themselves partially or wholly excluded from key WTO activities through deficient "internal" transparency. They believe that, notwithstanding the WTO's extensive schedule of formal committee and working group meetings, important matters are routinely discussed and decided in small, informal gatherings to which they are not invited or in which they lack the staff or expertise to participate. For some developing nations, the WTO often has the appearance of a "black box," an institution from which decisions affecting their interests emerge in a mysterious and unaccountable fashion.

Civil society groups also consider the WTO opaque. But their focus is on so-called "external" transparency—the ability of the public to obtain information about, and comment on, the WTO's deliberations. NGOs object to the remaining restrictions on the public circulation of Secretariat background papers, meeting agendas and minutes, and submissions by governments and others to dispute proceedings. They want dispute panel rulings to be distributed more rapidly—as do some governments—and some propose that NGOs be permitted to submit *amicus* briefs to dispute panels.

The WTO has taken modest but useful steps over the past few years to expand the scope of information about its activities available to the public and to give civil society groups opportunities to exchange views with Secretariat officials and national delegations. But the chief transparency demands of the NGOs have been staunchly opposed by developing country governments, principally because they view the interests of many of those stakeholders, particularly with respect to environmental or labour matters, as inimical to theirs. They are concerned that influential civil society groups are more effective than they are in working the WTO system. Many developing country WTO delegations are, indeed, outnumbered by the Geneva-based staffs of a number of NGOs, and some NGOs have closer links with industrial country WTO delegations than do developing country delegations.

One key to advancing both the WTO transparency concerns of civil society and the effectiveness of the WTO as an institution is to take steps to strengthen developing country capacities to participate in the WTO's proceedings. If these countries felt themselves better able to promote their interests in the WTO they might be more comfortable granting external stakeholders increased access to the organization. Enhancing developing country confidence in the WTO, therefore, may be a prerequisite for enhancing civil society confidence in the WTO.

This argument reinforces the importance of Director-General Moore's campaign, launched after the Seattle Ministerial, to substantially boost budgetary commitments for technical assistance to developing country WTO members. Developing countries need assistance in a wide variety of trade-related areas. They already benefit from substantial programmes organized by the WTO and a broad range of other multilateral and regional institutions. But they clearly need far more. Further assistance geared toward improving capacities to formulate trade strategy, to negotiate, to coordinate with like-minded countries, and to understand WTO rules and obligations would be especially useful in changing developing country perceptions of the balance of influence within the organization. Unfortunately, the response of industrial country WTO members to the Director-General's appeal so far has been disappointing.

Improving decision-making in the WTO

Significant changes will be needed in WTO decision-making procedures, not only to address developing country grievances but to enhance the organization's ability to conduct its business efficiently.

In her statement announcing the failure of the Seattle meeting, US Trade Representative Charlene Barshefsky put the matter quite bluntly, saying, "the WTO has outgrown the processes appropriate to an earlier time."[8] According to chief EU trade negotiator Pascal Lamy, events in Seattle suggested that "the [negotiating] process itself has to be reassessed and maybe rebuilt."[9] These sentiments were echoed in comments made by many other senior trade officials.

The crux of the problem is that the consensus-based decision-making system unofficially adopted at a time when the GATT had just a couple of dozen members has become unwieldy in an organization of almost 140 members. If consensus is to remain by default the preferred mode of decision-making—and there is no reason to believe that WTO governments will accept any other approach, especially one involving the wider use of voting—new mechanisms for improving the effectiveness and speed of consensus-building must be adopted.

Some variant of an executive committee arrangement could be the most promising mechanism for balancing decision-making efficiency and the requirement of consensus. The collapse of the Seattle Ministerial has prompted several proposals for an executive committee system. They deserve careful consideration and discussion by WTO members.

Under such a system, the majority of WTO members would delegate authority to a group of roughly two dozen governments to work on their behalf on matters before the General Council, both between and during Ministerial Meetings, and other formal sessions. The executive committee's role would be strictly limited to consensus-building on negotiating frameworks and solutions to specific problems. The executive committee would not have authority to make final decisions on behalf of other WTO members. All WTO members would still need to discuss and sign off on executive committee agreements. But if it were balanced in its composition, accountable, and trusted by WTO members, the executive committee should be able to expedite decision-making by the full membership.

The membership of the executive committee would have to be representative, and should reflect a combination of geographical balance, importance to the multilateral trading system (as measured by trade volume), and caucus size (as measured by the number of countries in a particular income grouping). A handful of major trading nations would have their own seats on the executive committee, but most nations would be represented by countries with which they have regional or economic ties. The members of these groupings would decide amongst themselves which delegation would assume the grouping's seat, a choice that might vary from meeting to meeting, depending on the subject matter.

One recent exercise came up with a roster of 20 country and regional members.[10] If a plausible executive committee can be designed with just 20 members, the challenges of finding a workable formula should not be insurmountable. Indeed, there are real-world models for this sort of arrangement. A geographically and developmentally diverse group of finance ministers, the so-called "G-20," has held out promise of productive discussions on reform of the international financial architecture. It may offer a helpful starting point for a discussion of a WTO executive committee.

Why should either developing country WTO members or Quad governments support an executive committee arrangement? The answer is simple. The interests of both sets of countries are not served by the status quo. Recent events suggest that, without some improved means of building consensus, future WTO negotiations are likely to be, at best, less productive and slower than they have been in the past, and deadlocks are likely to be more common.

The industrial countries will not be able to dominate trade discussions as they have in the past. An executive committee would provide Quad countries more assurance that trade liberalization could move forward. And, for the poorer developing country members, an executive committee would offer something that the current Green Room system does not: more hope that their concerns will be weighed in the WTO's most sensitive deliberations.

At present, the influence of this large group of underrepresented poor nations over WTO affairs is almost exclusively defensive or negative in character; it derives largely from their capacity to obstruct and oppose consensus. Countries wishing to advance a positive negotiating agenda need to engage with other WTO members in a more intensive and sustained manner. An executive committee offers a mechanism for that kind of engagement.

The final step that member governments must take to strengthen the WTO is to increase the institution's budget and the size of its staff. When the WTO agreements were being negotiated, nobody anticipated how active the dispute settlement body would be, or how large would be the demand for technical assistance. The WTO is by far the smallest of the Bretton Woods institutions. Its overburdened staff is unable today to respond to all member country requests for information or assistance. Rhetorical support for the WTO by some of its richest members has not been matched by resource contributions. The organization's staff does an astonishing amount with very little; several million dollars more funding would enable it to offer an even more impressive programme of research, consultation, and technical assistance. It should do so under an effective and efficient "integrated framework" with related institutions.

The WTO in the system of global economic governance

There is clearly much that WTO members can do, acting largely through their trade ministries, to make the WTO a more agile deci-

sion maker and to give key government and civil society stakeholders more confidence in its work. But there is just as clearly also a
limit to what WTO members can do *within* the organization itself.
If the challenges that face the organization are to be understood and
fully addressed, the WTO's place in the larger system of global economic governance will have to be considered.

It is obvious to many observers that the development of the world
economy is outpacing the capacity to govern it, at both the national
as well as the international level. Inadequate global management
makes it harder for governments and countries to take full advantage of the opportunities of globalization. It also threatens political
support for an open world economy. More effective management, in
turn, will require new policies, institutional reform, and a leadership
strategy consistent with the challenges ahead.

Governments currently have to deal with the challenges of the
twenty-first century through a set of institutions designed for the
world that emerged after World War II. It is important to recall,
however, that there was an underlying logic to the design of the
post-war economic system. What we might call the "logic of 1945"
was no less essential to the success of the world economy than were
its formal institutions and rules.[11]

Following the "logic" of 1945, the key institutions established
after World War II were each given a distinct role in a single overarching mission: to promote growth and stability through the
progressive liberalization of economic activity. The task of the International Monetary Fund (IMF) was to promote commerce by helping to maintain financial stability. The World Bank was responsible
for financing the reconstruction of war-damaged economies and the
development of capital-constrained countries. And the GATT, an
agreement that ultimately evolved into an institution, was designed
to expand trade through the elimination of tariffs and other trade
barriers. Each of these key institutions responded to a specific
perceived failure in the management of international economic relations between the wars.

Post-war leaders were convinced that a liberal international order
would maximize international economic stability and growth. But
they were concerned that the domestic impact of liberalization could

undermine political support for a liberal international system. The logic of 1945 emerged from this concern. It held that, to be successful, international liberalization had to be "embedded" in social compacts in which governments provided for the social welfare needs of their citizens in exchange for public support for an open world economy.[12]

At the heart of the logic of 1945, then, lay a historic compromise between international liberalism and domestic interventionism. Examples of this compromise could be seen in national measures to cushion the impact of the open world economy and in international rules that permitted countries to opt out of selected liberalization commitments. The GATT, for example, permitted certain "safeguard" actions to protect domestic welfare goals, such as current account stability. Controls on cross-border capital flows were commonplace, as national governments sought to defend the autonomy of domestic macroeconomic policy. The balance of payments support provided by the IMF—*international* intervention to stabilize *national* economies—also was consistent with this historic compromise, as was the establishment of the World Bank as the source of lending initially for reconstruction and then for development. (The ILO, which was established after World War I, was already responsible for labour conditions and employment.)

Two other convictions were shared by post-war leaders. One held that a sound international economy required the widest possible inclusion of nations from the ranks of the war-damaged and former enemies. The other held that national governments were the only international actors of any consequence, and that, therefore, economic diplomacy would be reserved for them and for the international economic institutions they controlled.

The impact of globalization has made the "logic" of the post-war period obsolete. This is not the place to argue the pros and cons of globalization. The important point is that it is now obvious that, in a variety of ways, the political authority of governments no longer corresponds to the geography of the markets and production networks in which firms and workers now operate.

When looked at from this perspective, it is apparent that the WTO is suffering from governance deficits and leadership deficiencies at the global level—and that it is not alone in that regard. The weakness of other multilateral institutions and the inadequacy of existing decision-making forums have increased the demands on the WTO to deal with issues not heretofore within its mandate.

Labour and environmental issues are the two most notable cases. As noted earlier, pressure for the inclusion in trade agreements of provisions on labour standards and the environment has been firmly opposed by developing country governments. The resulting tensions have damaged the WTO's effectiveness and played a significant role in stalling further liberalization efforts. These pressures have been brought to bear on the WTO not only because of the attraction of its unique enforcement power, but also because the institutions that might be expected to deal with labour and environment issues either do not exist or are weak.

On paper, the ILO should be the preferred institution in which to pursue discussion, research, and action designed to improve labour rights protections worldwide. It has considerable staff expertise on these issues, a unique tripartite governing structure that includes representatives of each of the main stakeholder groups (trade unions, business, and government), and an established programme of technical assistance on labour rights enforcement. Contrary to what many believe, the ILO even has enforcement power, although its system is certainly not as strong as the WTO's because it does not have the power to impose trade sanctions. But governments and trade unions generally view the ILO as an ineffective institution, and the ILO has, it must be admitted, not done enough to earn their confidence.[13] This has prompted labour advocates to turn their attention and their hopes to the WTO, whose only means of addressing the enormously complicated challenge of improving labour standards would be the threat or application of punitive trade sanctions.

Similarly, environmental activists have looked to WTO trade agreements for help in enforcing environmental standards that are not otherwise covered by environmental agreements. Their lobbying has prompted proposals for the creation of a "world environmental organization," a global institution with the power to enforce a range of environmental agreements.[14] Doubts about the prospects for such an organization have led to calls for the adoption of international agreements covering individual environmental problems, each with its own enforcement mechanisms, possibly even providing for the imposition of trade sanctions. Several such agreements already exist, but pressure to put the WTO in the service of environmental enforcement has not diminished.

As noted previously, pressure from environmentalists and others also is pushing the WTO in precisely the opposite direction, further complicating efforts to chart a course for the organization. In the view of some activists, as well as some of the most committed free-traders, the WTO has already been given excessive jurisdiction over issues that would have been better left to other multilateral institutions or decision-making mechanisms or to national governments. Environmentalists worry, for example, that WTO dispute panels are setting international environmental policy through their rulings. Some free trade advocates believe that intellectual property rights issues should not have been introduced into the WTO through the TRIPS agreement. In these and other areas, however, where there is a demand for multilateral policy-making, competent alternative institutions to the WTO do not exist.

The political pressures on the WTO and the weaknesses or absence of other institutions to deal with these issues highlight the need for a political process to allocate institutional responsibilities. Many issues can plausibly be described as "trade related," but unless its mission is radically changed the WTO will be well equipped to deal with only some of them, or certain portions of some of them.

Where, then, are decisions to be made about which issues should be the business of the WTO (and the national trade ministries that guide its work) and which should not? Certainly, the WTO itself cannot make those decisions, because these are ultimately matters of institutional competence, and, as in any well-managed system, effective decisions on institutional role and missions can be made only at a higher political level. But those discussions are not taking place and decisions are not being made. That has given well-organized advocates of various issues or causes ample opportunity to engage in "venue shopping." Because of its ability to levy trade sanctions, the WTO frequently has been the venue of choice.

Other key international economic institutions are suffering from the same deficiencies in multilateral governance. Over the past decade, the IMF and the World Bank have each come under simultaneous pressure both to expand and to contract their mandates. The Fund has been given a steadily expanding role in the prevention and management of financial crises, but it is also being pressed by a number of thoughtful critics to hand over some of its development-related lending to the World Bank.[15] The World Bank has been criticized for taking on too many issues (often with the encouragement of its major stockholders), and the division of labour between the World Bank and its regional counterparts is coming under increasing scrutiny. The current mandates of the institutions overlap in a variety of areas, wasting resources and perhaps undermining the effectiveness of both institutions. Every couple of years, the leaders of the Bank, the IMF, and the WTO pledge intensified collaboration on development-related matters, but their work with each other and with other organizations (e.g. UNCTAD or the ILO) has been disappointing. In June 2000, for example, the three institutions themselves concluded that their high-profile collaborative effort to deliver improved trade-related assistance to the world's least developed countries—the so-called "Integrated Framework"—had performed well below expectations.[16]

Weak or non-existent institutions, overlapping and ill-defined mandates, inadequate organizational cooperation, and the absence of a mechanism for deciding who does what—these are the global governance problems that are burdening the WTO and undermining the effectiveness of other important multilateral institutions and policy initiatives. But the impact of this "global governance deficit" is being felt even more deeply. The globalization of economic activity has outpaced the efforts of national and international policy makers to redraw the rules and standards necessary not only to ensure the stable and equitable expansion of markets, but also to deal with the economic and social dislocations that are inevitable in a globalized world economy. This gap between globalization and policy can be seen in the difficulty with which global financial authorities responded to the financial crises of 1997–1998 and the ongoing struggles of governments to adapt trade, intellectual property, and other laws to electronic commerce.

A Globalization Summit

If the promise of a global economy is to be realized, and the perils of globalization minimized, the existing economic, social, and political institutions will need some renovation, redirection, and a clearer division of labour. They also will require much more financial and political support than they now receive from some countries.

There is currently no supra-institutional decision-making process guiding such an effort. There is a need, therefore, for some high-level process to determine the appropriate division of labour among existing multilateral institutions, to decide when new organizations or capacities need to be created, to supervise the strengthening of existing institutions, to assign issues or problems to particular institutions, to adjudicate jurisdictional disputes, or to enforce cooperation among organizations.

These tasks clearly require concerted, broad, and high-level political leadership. Central bankers and ministers of trade, finance, labour, environment, and development must all play advisory roles, but only heads of government possess sufficient authority and prestige to make the necessary decisions. Existing mechanisms for organizing high-level economic leadership are inadequate. The G-8 is too narrow in its membership. The annual meetings of the World Bank and the IMF bring together the world's finance ministers and central bankers, but their discussions are preoccupied with narrow finance issues. WTO Ministerials are devoted solely to trade issues. The yearly gathering of heads of state for the opening of the UN General Assembly is too ritualized.

We propose a new mechanism for marshalling global economic leadership: a carefully designed summit meeting of heads of state— a Globalization Summit. The Globalization Summit would be dedicated to addressing the key governance challenges associated with globalization. The meeting would not be a negotiating session and would not supersede or replace any existing forum. It would involve a structured but informal discussion.

The goals of the summit would be to identify areas of common concern and to try to reach consensus on how to respond to them. The discussion would include an assessment of the adequacy of existing multilateral institutions and agreements. At the conclusion of the summit, the participating heads of state would decide whether to reconvene again. We believe they would find such a meeting sufficiently useful that they would choose to meet again. But the widest possible participation in the initial meeting requires, we think, that no government be asked to make a long-term commitment to a process of unknown value.

To be successful, the countries invited to participate in the Globalization Summit must be broadly representative of the world economy. Although it might be desirable, in principle, for the leaders of all the world's governments to take part in the summit, a gathering of that size would be a logistical nightmare. Two dozen heads of state would perhaps be the ideal size for such a meeting— large enough to allow broad international representation, but not so large as to prevent genuine give-and-take. In addition to heads of state, it would probably also be useful to include the heads of the World Bank, the IMF, the WTO, and the United Nations.

Which countries would participate in the Globalization Summit? Several selection schemes could be explored. One approach might be to use the memberships of the development and international monetary and financial committees of the World Bank and IMF as a guide. These include most of the major economic powers, plus constituency representation for smaller economies. Another option would be to include three groups of about eight nations each: all or most of the major industrialized countries; leaders of emerging market nations; and leaders of least developed countries. Priority must simultaneously be given to ensuring roughly equal participation from the world's five major geographic regions: Africa, Asia and the Pacific, Latin America and the Caribbean, North America, and Europe.

The precise agenda of the summit would be determined by the participating governments, but a committee of independent experts would be charged with preparing background material and a proposed agenda. The material prepared by the experts group would be used to structure the discussion. It might also include recommendations for action. This structured approach to discussion has been used successfully before, most notably in the context of Asia-Pacific Economic Cooperation (APEC).

We are realistic about the prospects for a gathering of this kind. A single meeting of a couple of dozen heads of state will not be able to make decisions on all of the difficult governance issues discussed here. But we also believe that a meeting of this kind would call forth an immense research and analytical effort on the part of specialists and institutions worldwide. Some of that work would feed into the preparatory process for the meeting. We also would expect that the run-up to the meeting and the meeting itself would generate intense media interest and public discussion, improving global public understanding of economic governance challenges. And if, as we expect, the summit initiates an international debate over how to reform the system of global economic governance, the first summit will probably not be the last.

The main message of this chapter is that the WTO has been very successful but that changes need to be made to increase its effectiveness in order to meet the challenges posed by globalization. It is important to understand, however, that the WTO is only one part of a system of global governance that now needs refurbishment and a clear definition of the functions of the various multilateral institutions. Only a combination of internal reforms and changes in the patterns of global governance will ensure that the WTO achieves its full potential.

Acknowledgements

The authors wish to acknowledge the extraordinarily helpful comments of ODC Senior Fellow Sylvia Saborio on various drafts of this chapter.

Notes

1. World Trade Organization, "Some Facts and Figures: Stats for Seattle," November 1999.
2. Development Division, World Trade Organization, *Background Note: High Level Symposium on Trade and Development,* Geneva, 17–18 March 1999.

3. World Trade Organization, "Some Facts and Figures: Stats for Seattle."
4. Committee on Trade and Development, World Trade Organization, "Participation of Developing Countries in World Trade: Recent Developments, and Trade of the Least-Developed Countries," WT/COMTD/W/31, 17 September 1997, p. 5.
5. Ibid.
6. William A. Diamond and Michael M. Hart, "Post-Modern Trade Policy: Reflections on the Challenges to Multilateral Trade Negotiations after Seattle," unpublished paper.
7. We focus here on labour standards, and not on the link between trade and environmental standards, because the debate surrounding the latter appears to be much further advanced, including in the WTO. For a thorough analysis of leading trade and environment issues, see Gary P. Sampson, *Trade, Environment, and the WTO: The Post-Seattle Agenda,* Washington, DC: Overseas Development Council, 2000.
8. "WTO Seattle Ministerial Fails: Talks to Resume at a Later Date," *WTO Watch* (Bureau of National Affairs), 3 December 1999.
9. Ibid.
10. The European Union, the United States, Japan, the People's Republic of China and Hong Kong (China), the Association of South East Nations, Canada, the European Free Trade Area and Turkey, Korea, Mexico, Australia and New Zealand, the Central European Free Trade Area, North Africa and the Middle East, South Asia, MERCOSUR (Southern Cone Common Market), the Andean Community, Israel, South Africa, the Central American Common Market (CACM) and the Caribbean Community (CARICOM), and two sub-Saharan African groupings. See Jeffrey J. Schott and Jayashree Watal, "Decision Making in the WTO," in Jeffrey J. Schott, ed., *The WTO after Seattle,* Washington, DC: Institute for International Economics, 2000.
11. The notion of the "logic of 1945" was developed by Ethan B. Kapstein in his book *Sharing the Wealth: Workers and the World Economy,* New York: W.W. Norton, 1999. Peter D. Sutherland discusses the relevance of the "logic of 1945" for contemporary global economic management in his 1998 Per Jacobsson Lecture, "Managing the International Economy in the Age of Globalisation," Washington, DC: Per Jacobsson Foundation, 1998.
12. John Ruggie, "International Regimes, Transactions, and Change: Embedded Liberalism in the Postwar Economic Order," *International Organization,* 36 (2), Spring 1992.
13. It should be noted, however, that the ILO Director-General, Juan Somavía of Chile, who assumed office in 1999, has provided dynamic leadership for the ILO and is taking promising steps to make it a more effective institution.
14. The most prominent advocate of a world environmental organization thus far has been French Prime Minister Lionel Jospin. Detailed proposals have been offered by Daniel Esty, of Yale University, and several other trade and environmental specialists.
15. "The Future Role of the IMF in Development," report of an Overseas Development Council task force, Washington, DC: Overseas Development Council, April 2000.

16. "Joint Statement on the Mandated Review of the Integrated Framework for Trade-Related Technical Assistance to Least-Developed Countries (IF) by the Core Agencies (IMF, ITC, UNCTAD, UNDP, World Bank, and WTO)" and "Heads of International Agencies Agree to New Approach on Trade-Related Technical Assistance for Least-Developed Countries," press release, 6 July 2000. The three other organizations sponsoring the Integrated Framework are UNCTAD, the UN Development Programme, and the International Trade Centre (itself a joint initiative of the WTO and UNCTAD).

6

Public participation in the World Trade Organization

Frank Loy
Under Secretary of State for Global Affairs, USA

We must build a trading system for the 21st century that honours our values as it expands opportunity.[1] . . . We must do more to ensure that spirited economic competition among nations never becomes a race to the bottom. We should be leveling environmental protections up, not down . . . Sustainable development is a stated objective and mission of the WTO. Achieving this goal will require greater inclusiveness and transparency in WTO proceedings to win the confidence of people around the world.[2]

(President William Jefferson Clinton)

Introduction

For the past 50 years, the World Trade Organization (WTO) and its predecessor organization, the General Agreement on Tariffs and Trade (GATT), have been—in common parlance—on a roll. The volume of trade governed by WTO rules during that period has grown 13-fold, reaching annual levels of US$5.3 trillion in merchandise and US$1.3 trillion in services in 1998. Tariff levels that in 1947 averaged 40–50 per cent of the value of goods, today average 4 per cent. Membership in the organization now boasts 139 countries, with 30 more aspiring to join.[3]

These successes have fulfilled many of the aspirations of the WTO's founders who, after World War II, saw a trade-liberalizing organization as a further insurance policy against the high tariff walls and resulting tariff disputes characteristic of the 1930s, which, they believed, had led to world conflict. The argument that these changes, overall, have both raised living standards and encouraged political stability seems overwhelmingly justified. It is an encouraging and good story—but it is not the whole story.

For these very changes (increased trade, low tariff levels, explosion of membership), plus other concurrent revolutions in our societies, have produced an urgent need to adjust the organization's way of doing business:

- As the volume of trade grows, more and more people will be affected directly by it, and even more will feel themselves affected. Not surprisingly, they will demand a higher level of understanding of this previously arcane organization, and some input into its policies.
- As tariff levels drop and competition among nations sharpens, subtler issues will come to the fore—such as the treatment of non-tariff barriers and intellectual property rights.
- As membership grows, and the club of mainly industrialized nations is transformed into a near-universal organization, two consequences become apparent: (i) the difference in the outlook between industrialized and developing countries will soon take centre stage—as it has in most international organizations, and (ii) the process of decision-making will have to be adjusted.

Although these changes in the organization by themselves have demanded reaction, developments in society as a whole add heightened urgency for change:

- the increased interdependence of the world economy and rapid globalization;
- the rise in membership numbers and the increased sophistication and political activism of the non-governmental organization community;

- the dramatic increase in the speed and ease of communication (which, among other consequences, has multiplied the influence of non-governmental organizations);
- the exponential increase in our understanding of the environmental impact of goods traded internationally, specifically considering consumption patterns and methods of production.

The birth of the WTO as successor to the GATT—a product of the Uruguay Round concluded in 1994—brought about some significant improvements in the workings of the organization, the most important of which was the dispute settlement system of 1995. But both the WTO proceedings as such and the dispute settlement system have taken only modest steps toward enabling the interested public—meaning principally non-governmental organizations (NGOs), the business community, and the media—to observe the WTO at work. The failure of the WTO to make itself more transparent has contributed mightily to the ignorance, suspicion, and hostility that the organization has engendered.

This chapter seeks, first, to explore the useful roles that NGOs could play in the WTO, and includes a look at their role in other institutions, past and present, and, second, to outline some specific, though modest, steps that the WTO could and should take promptly to remedy this "transparency deficit."

Defining a useful role for civil society—the NGOs

The NGO community clearly plays a role today as never before, but there is nothing new about non-governmental organizations attempting to influence government decision-making. As early as the 1800s, such organizations were actively promoting the passage of anti-slavery laws and treaties in England and elsewhere in Europe and, later in that century, they attacked human rights abuses in the Belgian Congo. By the turn of the nineteenth century, groups such as the Anglo-Oriental Society for the Suppression of the Opium Trade were part of an influential anti-drug movement that culminated in an agreement by states to approve the 1912 Hague Opium Convention. In 1945, NGOs were largely responsible for inserting human rights language into the United Nations Charter and, since then, have placed almost every major human rights issue on the international agenda.

In 1947, the drafters of the International Trade Organization (ITO) included a role for NGOs in the structure of the organization. The ITO was intended to be the third leg of the Bretton Woods institutions, alongside the World Bank and the International Monetary Fund. In the end, it failed to garner enough support, and the weaker GATT became an interim solution. The ITO framers envisaged that commercial and public interest NGOs would maintain regular contact with the ITO Secretariat, receive unrestricted documents, propose agenda items, and participate as observers and occasional speakers at conferences. The proposed charter for the ITO contained some of the same language as the WTO Charter, providing for "consultation and cooperation" with NGOs. Ironically, in the year 2000 the WTO faces requests from NGOs that could be met by adopting the standards for participation that the original ITO framers proposed a half-century earlier.[4]

The NGO community at the beginning of the twenty-first century looks very different from that of 1947. In recent times— roughly coincident with the birth of the WTO itself—the NGO community has grown in numbers, in its political influence, and in its capacity to make intellectual contributions to the problems it addresses.

Numbers begin to tell part of the story. In 1996, at the first WTO Ministerial Conference in Singapore, some 159 NGOs registered, of which 108 were present. In 1999, in Seattle, while more than 700 NGOs engaged in the Ministerial proceedings, 1,478 NGOs submitted position papers. The Union of International Associations, publisher of the Yearbook of International Organizations, now counts more than 50,000 international NGOs in its data base, up from just 6,000 in 1990.[5] The World Wide Fund for Nature (WWF) has some 5 million members, up from 570,000 in 1985, and, in the United States, the Sierra Club boasts 572,000 members, up from 181,000 members in 1980.

In other ways, the NGO community stands in contrast to what it was even 20 years ago. First of all, there are many more NGOs from developing countries. Secondly, present-day non-governmental organizations are linked to one another through broad networks and coalitions that render them more effective and sophisticated than their counterparts from earlier times. For example, the International Campaign to Ban Landmines (ICBL) was founded in 1992 by six concerned organizations based in a handful of countries. Today that network represents more than 1,100 groups in as many as 60 countries that are striving to implement the Landmines Convention and to ban antipersonnel landmines locally, nationally, regionally, and internationally. In 1997, the ICBL and its coordinator, Jody Williams, received the Nobel Prize.[6]

In 1996, the Coalition for an International Criminal Court (CICC) began a process to bring together a broad-based coalition of NGOs and international law experts as advocates for the creation of an effective court to try crimes against humanity. Today, the ICC Rome Statute has 97 signatories and has been ratified in 13 countries.

The ICBL and CICC are powerful examples of international networks operating over a multi-year period to accomplish specific objectives. Not all NGOs have such a record of accomplishment. Yet when one regards the full sweep of active NGOs—whose causes range from humanitarian to the environment, human rights, women's rights, free trade, and a host of other issues—it becomes apparent that they have redefined the political landscape the world over, and are a contemporary force with which leaders, locally and globally, must reckon more imaginatively.[7]

Contemporary NGOs, unlike their predecessors, are wellsprings of important scholarly efforts. Throughout the 1990s, members of the NGO community made significant intellectual contributions to the body of knowledge that underpins the field of trade and environment. For example, some of the most important thinking and writing about process and production methods emanates from the NGO sector, which includes, in particular, the work of Konrad von Moltke, of the World Wide Fund for Nature.

The London-based Foundation for International Law and Development, the US-based Center for International Environmental Law, the Environmental Defense Fund, and others have grappled adroitly with the issues that fall at the intersection of environmental policy and trade law. The World Conservation Union (IUCN) supplies objective, science-based information and analysis to various organizations—notably to the Convention on International Trade in Endangered Species of Wild Fauna and Flora.

Increasingly, the perspective of the developing South is presented with a good deal of vitality. The Centre for International Trade, Economics & Environment in Jaipur, India, and the Centre for Strategic and International Studies in Jakarta, Indonesia, are two examples of Southern NGOs that bring important perspectives to any discussion of trade and the environment.

The WTO and NGOs

The rules governing inter-nation trade often presage serious environmental consequences. Therefore, finding an effective role for NGOs in the WTO process has taken on new urgency. This relationship between the rules governing international trade and environmental consequences—unknown or at most marginal in 1947—has become a central and usually controversial element in international trade discussions and negotiations. The controversy starts with the proposition, advanced by environmental advocates and economists alike, that trade restraints and environmental degradation are costly— both reduce GDP—and, therefore, are worth addressing with parallel and equal determination. The environmentalists charge, with some justification, that this view has yet to pierce the parochial world-view of those who see trade not just as a means to the end of economic growth, but as an end in itself.[8]

Yet many object to the direct participation of NGOs in the WTO and charge that these organizations are not necessarily democratic, accountable, or even broadly representative, and are really nothing more than self-appointed representatives of themselves. Nonetheless, NGOs demand accountability and democratization of the WTO and insist that individuals have a voice in setting the international trade rules that they believe increasingly affect their lives.

Many of these individuals have multiple identities and do not necessarily identify solely with the geographic, political jurisdiction in
which they live. Instead, they also find common cause with NGOs
that cut across political boundaries and define communities of interest (human rights, animal welfare, opposition to trade in biotech
products, or any number of other issues). These citizens care first and
foremost about an issue and are likely to feel that their views are
better represented by an environmental NGO than by their own
governments.[9]

The events in Seattle in 1999 were fuelled by a vociferous coalition of NGOs built on the World Wide Web. Their voices placed
the public at the centre of a vital public policy discussion that was
traditionally dominated by governmental representatives in closed
meetings. As a result, the WTO has been forced to recognize other
actors on the international stage. Failing to do so would threaten the
viability of the trading system.[10]

Clearly, the way to develop a free trade constituency is to engage
the opposition and address their legitimate concerns. Intergovernmental institutions such as the WTO, which lack leverage with
individual legislators as in the United States, must make an effort to
satisfy and address the principal concerns of NGO groups by inviting
them in from outside the closed doors. As a central, new component
of its work, the WTO needs to continue to enhance its dialogue
with the NGO community.

Individual WTO members must also establish, at a domestic
level, broad consultative processes with civil society that provide the
public with opportunities to contribute to the formulation of
national trade policies. In the United States, for example, much has
been done to ensure that public opinion contributes to the formulation of trade policy. Through "notice and comment" rule-making
procedures, the public can weigh in on trade policy decisions. Trade
policy makers in the United States are advised not only by the rest
of the US government but also by public advisory committees.
Through successive trade legislation beginning in 1974 and again in
1984 and 1988, the US Congress mandated closer relations between
US trade officials and the "private sector"—viewed then and in this
context as consisting largely of trade and commercial interests. This

committee structure now includes a Trade and Environment Policy Advisory Committee, composed of business and environmental representatives, and the presence of NGO representatives on a large number of other committees that advise the government agencies responsible for foreign affairs and trade and commercial policies. Though not actually in the room sitting side by side with US negotiators, these "advisers" are just outside the door, where they are updated on offers and counter-offers.[11]

Since 16 November 1999, when President Clinton announced Executive Order 13141 on "Environmental Review of Trade Agreements," it is the policy of the United States to conduct "environmental reviews" of the trade policy decisions that are most likely to affect the US environment and, as appropriate, have an impact that is transboundary and global. Such policy reviews include decisions to participate in comprehensive multilateral trade rounds, bilateral or plurilateral free trade agreements, and major new trade liberalization agreements in natural resource sectors. These reviews, which assess the interlinkages between trade negotiations and the environment, involve public outreach at various stages in their preparation. This includes public notice of draft documentation and an opportunity to comment orally and/or in writing. In performing these reviews, it is the goal of the United States to complete them sufficiently early in the negotiating process that they can be taken into account in the formulation of national positions. The United States will continue to encourage its trading partners to conduct similar reviews and to exchange such information so that a global picture emerges of the environmental impacts of trade agreements. Though highly desirable, this process is not, by itself, enough, particularly when it comes to certain environmentally sensitive sectors.

Much of the mistrust and many of the misconceptions about the WTO stem from its lack of transparency. When members of the public are excluded from a process, they tend to imagine the worst. If it is so difficult to find out what the WTO is doing, then the organization is perceived as having something to hide. Very many of the complaints one hears could be addressed by providing accessible information on WTO activities. Except where this information would interfere with the end game of concluding a trade round, why not open up the proceedings? Policy formulation would benefit from well-informed contributions from public interest groups. If environmental groups that have felt excluded from the trade policy-making process consider that they are included in that process and have been given a fair opportunity to help shape decisions, they are much less likely to obstruct trade liberalization efforts.

The benefit of a strategy of inclusiveness was demonstrated during the course of the debate in the United States over the North American Free Trade Agreement (NAFTA) between 1991 and 1993. Both the Bush and Clinton administrations worked hard to ensure that environmental groups were briefed regularly, included in the public advisory committee groups, and given access to the negotiation process.[12] In the end, a number of large environmental NGOs endorsed the treaty as a net "positive" for the regional environment.

Today, the WTO is perceived as not being accountable or even responsive to public concerns. Currently, non-governmental representatives are not permitted to participate in or observe the processes of any regular WTO activities. This predicament needs to change.

Modest proposals for reform

The United States has long held that increased transparency and public participation should be integral components of WTO operations. At the May 1998 WTO Ministerial Meeting in Geneva, President Clinton formally urged the WTO to take every feasible measure to bring openness and accountability to its operations. He called for the WTO to embrace change boldly by opening its doors to the scrutiny and participation of the public. Since then, the Clinton administration has developed specific proposals designed to enlarge the "window in" through which the public can understand its functioning in all proceedings, including those of dispute resolution. Overall support for these proposals has been marginal, and in certain instances the overwhelming governmental reaction has been hostile. Nevertheless, headway could have been made in Seattle in December 1999 had the talks not collapsed. In the meanwhile, without waiting for the next global trade round to begin, the United States will continue to press for an agenda of reform.

A meaningful agenda of reform would include:

- expanding interaction and exchange of information with the public through the creation of consultative mechanisms;
- promoting the institution and its work through public awareness efforts;
- forging relationships with other intergovernmental organizations;
- providing timely access to a wider range of documents such as submissions to WTO meeting minutes;
- providing avenues for filing *amicus curiae* briefs;
- opening dispute settlement hearings in WTO disputes.

Creating mechanisms for better input from the NGO community

The WTO has some history of consultation and cooperation with NGOs where there have been concrete results. Article V.2 of the Agreement Establishing the WTO states that the General Council may make appropriate arrangements for consultation and cooperation with NGOs. Some of the architecture is already in place to begin this process. An Internet website has been created[13] and, as of October 1999, more than 200,000 people had logged on to the site—a 60 per cent increase since January of that year.[14]

In July 1996, the General Council established "Guidelines for Arrangements on Relations with Non-Governmental Organizations." These guidelines mention the need to make documents more readily available than in the past, require the Secretariat to engage actively with NGOs, and recommend the development of new mechanisms for fruitful engagement, including symposia on WTO-related issues. However, it is significant that the guidelines note there is currently a "broadly held view that it would not be possible for NGOs to be directly involved in the work of the WTO or its meetings."

The organization is nervous about giving NGOs an explicit role, as illustrated in the *Report (1996) of the Committee on Trade and Environment* prepared for the 1996 Singapore Ministerial. The report noted that "[t]he CTE considers that closer consultation and coop-eration with NGOs can also be met constructively through appro-priate processes at the national level where primary responsibility lies for taking into account the different elements of public interest which are brought to bear on trade policy-making."[15] Yet, even if the primary responsibility does lie at the national level, clearly the WTO has a secondary responsibility to allow consultation by inter-national NGOs—such as Consumers International or WWF International.[16]

Allowing NGOs into the workings of the organization worries members because they believe that the WTO is a special case. They justify their reluctance on the grounds that the WTO differs from many multilateral organizations. And it does. For trade negotiations to conclude successfully, national representatives must subordinate certain national interests in order to achieve marginally acceptable or " sub-optimal" compromises that, by definition, require trade-offs. Thus, one seems justified in asking if the system can still work if these trade-offs are open to scrutiny by the very special interests that would have opposed them.

However, the WTO is by no means the only international organ-ization that strikes compromises among competing points of view. Such compromises occur in truly every negotiation, whether the negotiations concern the environment, human rights, or any other issue. No one seriously disputes the need for governments to conduct actual negotiations through government-to-government exercises—which means, among other things, that many sessions will be closed to non-governmental actors.

The WTO could begin by looking at some negotiations conduc-ted under the auspices of United Nations specialized agencies. Consider the Montreal Protocol on Substances that Deplete the Ozone Layer, signed in 1987. Substantial business interests were affected, and the agreement brought marked change to an entire industry. Interestingly, the experience also brought change to the community of environmental organizations. The negotiations in fact spawned an international network of NGOs linked by electronic media, which today regularly consult, coordinate positions, and work jointly to influence government positions on international environmental issues and negotiations—including WTO negotiations. In the Montreal Protocol, the influence of NGOs proved of critical importance in pushing the parties toward ever-stronger controls over ozone-depleting substances.[17]

The Convention on International Trade in Endangered Species of Wild Fauna and Flora (CITES) also operates with particularly vigorous NGO participation. In spite of the objections of some parties, the collaboration has intensified over the years. This participation ranges from rather straightforward, generally quite informal lobbying by organizations, such as Safari Club International and animal rights organizations, to the scientific and legal work of the IUCN, which operates more as an in-house think tank.

The negotiations of the International Framework Convention on Climate Change and the follow-on Kyoto Protocol provide another example. Throughout the negotiations, NGOs such as the Environmental Defense Fund and the World Business Council for Sustainable Development (to name just two) crafted compromise proposals that were designed to help negotiators reconcile environmental and commercial interests.[18]

Conversely, the initial lack of effective NGO participation in the Intergovernmental Panel on Climate Change raised questions of its legitimacy and led to the establishment of an ad hoc working group to encourage greater developing country involvement. Because participation contributes to popular legitimacy by giving stakeholders a sense of ownership in the process, restricted participation can provoke dissatisfaction on the part of those excluded, creating the basis upon which a regime's legitimacy can be challenged.[19]

It is a well-known irony that the strongest opposition to NGO participation comes from developing countries—even as those very NGOs purport to promote their countries' interests. The explanation is not too subtle. For one thing, the environmental agenda is viewed by most developing countries as counter to their development agenda. But there is a second reason. Developing country NGOs at times are lacking and, when they do exist, they often do not have the financial resources to attend negotiating meetings. Therefore, the NGOs that do attend will be those from industrialized countries, which may appear to stack the deck even more.

In the past, WTO members have left it to the Secretariat to find special funds to help bring G-77 NGOs to WTO symposia, and have not been prepared to provide for this in the regular WTO budget. WTO members need to explore ways of funding such initiatives to ensure that Southern NGOs are also properly represented.

Regular briefings for NGOs on WTO activities have begun and NGO-produced documents are made available to WTO members. In the last several years, representatives from the secretariats of the major multilateral environmental agreements have reported to the WTO Committee on Trade and Environment (CTE) on the workings of these conventions, as well as recent developments, and have engaged in discussion of the trade implications of their activities.

In May 1998, President Clinton called for "a forum where business, labour, environmental and consumer groups can speak out and help guide the further evolution of the WTO."[20] Later that year, the WTO Secretariat organized seven regional trade and environment seminars in developing countries, two of which concluded with meetings between government and NGO representatives. The objective was to improve policy coordination. Indeed, some participants indicated it was the first time they had actually met their trade or environment ministry counterparts.

In March 1999, the WTO hosted a High Level Symposium on Trade and Environment which governmental and non-governmental participants from the trade and environmental communities attended. In September 1999, in Geneva, Switzerland, a privately sponsored high-level Forum on Trade and Environment was held where trade and environment ministers, heads of various environmental and business NGOs, and international trade and environment and development organizations sought to identify areas where progress might be made at the Ministerial Conference in Seattle.

Earlier derestriction of WTO documents

In 1996, the WTO took initial steps to improve public access to documents. In July 1998, WTO members continued to address the issue of transparency when they began devising additional WTO procedures involving earlier derestriction of documents, including minutes of WTO meetings. Although the WTO must be applauded for the extent to which it has already managed to increase the availability of documents to the public, current derestriction procedures have significant shortcomings. The delay in derestriction seriously limits the value of documents as public information and makes it more difficult for WTO members to explain clearly to domestic constituencies the basis for national activities regarding the WTO. These artificial delays have no real rationale other than traditional practice. That is why the United States and Canada extended a proposal to the WTO General Council that would greatly improve public access to WTO documents. There ought to be a general presumption under which most types of WTO documents are immediately derestricted unless a compelling reason is put forward.

Public participation in the WTO

In some quarters of the trade community, proposals for public observation of and participation in WTO meetings, including committee meetings, tend to generate widespread anxiety that this level of involvement might negatively affect the intergovernmental character of the WTO. The ideas put forth by the United States in Seattle maintained the government-to-government nature of the WTO as an institution. Several bodies of the United Nations that are essentially governmental in character appear largely unaffected by a liberal approach to transparency, public observance, and even public participation; and their work continues unimpeded. For example, at the conclusion of a discussion during negotiations within the UN Environment Programme, NGO statements are generally viewed as a useful way to transmit information to negotiators that helps them to make the right decisions.

WTO committees should always be able to go into executive session as their work demands it. Indeed, one should question the wisdom of opening negotiation sessions where the actual horse-trading occurs to persons other than those representing WTO member governments.

Transparency, public observation, and participation in WTO dispute settlement proceedings

Since the WTO Understanding on Rules and Procedures Governing the Settlement of Disputes (DSU) was agreed in 1995, a number of high-profile environment-related disputes before the WTO have led to changes in the environmental and conservation laws and regulations affecting WTO members, including the United States. These cases can be complex and difficult to resolve. Environmental, health, and safety measures can be protective of the environment and reflect genuine public concern for the environment, human health, and safety and still be unduly trade restrictive or a disguised barrier to trade.

The very first case to be heard by the new DSU is a good example: the United States reformulated gasoline rules that were successfully challenged by Venezuela and Brazil. In another case, the European Union moved to ban the importation of US meat from animals treated with hormones. Its desire to protect the agricultural sector clearly dovetailed with deeply seated public fears—scientifically justified or not—about the possible effect of beef hormones on human health. In a number of countries, domestic trade measures reflect local concerns that are religious, ethical, related to animal rights and other issues, and seem to be inconsistent with WTO guidelines.

Environmentalists and health advocates, among others, have thus been led to scrutinize the dispute settlement system. Public mistrust of the system, fuelled by the manner in which these disputes are resolved generally, undercuts public support for the WTO and for trade liberalization. President Clinton understood this danger when, at the 1998 Geneva Ministerial, he urged that WTO dispute settlement procedures be updated to make, the institution more transparent and accountable and to strengthen public confidence in trade agreements. Clearly, as the WTO takes on more difficult and controversial cases, there is an ever-increasing need for transparency in dispute settlement proceedings. Lack of openness and public access can complicate a negotiator's job in resolving disputes. Because private stakeholders become suspicious, this non-transparent process can make it more difficult to find practical solutions.

In accordance with President Clinton's call for greater transparency in WTO dispute settlements, the United States, during the five-year review of the DSU beginning in 1998 and 1999, has advocated the derestriction of country submissions to disputes simultaneously with their submission—except for confidential business information. The United States has also supported maintaining a public docket, open for inspection, of all submissions to dispute settlement panels and the abolition of any "hold" on panel or Appellate Body reports, once these have been issued to the parties to the dispute.

Procedurally, those who believe that they have an interest in the outcome of decisions should have an opportunity to be a part of the decision-making process. Opportunities should be offered to submit views and to observe how a particular outcome is reached. The United States, in advance of the 1999 Seattle Ministerial, argued that panel and Appellate Body proceedings should, as a general matter, be open to public observers on a first-come-first-served basis. Current practice involves hearings that take place behind closed doors and exclude all but the parties to the dispute. The US proposal is to permit the public to observe—but not to speak—at the hearings. The panels would not be compelled to admit observers without limit and the WTO could establish rules concerning their conduct. Such reforms, if instituted, would place WTO proceedings on a par with national court proceedings in many countries and with proceedings before international adjudicating bodies such as the International Court of Justice (ICJ) at The Hague and the European Court of Justice (ECJ) at Strasbourg, both of which are open to the public and to the press. In recent years, television cameras have been allowed at these institutions, and the ICJ has prepared full transcripts of all hearings, which are made available to the public promptly. The fact that any interested party may attend proceedings that are just as sensitive as those before the WTO has not interfered with the government-to-government nature of the disputes handled by either the ICJ or the ECJ.

The United States and the European Union, the two most active users and beneficiaries of the WTO dispute settlement mechanism, should continue to discuss opening to the public, on a trial basis, those disputes to which they are party. Opening disputes on a trial basis would permit logistical problems to be identified and resolved. This would also be of benefit to developing countries that wish to build greater expertise in this area and gain knowledge about the dispute resolution process. Today, a developing country member wishing to have a window into a particular dispute must bear the expense of intervening as a third party. The new proposal would permit that country to observe the proceedings without having to take a stand or prepare papers.

A workable procedure must be found through which panels would publicly offer interested outside parties opportunities to submit *amicus curiae* briefs.[21] The United States has suggested a mechanism for panels to receive summary (three-page) requests from civil society to provide input. The panel would then exercise the discretion that it already has under existing dispute settlement procedures to seek further information or advice from the submitter. The panel could set page limits on submissions, as well as deadlines giving ample time for the parties to respond. Organizations based in developing countries could even receive more time to prepare their input. These new procedures could be instituted on a trial basis and would not give the right to be heard at panel meetings to anyone other than the parties or third parties.

Because the WTO still faces serious questions about its capacity to deliver substantively correct decisions on trade and environment issues, WTO panellists should be strongly encouraged to seek outside expertise in all disputes involving significant environmental issues that are beyond their principal competency. They are admonished to do so under Article 11(2) of the Agreement on the Application of Sanitary and Phytosanitary (SPS) Measures, but only permitted to do so under Article 14 and Annex 2 of the Agreement on Technical Barriers to Trade (TBT). In addition, Article 13.2 of the Dispute Settlement Understanding allows for technical contributions by experts. In practice, WTO panels have requested such contributions in only very few instances. In the Shrimp-Turtle dispute, the panel did request advice from a group of outside experts, including some affiliated with the IUCN, an international NGO.[22]

Such expert recommendations, whether the experts act as a body or each advises the panel individually, should be released to the pub-

lic together with the Report of the Panel. It would be valuable for
the public to see plainly the extent to which the experts agreed and
the panellists followed their recommendations.[23] In addition, options should be explored for including technical experts on WTO
panels when they are called upon to grapple with environmental or
conservation measures alleged to have run afoul of trade rules.

Resistance to most of these reforms is widespread, particularly
among developing countries, which fear, among other things, that
highly capable developed country NGOs could exert extraordinary
influence over panel deliberations if they were given greater access
to dispute proceedings. Even some developed countries feel that
amicus briefs and public observers would delay and politicize proceedings. But these are not the necessary results of such transparency,
nor are the fears of harm to the process balanced against the likely
benefits to the institution. Indeed, panels should always have the
ability to meet in executive session if they desire.

There is also, it would seem, a legitimate resource concern. The
number of dispute settlement proceedings is ever expanding. If this
is coupled with the burden of taking into account large numbers of
amicus submissions by NGOs and other private parties, even in summary form, and of systematic resort to scientific experts by panels,
then attention should be given to assessing the additional resources
that would be needed so that WTO panels of the first instance and
the appellate panels can do their jobs well. The number of appellate
panellists on the WTO roster currently stands at seven. Perhaps that
number should be increased. In addition, perhaps, there is a need for
judicial clerks and other support staff for panels. The WTO staff is
small, as is its budget, which stands at only US$80 million per
annum, the equivalent of the IMF travel budget.[24]

Keeping civil society informed

How are the public, the international environmental community,
and even decision makers to be kept abreast of the progress of trade
negotiations that directly affect them? In the run-up to Seattle, the
United States proposed that the WTO Committee on Trade and
Environment be used as a forum to discuss and highlight the envi-

ronmental implications of negotiations taking place in the other groups and to identify the links between areas of negotiation and environmental protection. Indeed, by its own terms of reference, the CTE mandate is to improve the transparency of WTO operations. In proposing such a role for the CTE, the United States intended that the CTE monitor and report on environmental issues raised at the negotiations in order to ensure that such issues would be aired in a systematic and transparent manner. It was never the intention of the United States for the CTE to oversee the negotiations or to serve as a forum for the negotiation of specific text. One expects that the work of the CTE would be valuable because it would provide input to deliberations at the national level on positions to be taken in the actual negotiating groups. Members could then consider whether or how they would weigh in at the negotiations. This committee would serve as a window onto the entire process.

Expanding institutionalized interaction between trade and environment policy makers

Greater transparency and public involvement at the WTO should be accompanied by renewed efforts on the part of WTO member states to include both trade and environmental policy experts in their internal processes of international trade and environmental policy decision-making. Environmental experts should be on the delegations that conclude trade arrangements whenever environmental issues are involved. They should attend international meetings where the impact of national or global environmental regulations on the world trading system is discussed. It is equally important to include trade experts along with environmental experts on delegations to conclude multilateral environmental agreements (MEAs). These experts would represent governments. More thought should also be given to the role that NGOs might play on national delegations.

At the WTO Committee on Trade and Environment, many countries have not fielded environmental experts along with their permanent Geneva trade representatives. To date, this has created at least part of the problem that the CTE has faced in reaching consensus on how to manage perceived trade and environmental conflicts. It is noteworthy that at Seattle a number of member states had environment ministry representation on their delegations and several environment ministers were in attendance. The WTO Secretariat should build upon the work it has already done to bring trade and environment decision makers together to air views that help to de-mystify policy goals and choices. One person's environmental, health, or safety regulation is often another's unfair, unnecessary, or too restrictive non-tariff trade barrier. At environmental agencies in member countries, trade considerations and a review of WTO rights and obligations should always be an integral part of the domestic environmental regulatory regime. At the trade and commercial agencies, those who make policy should engage, routinely and systematically, regulators concerned with the environment, conservation of natural resources and human, plant, and animal life, health, and safety.

Increasingly, the negotiation of MEAs is attracting trade and commercial ministry representation. This is important if the achievement of identified global environmental goals through the use of trade-related measures is to be consistent with countries' WTO obligations, and if painful conflicts before the WTO dispute settlement bodies are to be avoided as much as possible.

Increasing cooperation between the WTO and international environmental institutions

Cooperation needs to be strengthened between the WTO and international organizations concerned with environmental matters. One of the few concrete outcomes of the 1999 Seattle Ministerial was a memorandum of understanding, concluded at the conference, which provides a mechanism for the WTO and the United Nations Environment Programme (UNEP) to work more closely together on matters of common concern. Beginning in 1999, UNEP has undertaken a series of environmental review projects. These country studies focus on a single environmentally sensitive sector of the national economy and constitute the first phase of a project entitled "Capacity Building for Integrating Environmental Considerations into Development Planning and Decision Making."[25] It seems that there would be opportunities for UNEP to work with the WTO to gather and make available information and data on the likely environmental impact (positive and negative) of WTO initiatives on sectors widely perceived to be "environmentally sensitive." In this way, a global picture may begin to emerge. Any representations of free trade—its benefits and its costs (such as its potential harm to the environment)—should never be based upon conjecture, uninformed by hard data.

The secretariats of those MEAs employing trade measures to accomplish environmental objectives would benefit greatly from observer status at the WTO. Certainly, presentations by MEA secretariats at the WTO Committee on Trade and Environment have helped to create a greater appreciation, and even acceptance, of the use of trade measures in certain MEAs. One might look to the example of CITES, where the IUCN—which was working to draft CITES—asked the GATT Secretariat whether the trade measures being contemplated in CITES were acceptable under GATT Article XX, to which the Secretary gave them an answer that sounded affirmative. Routine consultation between the WTO and relevant MEA secretariats could thereby help avoid the needless use of overly restrictive trade measures, while enhancing the understanding of the necessity of certain measures for the protection of the environment.

Conclusion

Reaching the right formula to render the WTO a more environmentally sensitive institution is challenging because, in truth, both trade and environmental policies are intended to improve human welfare. In most societies, the public at large does not really wish to choose between development and free trade on the one hand and protection of the environment on the other; it wants both. And the WTO should be able to serve both.

The benefits of free trade include the additional resources that may be generated for the purposes of environmental protection. Within developing countries, the best hope for creating the resources and building the capacity to confront continuing environmental degradation is a liberal world trading system combined with sound national, regional, and global environmental management regimes. Therefore, we must apply rigour, will, and wallet to what might be called the institutional or "horizontal" problems faced by the WTO. If countries can muster the same resolve they demonstrated with respect to issues such as the protection of intellectual property rights during the Uruguay Round, we could make significant progress in the coming years as the next round of global trade negotiations is launched.

Notes

1. H.E. Mr. William J. Clinton, President, WTO Ministerial Meeting, Geneva, 18 May 1998; online at http://www.wto.org/english/thewto_e/minist_e/min98_e/clinton.htm.

2. Statement of the President of the United States, High Level Symposium on Trade and Environment, Geneva, 15 March 1999; online at http://www.wto.org/english/tratop_e/envir_e/dg_clin.htm.

3. See http://www.wto.org/english/thewto_e/whatis_e/whatis_e.htm.

4. P. J. Simmons, "Learning to Live with NGOs," *Foreign Policy,* Fall 1998.

5. "Citizens Groups of Non-Governmental Order," *The Economist,* 11 December 1999, p. 21.

6. See http://www.icbl.org.

7. See http://www.iccnow.org.

8. Jessica Matthews, "Environmentally Challenged," *Washington Post,* 14 October 1996.

9. Daniel C. Esty, "Environmental Governance at the WTO: Outreach to Civil Society," in Gary P. Sampson and Bradnee Chambers, eds., *Trade, Environment, and the Millennium,* Tokyo: United Nations University Press, 1999, p. 102.

10. Ibid.

11. Claude E. Barfield, "The Role of Interest Groups in the Design and Implementation of U.S. Trade Policy," in Alan V. Deardorff and Robert M. Stern, eds., *Social Dimensions of U.S. Trade Policy,* Studies in International Economics, Ann Arbor: University of Michigan Press, 2000.

12. Esty, "Environmental Governance at the WTO," p. 102.

13. http://www.wto.org.

14. Gary P. Sampson, "Trade, the Environment and the WTO, a Policy Agenda," Policy Paper of the Overseas Development Council, Washington, DC, November 1999, p. 8.

15. World Trade Organization, *Report (1996) of the Committee on Trade and Environment,* WTO Doc. WT/CTE/W/40, 12 November 1996.

16. Steve Charnovitz, "A Critical Guide to the WTO's Report on Trade and Environment," *Arizona Journal of International and Comparative Law,* 14(2), p. 367.

17. Richard Elliot Benedict, *Ozone Diplomacy: New Directions in Safeguarding the Planet,* 2nd edn., Cambridge, MA: Harvard University Press, 1998.

18. Simmons, "Learning to Live with NGOs."

19. Daniel Bodansky, "The Legitimacy of International Governance: A Coming Challenge for International Environmental Law," *American Journal of International Law,* July 1999.

20. Statement by H.E. Mr. William J. Clinton, President, WTO Ministerial Meeting, Geneva, 18 May 1998.

21. The Appellate Body ruled in the Shrimp–Turtle and countervailing duty disputes that panels and the Appellate Body have the right—but not the obligation—to accept non-requested submissions from non-parties, including NGOs.

22. "Accreditation Schemes and Other Arrangements for Public Participation in International Fora," International Centre for Trade and Sustainable Development, Geneva, November 1999, p. 5, n. 6.

23. In the NAFTA Science Advisory Boards (which advise), the panels on technical scientific issues that arise in SPS and TBT disputes under the NAFTA are made publicly available at the same time as the final panel decision.

24. "Trade at Daggers Drawn," *The Economist,* 8 May 1999, p. 20.

25. United Nations Environment Programme, *Capacity Building for Integrating Environmental Considerations into Development Planning and Decision Making,* 1999.

7

The relationship between trade and environment regimes: What needs to change?

Claude Martin
Director General, WWF International

Over the past 50 years, the volume of world trade has grown an average of 6 per cent every year. At present, it is 18 times the level it was in 1948, owing in large part to the elimination of trade barriers, such as import tariffs, quotas, and other trade restrictions. Although this trade expansion has helped bring about global economic prosperity, the benefits have not been evenly shared. Income disparities between the rich and the poor continue to widen, biodiversity has declined, pollution has increased, and the world's natural resources have been seriously depleted. It has been estimated that, since 1970, 30 per cent of the earth's natural wealth has been destroyed as the result of alarming trends such as increasing greenhouse gas emissions, deforestation, soil erosion, and overfishing.

In short, governments have done a good job in creating a global marketplace, but not one that is yet producing sustainable outcomes for the world's environment or for many of its poorest communities. As international trade and investment become increasingly important factors shaping our lives, the way in which we trade and invest across borders has profound implications for the health of our planet.

The World Wide Fund for Nature (WWF) and other environmental campaigners cannot but be concerned about the impacts of trade on environment and sustainable development; hence their involvement in the World Trade Organization (WTO) process. Trade liberalization is not limited to paring tariffs and tearing down trade barriers. It also involves negotiations about regulations, some of which directly relate to social and environmental rules and principles. The environmental impacts of free trade—in the widest sense of including social and development effects—must be considered alongside economic issues. The challenge is to ensure that trade and trade liberalization not only broadly benefit people and the planet, but also support sustainable development.

More importantly, trade and trade liberalization processes must take into account the real interests and concerns of developing countries. WWF's long-standing commitment to make conservation work for local communities reflects an understanding that paying close attention to developmental imperatives is an absolute prerequisite to durable conservation. The majority of the world's poor depend directly on the environment (water, soil, and forests). Environmental and sustainable resource use is an important dimension in any development strategy of a country that aims to attain economic growth in order to provide for the needs of its citizens. Sustainable indigenous resource use and management must be encouraged. Appropriate technology and financial resources must be transferred and industrial countries must make a commitment to greater support for regulatory capacity.

Proposed environmental reforms in support of sustainable trade

The world's resources are limited and their gradual attrition through unsustainable policies and practices will have massive repercussions on a country's prospects for long-term economic growth. A trade policy that puts profit before resource management and the provision of sustainable economic activity for poorer countries can benefit only those already rich—and then merely in the short term. There are six key elements of reform that will help to reassure people that the WTO will not liberalize trade at the expense of other vital concerns. These key reforms call for ensuring that:

1. the environmental and social impacts of trade practices are assessed;

2. the trade liberalization of environmentally friendly products is prioritized;

3. trade measures are accompanied by appropriate and necessary environmental and sustainable development policies;

4. the interests of developing countries are taken into account;

5. the WTO cooperates effectively with other multilateral agencies;

6. the WTO does not extend its remit to investment and other areas of commerce.

These WTO-directed reforms involve processes that are not necessarily confined to the WTO itself. Most of them call for reform activities at the national level, the involvement and participation of a broad range of stakeholders, and more policy coordination between ministries at the national level and intergovernmental organizations at the international level. Only by making better use of these parallel avenues will reform in the WTO be feasible in the long run.

Reform 1: Carefully assessing the environmental and social impacts of trade practices before proposals for liberalization are pursued

In negotiating trade agreements, implementing trade rules, and settling disputes, the WTO must adopt a broad approach that considers economic, social, and environmental concerns. There are at least three ways by which the WTO can fully incorporate environmental and social considerations potentially affected by trade: (a) by supporting the process of sustainability assessments of trade agreements; (b) by adopting, where relevant and necessary, a precautionary approach; and (c) by broadening the framework of its dispute settlement procedures.

Sustainability assessments

The idea of assessing the effects of trade policies on the environment and development is not new. Calls for the assessment of trade-related measures were made in early 1994 at the Third Session of the UN Commission on Sustainable Development (CSD III). Recently, the term "sustainability assessment" (SA) was coined to reflect the objective of measuring and evaluating the economic, social, and environmental effects of trade agreements in an integrated manner. This assessment process has emerged as a useful tool to address the linkages between trade liberalization and environmental and social change.

At an international experts meeting held in March 2000 in Quito, Ecuador,[1] participants recognized that sustainability assessment could help improve the quality of political decision-making by enhancing understanding of the links between trade and sustainable development. By informing policy makers about the potential economic, social, and environmental effects of the trade agreement they are to become a party to, the objective is to help these negotiators identify where their country's interests lie and how different negotiating outcomes will affect their domestic economies. As a result, assessment processes will contribute to more coherent policy responses that integrate these different sets of objectives. It is clear that sustainability assessment should also be applied retroactively to both trade-liberalizing and trade-restricting policies currently in place, so as to determine whether existing trade flows are sustainable or not.

Individual countries are responsible for defining and interpreting SA based on their own circumstances. The priorities and specific aspects to be included depend on the circumstances of each country, their differing degrees of development, and the issues under assessment. Although SA is essentially a national process, the WTO as a body should encourage member countries to carry it out and should provide technical and financial assistance for less-resourced countries, in cooperation with other relevant intergovernmental bodies such as the United Nations Conference on Trade and Development (UNCTAD) and the United Nations Environment Programme

(UNEP). In including SA in its *modus operandi,* the WTO needs to ensure that it does not become another conditionality for trade or a disguised trade-restrictive measure. The purpose is not to raise new barriers to trade and market access but to make trade more sustainable and increase its benefits to exporting countries.

In this respect, it is important to involve a broad range of stakeholders in the design and application of SAs. Much of the relevant information, as well as skills to undertake SAs, is in the hands of private actors, civil society, and academia. Early involvement will contribute to their ownership of the process and ensure that conclusions are as well informed as possible. It will also enhance the applicability and effectiveness of policy measures and help build capacity.

The WTO and the precautionary principle: A way forward

Recent disputes in the WTO, such as the Beef Growth Hormone case, have concentrated attention on how a rules-based trading system should deal with goods where their safety or environmental impact are "scientifically uncertain." The Technical Barriers to Trade and Sanitary and Phytosanitary agreements in the WTO require that technical regulations and health and safety laws are not more trade restrictive than necessary to achieve their legitimate objectives, and do not create unnecessary barriers to trade. In assessing whether trade restrictions meet these criteria, due consideration ought to be given to available scientific and technical information. These rules characterize precaution as a temporary response to a lack of scientific knowledge, and assume ignorance can be remedied by further research in the short term.[2] The problem arises when there is conflicting evidence: does the environment get the benefit of the doubt, or does trade; how is this decided and who decides?

The widely accepted precautionary principle counsels that environmental measures must sometimes be adopted when scientific information is incomplete. It offers a sound framework for accommodating both the inputs of scientific, economic, regulatory, and ecological data and the more subjective values surrounding risk and uncertainty.

The multifaceted nature of risk means that differences between countries' cultural norms and ideological beliefs will affect any decision involving uncertain impacts. Rational parties with honourable intentions can indeed have opposing views about the acceptability of technology. In fact, research in Europe suggests that countries with high levels of scientific literacy tend to take a more precautionary approach to new technologies.[3] Basic scientific information and risk assessment methods do not encapsulate these subjective cultural elements and so ignore critical differences.

Differences also exist in countries' regulatory culture and capacity to regulate. Objections by the United States to a proposed European Union ban on cadmium batteries suggested the alternative of improved recycling. However, EU regulators see a ban as a more efficient and reliable response and one acceptable to their citizens.

The use of the precautionary principle and other risk-based approaches must be clarified in a transparent, democratic, and inclusive manner. The WTO, as it currently operates, does not provide such a context. In addition, unlike national regulators, the WTO cannot appeal to—or be reformed by—direct democratic oversight, and consensus decision-making means reforms tend to be blocked by parties that currently benefit from the flawed system.

The conclusion of the Cartagena Protocol on Biosafety in Montreal in January 2000 was a welcome step in addressing the issue of how to operationalize the precautionary principle. The text strikes a reasonable balance between ensuring that national governments can take precautionary decisions that are consistent with the risks acceptable to their citizens while also making sure that the precautionary principle is used in a transparent manner and includes an evaluation of available scientific evidence. However, further debate on the precautionary principle is both necessary and inevitable, especially in terms of defining how it is applied in a trade context and more specifically in relevant WTO agreements.[4]

Nonetheless, the progressive interpretation of the precautionary principle in the Protocol makes it the first international treaty explicitly to address both environment and trade since the creation of the WTO. It is an important signpost on the road to more enlightened trade policy-making in terms of striking a better balance between trade interests, the environment, and other public policy objectives outside the WTO context.[5]

Broadening the framework of WTO dispute settlement

The WTO dispute settlement mechanism has the binding character of WTO obligations supported by a compliance mechanism that provides for the payment of compensation and the application of sanctions in the event of non-compliance. WTO panel decisions are automatically adopted by the WTO member countries unless there is consensus against doing so. The speed, power, and efficiency of the system are both frightening and fascinating to environmental groups. It is the very power and authority of the system that has led to calls for reforms.

Given the growing economic and environmental interdependencies, more trade and environment issues are expected to be negotiated at the WTO. However, the handling of dispute cases so far has shown that the dispute settlement procedures are not broad enough to take into account the complexities brought about by environmental and social factors.

The Shrimp–Turtle case is a good example of this. The case raised questions about the extent to which countries can restrict the importation of products that are produced by processes that have negative environmental consequences. It also illustrates that, because of its adversarial nature, formal WTO dispute settlement may not be the best means to resolve disputes of this kind. The trade ban and its ensuing dispute damaged the parties' relationships, undermined cooperation in multilateral trade and environmental forums, and failed to address adequately the underlying environmental problem (the protection of endangered sea turtles). The dispute suggests the need for an alternative method of solving trade–environment–development conflicts. Dispute prevention is one such approach.

Preventing these conflicts from occurring or from escalating into full-blown trade disputes at the multilateral level requires the creation of a more integrated approach to dispute settlement. This would involve utilizing policy mechanisms beyond those available in the trade arena and promoting dialogue whereby different stakeholders can constructively explore their various viewpoints of the conflict and collectively search for creative and integrated solutions.

WTO members should explore the establishment of multi-stakeholder consultative processes in which relevant facts could be put on the table by all interested parties from governments, non-governmental organizations (NGOs), industry, academia, local communities, etc. Should the WTO refuse to conduct such consultations, there is no reason why such multi-stakeholder consultation processes could not be established outside of the WTO.

The lack of transparency and openness in the current "closed door" dispute settlement processes makes environmentalists doubtful whether environmental concerns are given proper consideration. Many consider and request that the hearings be open to public scrutiny and observation. This could very well be taken into account in multi-stakeholder consultation processes.

The time has come for the WTO to adopt a broader vision of a sustainable trading system. This broader vision would lead the WTO to adopt trade measures that discriminate between different production processes and trade rules that encourage the use of environmentally friendly technologies. WTO dispute settlement procedures need to be reformed so that trade disputes with social and environmental components can be resolved in a more multidisciplinary, more open, and less partisan forum.

Reform 2. Prioritizing liberalization measures that offer direct and immediate environmental benefits

A concrete step that the WTO can take in the context of trade and environment issues is to encourage and work with countries to eliminate environmentally harmful subsidies. The WTO can and should engage in negotiations about the elimination of subsidies in energy, agriculture, forestry, fisheries, and other areas that constitute trade barriers and are destructive to the environment.

For example, many of the world's fishing fleets are simply too big. Estimates suggest that fishing power worldwide is two and a half times greater than is considered "sustainable." This is bad news not only for ocean wildlife, but also for fishing communities. As more and more boats chase fewer fish, fishers are finding it harder and harder to make a living. Nations with fleets fishing in distant waters have created a whole range of subsidies for their fishing industries. These include direct and indirect fishing subsidies that maintain many fleets at levels that result in overfishing and make little economic sense. Tens of billions of dollars are spent each year on subsidies to the fishing industry. Elimination of such subsidies would increase developing countries' market access and at the same time reduce pressure on the environment.

More proactively, the WTO should focus its efforts on liberalizing trade in products that are produced by environmentally friendly methods. Case studies indicate that exports that serve sustainable production and consumption are moving out of small niche markets into the mainstream in terms of volume and consumer acceptance. The WTO should encourage this type of sustainable trade.[6]

The case studies demonstrate how developing country enterprises and sectors covering manufacturing (environmentally preferred dye in textiles in India, CFC-free refrigerators in South Africa and Egypt), tourism (greening mass tourism in Senegal and Jamaica), forestry (sustainable timber harvesting in the Solomon Islands; sustainable non-timber forest products in Ecuador), and agriculture (organic fruit production in Chile, organic coffee production in Costa Rica, organic cotton production in Uganda) have turned tighter environmental regulations, new corporate practices, and changes in consumer values into economic and environmental advantages. Pioneering companies, non-governmental organizations, communities, and cooperatives can make a difference, often ahead of regulation or customer demand. Partnerships along the product chain are central to success for all producers, whether big or small, and new commercial relationships can emerge as a result. The case studies also show that the benefits of higher social and environmental performance of exports are many and diverse, including economic gains such as premium prices and increased sales, social benefits such as job creation and environmental improvements, as well as enhanced security through longer-term trade relations.

Admittedly, these cases of sustainable trade constitute only a small proportion of total trade flows and are exceptions, rather than the norm. But they offer a sense of what is possible. They illustrate that environmental policies can create export opportunities for developing countries. In this context, the WTO should encourage the development and application of rules to reduce the barriers faced by exporters of environmentally friendly products, such as tariffs and non-tariff barriers that provide unfair advantages to polluting industries. Clearly, liberalizing trade in commodities that are produced sustainably should be a priority of any upcoming negotiations.

Reform 3. Accompanying liberalization by improved environmental and sustainable development policies

It is generally accepted that trade liberalization contributes to increased economic activity and that countries that open up their markets and adopt trade and investment liberalization policies experience higher rates of economic growth. At the same time, there is growing recognition that trade liberalization and trade policy cannot be viewed in isolation from other areas of economic, environmental, and developmental policies. Though the objectives of these three policy spheres are not identical, they often overlap. Trade liberalization policies may have important repercussions on environmental and developmental imperatives. A sound analysis of the interface between the different spheres will help determine where synergies, trade-offs, and conflicts lie. For example, a particular production process may be beneficial for development but harmful for the environment, or a specific trade pattern may be environmentally friendly but inadequate for development. A set of policy instruments will then be designed to deal with a particular sectoral problem or to form an integrated package to tackle a more general set of trade–environment–development concerns.

At the very least, environmental and developmental impacts should be considered when formulating and negotiating trade policies, and flanking policies should be developed to minimize or to avoid the negative effects of trade. Ecolabelling is an example of a win–win parallel policy, being good for both trade and environment. It deals with legitimate health, safety, and environmental concerns, and harnesses market power to generate environmental benefits. Labels alert consumers to the conditions under which products are produced (e.g. tuna cans saying they are dolphin safe, timber certified as harvested from "sustainable forests," refrigerators labelled as CFC free), and allow them to vote with their pocketbooks in deciding which environmental conditions they want to see continued and which ones they do not want to see continued. Moreover, ecolabelling is a relatively inexpensive and straightforward strategy to implement.

At best, an integrated policy package should be designed to satisfy the objectives of all three policy spheres and minimize conflicts among them. (See the box on pages 148–9 for an example of an integrated policy package for sustainable forest management).

Integrated policies are especially important in enabling developing countries to adopt minimum environmental standards. Developing countries are justifiably concerned about any discussion on minimum environmental standards because these standards are usually what are right for people in relatively wealthy countries. The disparities in income and quality of life must always be kept in mind. In the United States, per capita income is about US$31,000. In Niger, Sierra Leone, Burkina Faso, and Ethiopia, per capita living standards are in the order of US$400–600. Life expectancy in industrialized countries is about 77 years, in Rwanda, 28 years, in Sierra Leone, 35 years. Differing levels of development must be taken into account when setting environmental standards. Technical and financial assistance must also be provided to help poorer countries meet these environmental standards and adopt environmentally friendly methods of production. Direct assistance to enable developing countries to "leapfrog" the dirty technologies that the industrialized countries used to enrich themselves should not hinder the development of environmentally friendly indigenous processes and production methods. These methods must be encouraged and supported as well.

Integrated policies: Sustainable forest management and forest certification

Certification aims to promote the sustainable management of forests and improved access for sustainably produced forest products to consumer markets. As a policy tool, certification belongs to the group of market-based instruments. It has impacts on a broad range of issues in the trade–environment–development interface. Among these issues are: market access and trade barriers, full-cost internalization and market transparency, ecological stability, the security of tenure of resources, the well-being of forest-dependent communities, and the care and safety of workers. In order for certification to maximize its potential net benefits and avoid unnecessary adverse impacts, this policy tool needs to be supported by a set of interrelated policies.

Land-use policies

A comprehensive land-use policy for forests and nearby areas is necessary clearly to demarcate forest lands that can be used for production forests, for protection, for conversion to plantation forests or other agricultural uses, and for industrial and other uses. Programmes will have to be designed to manage these conversions over time, including the design of infrastructure plans to support designated land use, roads, parks, irrigation, etc. This should be a dynamic process, revised and reviewed regularly and based on scientific studies and environmental audits as appropriate.

Forest sector policies

Concession agreements that provide for sustainable management opportunities and responsibilities should include the following:

- a clear commitment to sustainable forest management by owners and shareholders;
- local partnerships;
- monitoring systems;
- levels of fees;
- permissible technologies.

Cross-sectoral policies

These are intended to:

- create and/or strengthen regulatory policies that stimulate and support off-farm jobs;
- provide incentives for businesses to develop economically viable off-farm employment;
- ensure that infrastructure development is subject to stringent environmental safeguards;
- establish mechanisms for inter-agency coordination.

International cooperation

International support and development assistance need to be secured for:

- local capacity-building in developing forest management programmes, designing forest policy, and implementing that policy;
- facilitating appropriate technology transfer and change;
- supporting pilot initiatives on certification to show its viability;
- establishing a forum for continuous information exchange;
- developing suitable financing schemes and other incentives to promote sustainable forest management, which include certification as a complementary instrument.

Reform 4. Taking into account the concerns of developing countries

The débâcle at the third Ministerial Meeting of the WTO in Seattle exposed what is perhaps the most serious problem concerning the legitimacy of the WTO. It is dominated by a few powerful countries fighting for their own interests, so that African, Latin American, and Caribbean countries feel they have no chance of being heard.

Negotiations took place in closed sessions involving 20–30 countries (depending on the issue), with the rest of the 135 member countries sidelined. It is not surprising, therefore, that excluded countries complained so vehemently in Seattle, the Organization of African Unity leading the way with an unprecedented attack on the WTO's lack of transparency and a threat to reject any statement that might come out of the talks.

In order to restore its legitimacy, the WTO will need to give priority to the needs and concerns of developing countries. In the area of trade and environment, the WTO can achieve this prioritization by reforming the WTO's Agreement on Trade-Related Aspects of Intellectual Property Rights (TRIPS), providing special and differential (S&D) treatment to developing countries, and giving technical and financial assistance to increase developing countries' presence and representation in negotiations and their ability to negotiate effectively.

The TRIPS reform is an important concern to developing countries. It is necessary to extend its transition periods and identify actions or specific reforms to make the agreement support rather than undermine the Convention on Biological Diversity (for example on technology transfer, access and benefit-sharing from trade in genetic resources, and protection of traditional knowledge).

Enhancing and operationalizing the S&D provisions of the WTO would play an important role in reshaping trade flows and capturing the benefits from trade for developing countries. These include strengthening the food security exemptions from WTO rules; enabling developing countries to participate in international standard-setting bodies to help improve domestic environmental regulations as well as facilitate trade; and providing incentives to promote the dissemination and transfer of environmentally sustainable technologies.

A substantial amount of capacity-building is required to enable developing countries to participate effectively in the WTO. Delegations from developing countries often lack the technical and financial resources to undertake thorough analysis of their own trade and environment issues, and the expertise to formulate, articulate, and defend their own interests and needs in highly complex trade talks. Efforts at capacity-building will go a long way to increasing the quality and fairness of WTO negotiations.

Reform 5. Cooperation with other multilateral institutions

Since international trade has significant environmental and social implications, trade policy cannot be made in isolation from other areas of public policy. The WTO has a responsibility and an obligation to cooperate with relevant international organizations working on trade and sustainable development such as UNCTAD, UNEP, and the United Nations Development Programme. Thus far, a mandate has been established for the WTO to work jointly with the International Monetary Fund and World Bank in order to achieve greater coherence in economic and development policies. Although some collaboration is taking place with other UN agencies, there is a clear need to formalize such partnerships. This would entail, for example, that the WTO fully respect the authority of multilateral environmental agreements.

It has often been pointed out that the trade and environment regimes are of a very different nature. On the one hand, the trade regime is "centralized" in one institution—the WTO—which is equipped with a dispute settlement system that is largely regarded by governments as functioning well. In short, the threat of trade sanctions, whether justified or not, makes it a powerful compliance mechanism. On the other hand, the environment regime is spread among more than 200 multilateral environmental agreements, ranging from toxic substances to the protection of elephants and the prevention of biodiversity loss. In contrast to the trade system, coercion is not a sound basis for the development of environmental policy and MEAs are usually based on consent. In effect, this has resulted in serious imbalances between the trade and environment regimes and in sweeping generalizations that the trade system works whereas environmental regimes are either weak or do not work.

Although there may be some truth to such allegations, it should be emphasized that the "supremacy" of the trade regime has often resulted in a "chilling" effect on other intergovernmental processes dealing with trade and environment. This suggests that effective measures need to be taken to define where the WTO's mandate starts and stops on non-trade-related matters, and when cooperation with other international organizations in their areas of competence is required and necessary. The WTO cannot continue to work in isolation and in ignorance of the constraints it is imposing on important intergovernmental bodies that have a crucial role to play in the building and achievement of a sustainable global economy. Clarification of competencies and effective cooperation are urgently needed.

Reform 6. Keeping within the limits of the WTO's competence

Research by WWF shows that the interactions between foreign direct investment (FDI) and the environment are complex: they can be both positive and negative. FDI can bring cleaner, more efficient technologies and working practices to foreign countries, or it can create irreversible environmental damage if the investment takes place at such a scale and pace it overwhelms host country regulatory capacity. The negative impacts are most prevalent in the natural resource sectors, which form the largest proportion of investment flows to the least developed countries.[7] Any agreement on investment must recognize the necessary limits to liberalization in a systematic and coherent manner that subordinates investor rights to legitimate national sovereignty and the achievement of sustainable development.

Actual FDI flows are highly liberalized in most countries. Problems arise because FDI is under-regulated and countries are damaging themselves to attract new investment. The most urgent areas for international negotiation are: binding standards for the behaviour of multinational corporations; the prevention of harmful competition for FDI—including lowering environmental and core labour standards; cooperation on market governance of FDI; and active promotion of appropriate FDI to less developed countries.

The strategic task of agreeing on a broad framework for regulating FDI and deciding on priorities for negotiations is not within the competence of the WTO. The investment regime is a dynamic process that goes beyond the trade regime's system of rules applied by governments and supported by a compliance mechanism. The investment time-frame and the nature of the relationship between an investor and a host country are very different from those between exporters of goods and services and importing countries.[8] The FDI framework should be negotiated in a transparent UN-sponsored forum that supports the active participation of the widest number of countries possible. The High Level Intergovernmental Event on Financing for Development offers an appropriate forum for such an approach and process to be discussed.

This approach will need to be complemented by other initiatives and regulations, negotiated at the national and international levels, if the goal of fair and sustainable investment is to be achieved. National export credit agencies, business and industry, investment agents, and fund managers must all be encouraged to promote environmentally and socially responsible investments.

Conclusion

The main lesson to be learned from the failure of the WTO meeting in Seattle is that the diverse needs and interests of developing countries should be better taken into account in international negotiations. Otherwise, the global trading system is likely to experience enormous pressures in the next few years. Some of the trickiest and most emotive of these needs and interests concern the environment. The relationship between trade and environment is quite thorny. Developing workable international rules that protect the environment but do not restrict trade and development is a difficult challenge.

The search for solutions to these challenges does not lie within the WTO alone. Other avenues for making trade more sustainable include domestic trade policy-making, regional and bilateral forums, and other intergovernmental institutions that deal with the broader concerns of sustainable development. Other avenues for reform include the growing body of experience in trade and environment reforms outside of the WTO, such as those that promote sustainable consumption and production patterns and those that prioritize win–win solutions that both generate environmental benefits and secure market access.

The WWF has no illusions that its proposed six key reforms would be easy to implement. But the Seattle fiasco gave the clear message that the WTO must not shy away from this challenge. It must face it by considering and coordinating with parallel approaches. This challenge is here to stay and we can expect that trade and environment issues will be at the top of the agenda in future world trade negotiations.

Notes

1. Over 100 individuals from 30 countries attended the meeting, equally balanced between industrial and developing countries and coming from a cross-section of stakeholders. It was a unique opportunity to exchange views and experiences about the role and utility of SAs and to identify concerns about and potential obstacles to the further development of this tool (notably, the need for trust among countries as well as practical steps that would facilitate the application of SAs).
2. Nick Mabey and Richard McNally, *The Precautionary Principle: The Rational Guide to Policy Making under Uncertainty,* WWF-UK Discussion Paper, November 1999.
3. Economic and Social Research Council, "The Politics of GM Food: Risk, Science and Public Trust," Special Briefing No. 5, October 1999.
4. For a full discussion of the Cartagena Protocol and the precautionary principle, see Michelle Swenarchuk, "The Cartagena Biosafety Protocol: Opportunities and Limitations," Toronto: Canadian Environmental Law Association, February 2000, online at http://www.cela.ca/Trad&Env/biosafe.htm, accessed 25 September 2000; Aaron Cosbey and Stas Burgiel, "The Cartagena Protocol on Biosafety: An Analysis of Results," IISD Briefing Note, Winnipeg: IISD, February 2000, online at http://iisd.ca/trade/pubs.htm, accessed 25 September 2000; Pete Hardstaff, "Science and Precaution in Trade Regimes," RIIA conference on Sustainability, Trade and Investment: Which Way for the WTO?, London, March 2000.
5. Ibid.
6. Nick Robins and Sarah Roberts, *Unlocking Trade Opportunities: Changing Consumption and Production Patterns,* London: International Institute for Environment and Development, May 1997.
7. Richard McNally, *Foreign Direct Investment and Sustainable Development,* WWF-UK Discussion Paper, 2000.
8. Konrad von Moltke, "An International Investment Regime? Issues of Sustainability," draft, IISD, Canada, 2000.

8

Trade and environment at the World Trade Organization: The need for a constructive dialogue

José María Figueres Olsen, José Manuel Salazar-Xirinachs, and Mónica Araya

Former President of Costa Rica and Managing Director, World Economic Forum; Chief Trade Advisor and Director, Trade Unit, Organization of American States; and Director, Sustainable Americas Project, Yale Center for Environmental Law and Policy

There is no better way for sustainable development to be implemented than by linking its economic, human development, and environmental cornerstones. It is at this intersection where benefits—such as improved living conditions—can be maximized. Moreover, sound environmental policies can create new business opportunities, and these in all likelihood increase trade. Thus, links between trade and environment not only are necessary, but could also be extremely beneficial. In the context of the "trade and environment linkages" debate it becomes essential to ensure that our commitments to trade and investment liberalization, together with their rule-making, take into account other equally important global objectives, such as environmental goals.

The underlying premise of this chapter is that environmental concerns are among the critical issues that the World Trade Organization (WTO) needs to address successfully in the process of strengthening its credibility. Clearly, the WTO is not an environmental forum—and should not become one—but it should do its best to promote a trading regime that is environmentally sensitive and responsible, thereby contributing to other common global goals.

As a general trend, developing country scepticism prevails vis-à-vis the calls for expanding the scope of environmental issues within the WTO. However, two clarifications seem necessary. First, the Southern community in the WTO is not monolithic. As a result, the agendas of Southern countries in the WTO reflect a variety of priorities according to their needs and regional realities. For instance, whereas some Latin American countries have focused on Northern protectionism as a major issue, some African countries have placed poverty and development dilemmas at the centre of their agendas. By the same token, their stakes concerning the WTO trade and environment agenda are not identical. In fact, they are likely to become more distinctive in the future.

Secondly, although Southern scepticism has contributed to the slow pace of the WTO trade and environment agenda, other factors also raise hurdles to further progress. Above all, the process faces a lack of leadership. One reason for that might be the failure of developed nations—the main supporters of such debate—to bridge their own differences in this field. Without such leadership, closing the gaps between concerns from environmental constituencies and environmental-related concerns from developing countries becomes even more challenging. Thus, even if it is not the focus of this chapter, the role of developed nations is as crucial for a successful dialogue on trade and environment issues as the developing country role.

The reason for our focus on developing countries is the unexplored or inadequate debate on why they should engage more positively in the trade and environment agenda in the WTO. This chapter argues that it is in the best interests of the developing countries to contribute— not oppose—such an agenda. Instead of resisting a deliberation that is unlikely to fade away (quite the contrary), these countries should make their own case for a more environmentally sensitive trade regime on terms that meet the needs of the South.

The chapter is organized as follows. First we outline the ongoing context in which the "trade and environment" debate is taking place. Then we address some of the WTO "trade and environment" institutional efforts and the controversial issues that have emerged in the process. We follow this with a discussion of why it is in the interests of the developing countries to participate in this debate. After identifying the limitations that developing countries must face in the process of engaging in the multilateral debate, we suggest the need for a new approach to promote free trade and environmental protection. The chapter concludes with some general remarks.

Background

The "trade and environment" debate is complex and manifold. Furthermore, it involves some of the most fundamental WTO principles and rules, such as the concept of non-discrimination or the definition of "like products." Additionally, as the number of new issues and participants in the debate increases, arriving at satisfactory answers becomes more difficult.

There seems to be a consensus that responsibility for addressing the problems of global environmental policy should not be transferred to the multilateral trading system. In fact, some analysts have argued that there is a case for a Global Environmental Organization that would complement and counterbalance the WTO.[1] Although this is clearly a long-term goal, several international leaders seem to be increasingly supporting it.[2]

In the absence of such a global counterpart, the WTO increasingly faces the challenge of building confidence in the ability of the multilateral trading system to promote trade while responding to legitimate concerns in the area of environmental protection. As past years have shown, this challenge goes beyond achieving an understanding between the trade and environmental communities. In fact, during recent years these communities have come closer, leaving the WTO with a better "environmental track record" than the one inherited from its predecessor, the General Agreement on Tariffs and Trade (GATT).

However, despite the progress made by bridging some of the gaps between the free-traders and environmentalists, the North–South divide has become critical enough to threaten further progress on the "trade and environment" agenda. It is important to understand the major impulses behind the South's resistance.

At least three central ideas underlie the current debate on trade and development. One is that developing countries' growth depends on the rate of economic expansion and the import demand of developed countries. Secondly, developing countries need finance, investment, and technology from abroad to complement their national resources in order to achieve their full growth potential. Thirdly, open trade is an essential ingredient of development. However, there is an increasing awareness that, beneficial as trade and investment may be as engines of growth, they are not a panacea. To generate true development they have to be complemented by the right kind of domestic economic, social, and environmental policies.[3]

In general, the developing world feels a high degree of frustration over unmet promises of prosperity.[4] In particular, there is the sense that commitments made at the Rio Earth Summit in 1992 and in the context of the Uruguay Round have not been kept. For example, they point to the lack of success of Agenda 21—a key product from the Earth Summit—in fostering a North–South partnership to achieve sustainable development in a framework of common but differentiated responsibilities. This claim seems to be supported by recent assessments that show little progress in the implementation of Agenda 21, especially on issues such as finance and access to environmentally sound technologies.[5]

With respect to the Uruguay Round, developing countries also doubt the credibility of key commitments made by developed countries. One common criticism involves the slow progress in dismantling the Multifibre Arrangement and the goal of phasing out quotas on textiles and apparel gradually over a period of 10 years.[6] It has been argued that, although 70 per cent of the transition period is complete, as of 1999 only 6 per cent of the items in value terms have been liberalized.[7]

More recently, the collapse of the trade talks during the WTO's Ministerial Meeting in Seattle dramatically illustrated this generalized sense of developing country disappointment with respect to both procedural and substantive issues.[8] There, the North–South divide loomed large, especially as developed countries were reluctant to eliminate their own barriers to trade (i.e. agricultural subsidies) yet targeted protectionism in the developing world. While industrialized countries demanded timely implementation of trade commitments by developing countries (in particular, on intellectual property rights and investment measures), the latter resisted new concessions until developed countries fulfilled the trade reforms undertaken in the Uruguay Round and complied with WTO rulings and the "best efforts" commitments to encourage technology transfer.[9] Equally significant was the message coming from the tenth session of the United Nations Conference on Trade and Development (UNCTAD X). Once again, developing countries complained loudly about the lack of balance in a trade agenda that they claim has ignored their concerns.[10]

As a result, the consensus among developing countries seems to be that, until development and equity concerns are taken into account in the multilateral trading system, other issues that in their view threaten this agenda—such as environmental protection—are not welcome, at least in the short term. In the context of the WTO trade and environment debate, the core concern among developing countries is that broadening the organization's scope for addressing environmental concerns would only reinforce the existing imbalance in the trade talks. In particular, these countries fear that higher environmental standards—by creating new non-tariff barriers to trade—could trigger a new wave of protectionism, offsetting the gains from decades of trade liberalization efforts and negotiations.[11] These fears have led to a highly polarized debate within the WTO, which clearly reduces the prospects for a constructive dialogue. Recent developments in this debate will be outlined in the next section.

Addressing trade and environment issues at the WTO

Addressing trade and environment linkages at the WTO is one of its most challenging tasks. On very few occasions in the history of the post-war global trading system have governments assembled to start a negotiation and failed to do so. As Jeffrey Schott remarks, "never before had the failure involved questions about the legitimacy of the trading system itself."[12]

Throughout 2000, strengthening trust inside and outside the WTO while building consensus among a growing—and increasingly active—WTO membership has proved to be harder than ever. Particularly difficult to address is the belief by many developing countries that the playing field of international trade is not level but sloped against them. Some North–North differences that are part of the reasons for the Seattle failure also continue unresolved. These developments affect the possibilities for progress in trade and environment issues.

However, it is fair to say that, in the past few years, some progress has been made in addressing these issues inside and outside the WTO. We shall not attempt to summarize the entire debate; instead we shall highlight how recent WTO developments have increased North–South tensions in the process of showing higher sensitivity to environmental concerns.[13]

Institutional issues

The WTO Committee on Trade and Environment (CTE), established in 1995, has a broad-based mandate that covers goods, services, and intellectual property rights.[14] It has worked on 10 items based on a "cluster approach" in the areas of market access and the linkages between the multilateral environment and trade agendas.[15]

The CTE has been a step forward in the process of formally establishing a multilateral forum for the discussion of the trade and environment issues. But, despite years of important discussions, its findings have had no real impact on the multilateral trade agenda. Southern opposition to progress in trade and environment linkages has led to a highly polarized debate, which has affected the CTE dynamic. The lack of substantial progress in turn has left the CTE vulnerable to criticism by members from the environmental community, who feel that the lack of "tangible results" is evidence that this forum has failed to make the trading regime more environmentally sound. Furthermore, they complain that the WTO has isolated the debate within a committee that they see as "sterile" or "moribund."[16]

The WTO also created the Trade and Environment Division to provide service and support to WTO committees dealing with trade and environment and technical barriers to trade.[17] In addition to the work of the CTE, two of the most important institutional issues are participation by NGOs in some proceedings and transparency. As regards participation, owing to pressure from several members and outside organizations to move the WTO away from the GATT's secretive culture, the WTO Secretariat has engaged in a "trade and environment" dialogue with non-governmental organizations (NGOs). Since 1994 the WTO Secretariat has organized an annual Symposium on Trade, Environment, and Sustainable Development (with the exception of 1995).[18]

These opportunities for dialogue have clearly exposed the sharp differences among trade officials from the developed and developing countries. For example, during the WTO High Level Symposium on Trade and Environment in Geneva in March 1999 (a major trade and environment event), the United States and the European Union outlined their goals for expanding the WTO's environmental agenda as part of a new trade round—in an effort to address complaints from the environmental community—whereas developing countries such as Brazil, India, and Mexico voiced their opposition to any expanded scope for environmental issues in the WTO agenda.[19] One of their core arguments was that the trade body's rules were already capable of dealing with trade-related environmental concerns. Other initiatives in this field include several regional seminars on trade and environment for government officials from developing countries, least developed countries, and economies in transition.

With respect to cooperation with other organizations, the WTO has granted observer status in the CTE to intergovernmental entities, five of them working on environmental issues: the Commission on Sustainable Development, the Convention on Biological Diversity, the Convention on International Trade in Endangered Species, the Framework Convention on Climate Change, and the United Nations Environment Programme. UNEP has also requested observer status in the WTO General Council.[20]

Other institutional issues have been more controversial. One notorious example is the question of NGO input into WTO proceedings. For instance, the proposals for NGO submissions of *amicus curiae* briefs to dispute settlement panels have not been welcomed by many members, especially developing countries. They are concerned that such input will in practice accentuate disparities in the trade agenda.[21] Although these issues are part of the trade and environment debate, they belong to a much broader discussion on institutional reform within the WTO in order to make its operations more open and transparent, including the dispute settlement process.[22]

Another trade and environment initiative that the WTO has undertaken involves a comprehensive analysis of the relationship between trade, economic growth, and the environment, taking stock of economic and political economy research. According to the report, economic integration has important environmental repercussions, not all of them favourable. It has, or at least is perceived to have, diminished the regulatory power of individual nations. The WTO therefore argues that, in a world of ecological interdependence and dismantling of economic borders, there is a growing need to cooperate on environmental matters.[23] Rather than blocking free trade, the WTO suggests that countries need to tackle some of the institutional and policy challenges. In particular, they need to support the "institutional and democratic reforms that go hand in hand with increased income, which are necessary to allow citizens to articulate their preference for environmental quality and influence the political decision-making process."[24] What was new about the WTO findings was the recognition that, in the absence of proper environmental policy and institutions, trade can have negative impacts on the environment. An admission of this nature impressed some, including members from the environmental community.[25]

However, it would be mistaken to suggest that such empirical findings have changed the developing country position on trade and environmental issues in the WTO debate. As we shall show, several fundamental issues still remain unresolved.

Major contentious issues

Before discussing why developing countries should participate more actively in the trade and environment dialogue, it would be useful to point out which issues these countries are most concerned about and why. Three proposals have faced particular opposition:

- a review or reinterpretation of GATT Article XX to provide further accommodation of trade measures pursuant to multilateral environmental agreements (MEAs);
- accommodation on environmental grounds of trade measures based on non-product-related process and production methods (PPMs)—this debate has emerged in the context of the discussion on ecolabelling schemes;
- greater scope for the use of the precautionary principle.[26]

There has been a well-documented debate on each of these issues.[27] In general, developing countries reject such proposals because of their concern that they will provide an opening for unilateral trade measures and market access restrictions under the guise of environmental protection.[28] They are worried that further accommodation of trade measures pursuant to MEAs could offset some of the trade rights to which countries are entitled by virtue of the WTO system.[29] Leading developing countries have made the case that the trade regime already provides sufficient accommodation of such measures, so no further accommodation is necessary. In particular, they stress that only 10 per cent of MEAs contain trade-related provisions and, thus far, there has been no legal challenge in the WTO to MEAs. With respect to PPM-based discrimination, developing countries have also expressed concerns about market access. They support the maintenance of the customary trading regime approach: WTO rules should accept PPM-based discrimination only when the PPMs affect the characteristics of the product itself. Finally, an expanded scope for the precautionary principle in the WTO also arouses resistance because of the fear that it could trigger extremely strict sanitary and phytosanitary measures, leading to new forms of protectionism in the name of precaution. We will come back to these points later.

With the prospect of a new round of negotiations, new trade and environment proposals have emerged since 1999. For example, the United States—focusing on win–win situations that benefit both trade and environmental goals—has suggested the removal of certain subsidies (for example, in fisheries and agriculture) that distort prices and are environmentally harmful, and the elimination of restrictions on trade in environmental goods and services.[30] Other proposals on behalf of the United States, the European Union, Norway, and Canada have suggested the need to carry out environmental impact assessments of future trade negotiations. These proposals have been less controversial from a developing country point of view, as long as they remain a voluntary—not a mandatory—commitment.[31]

Several developing countries have presented proposals on other items of the CTE agenda. Two issues in particular have received attention: (a) the provisions of the WTO Agreement on Trade-Related Aspects of Intellectual Property Rights (TRIPS) that are relevant to environmental issues, a discussion led mainly by India;[32] and (b) the export of domestically prohibited goods, led by several African countries.[33]

Notwithstanding the efforts in these fields, the developing country input to the trade and environment debate is low. The next section will focus on the need for a more proactive engagement in the process of creating a more environmentally sensitive multilateral trading system.

The need for constructive engagement in the trade and environment agenda

There are at least four reasons why it is in the interests of the developing countries to engage proactively at the national and international level in the trade and environment debate in order to ensure that environmental concerns are properly addressed in the WTO and that trade liberalization and environmental protection efforts reinforce each other. First, social welfare could be maximized if both trade and environmental goals are strengthened; secondly, an effective trade and environment approach at the WTO would help maintain momentum for trade liberalization and restore confidence in the organization; thirdly, by dismissing the need for this debate, many "win–win" opportunities remain unexplored, including those that could potentially benefit exporters in developing countries; lastly, it is preferable to try to influence the debate rather than to have the difficult issues resolved through the dispute settlement mechanism.

Enhancing social welfare

Trade liberalization is not an end in itself. Rather, open markets and economic integration provide a promise of social welfare gains through economic growth. Environmental protection efforts also seek to increase social welfare. More progress towards the fulfilment of this common objective could be made by linking trade and environment and realizing the synergies created by their interaction. On the contrary, if trade liberalization proceeds in developing countries without regard for its effects on the environment, there is a high probability that some of the economic gains from trade will be consumed, and in some specific sectors or products the environmental costs will perhaps turn out to be higher than the economic gains. In other words, although poor countries may gain some material advances from trade liberalization, they will simultaneously have losses from environmental harms.

Supporting trade liberalization

Developing countries need a rule-based multilateral system. Some argue that they probably need it more than the developed countries because they are much weaker.[34] Hence, lack of support for the WTO from key countries could be detrimental for the South.

This leads us to the second reason why developing countries should not oppose the WTO's efforts to address environmental concerns. Clearly, environmental destruction threatens the ongoing commitment to trade liberalization—and to the WTO in particular—especially in the developed nations. Trade liberalization might not be irreversible and the question of what it takes to maintain support for such an agenda deserves considerable attention. The coalition in favour of free trade is increasingly vulnerable, especially in developed nations where there is a growing public perception that the costs of trade liberalization could end up outweighing the benefits.[35]

There is a growing sense of nervousness, especially in the United States and several European countries, about the unintended consequences of globalization, especially for the environment and domestic wages.[36] The argument that the WTO has sacrificed health, safety, and environmental standards for the sake of trade, although highly controversial, has been used with some effectiveness in a majority of the anti-trade campaigns. The opposition of the US environmental community—among other sectors—to granting fast-track authority to President Clinton is perhaps the major example of the loss of momentum for new trade initiatives in the United States.[37] However, the approval in May 2000 by the US Congress of Permanent Normal Trade Relations with China and of the African and Caribbean Trade and Development Act was a positive sign for trade policy in the otherwise bleak post-Seattle atmosphere.

The ill-fated Multilateral Agreement on Investment (MAI) at the Organisation for Economic Co-operation and Development (OECD) was a precedent-setting illustration of the difficulties developed countries face in their attempts to negotiate new global rules. The MAI negotiations were officially suspended in December 1998, having revealed a similar dynamic to that in Seattle: unresolvable differences among the negotiators combined with strong and organized resistance outside the process.[38]

Since then, attacks on global trade and investment have become even more vociferous and—most important—much better organized. For example, prior to Seattle, Friends of the Earth in Britain led over 570 NGOs from more than 60 countries in a campaign to stop the WTO negotiations on environmental grounds.[39] During the WTO Ministerial Meeting, the NGO protests were carefully planned;[40] in fact, *The Economist* remarked that these organizations "were a model of everything the trade negotiators were not. They were well organized. They built unusual coalitions. They had a clear agenda—to derail the talks."[41] In the aftermath of the collapse of the global talks, which in fact empowered many of the anti-globalization organizations, public scrutiny of the WTO can only be expected to increase.

In the South, where—as highlighted earlier—populations are even more exposed to the impacts of environmental degradation, a trade agenda that continuously ignores or dismisses its environmental consequences is unlikely to survive politically in the long run.

The potential for win–win opportunities

The third core argument for developing nations not opposing the trade and environment debate relates to the potential for some trade and environmental objectives to overlap and, in fact, reinforce each other.

The most classic example is the elimination of subsidies in agriculture, energy, fisheries, and timber. Not only do subsidies distort prices and disrupt trade, but they also cause environmental harms. In the case of fisheries, which is the sector that has recently received more attention in the WTO, some experts have estimated that the world's fishing fleets have nearly two and a half times the fishing capacity required to harvest fish stocks in an economically optimal and environmentally sustainable manner; in many cases, what keeps the boats afloat is the subsidies, which are in open violation of the existing international trade rules.[42]

But there are many other areas that offer opportunities for win–win situations for both trade and environmental objectives. Ecolabelling, for example, represents a clear intersection between market opportunities and environmental protection because it relies on market forces to promote environmentally friendlier products.[43] Unfortunately, in the WTO context developing countries have focused so heavily on the potential discriminatory implications of labelling schemes that they have blocked further progress on the specifics of an environmental initiative that could benefit some exporters. A more effective way to approach concerns about ecolabelling schemes would be to propose specific steps for developing country participation in the selection of the criteria for the schemes themselves.

Developing countries could win by addressing their trade-related concerns, and also win by taking advantage of "green" opportunities abroad. Under the current approach they lose because, by polarizing the debate, their concerns have less chance to be taken seriously, and they lose again because delaying progress on ecolabelling hinders potential business opportunities.

Unfortunately, other win–win possibilities and how to ensure the producers in developing countries take advantage of them still remain unexplored. Simply put, developing countries need to discover specific market opportunities that are beneficial to the environment—a topic to which they have given too little attention.

Pressure on the dispute settlement mechanism

The fourth reason for developing countries to join the effort to advance the trade and environment debate is that it is preferable to try to influence the debate rather than the issues being decided through decisions from the dispute settlement mechanism.

Trade and environment experts have argued that, especially in the absence of a new trade round where some issues could be negotiated, the responsibility for resolving conflicts in these two areas will continue to be placed on the trade body's already overburdened dispute settlement system.[44] As James Cameron has suggested, "it is the dispute settlement that is stepping in to do the job that the negotiators failed to do."[45]

In the field of trade and environment, the WTO dispute settlement system has focused on interpretation of Article XX of the GATT, which allows countries to impose trade-restrictive measures if they are considered necessary to achieve certain objectives (such as the protection of non-renewable natural resources or public health). In a landmark decision in 1998, the Appellate Body concluded, on the basis of Article XX(g), that the United States had the right to impose a ban on shrimp imported from countries that failed to protect endangered sea turtles.[46] The ban violated the WTO rules because it was imposed in a discriminatory manner, but the decision gave a blessing to discrimination against products on the basis of non-product-related PPMs. As highlighted earlier, developing countries had strongly objected to further progress on this issue and, as a result, they harshly criticized the decision (particularly Thailand, Malaysia, and Pakistan).

A new decision in July 2000 is expected to have major implications for the use of trade measures to support environmental or public health goals. A WTO panel upheld a French ban on imports of chrysotile asbestos based on GATT Article XX(b), which allows an exemption to WTO rules for measures necessary to protect human health, among others. This is the first time that the WTO has allowed a member to impose a ban on imported goods based on Article XX(b).[47]

These four arguments all support a case for more constructive Southern participation in the trade and environment debate as the best way both to address developing countries' fears and to explore the opportunities of this issue while strengthening the WTO.

Effective participation in the WTO trade and environment debate

Even if resistance by developing countries to trade and environment issues were dropped, there would still be important constraints on proactive participation in the debate. Trade and environment expertise is scarce in the developing world. Most Southern governments have invested in the creation of either a team of trade experts or a team of environmental experts, but expertise in both fields is rare. Although this situation occurs in the developed countries as well, it is in the poorest nations where some sort of policy dialogue is least likely to occur, at least in the short term.

Building trade and environment teams cannot happen overnight. Furthermore, the linkage between trade and environment has not been a national issue, so most countries in the developing world also lack independent trade and environment authorities, research centres, think-tanks, or universities that could lead an effort to develop a domestic agenda addressing the main concerns and identifying the potential benefits.

For instance, academia could—and should—play a leading role in the debate. A promising approach has been developed in Central America. Several professors working on economic policy and sustainable development issues have led a Costa Rican working group addressing the question of what a national trade and environment agenda should focus on. The discussions have involved some well-known leaders from the business sector, highly respected individuals working on environmental issues, officials from specialized institutions, academics, and representatives from NGOs. The ultimate goal of this forum is to arrive at concrete proposals on key issues for domestic constituencies. These will eventually be presented to the government. Fortunately, this is not an isolated case. Similar national dialogues have also started in Guatemala, El Salvador, and Panama.

The foregoing points to several ways of contributing to a less polarized WTO trade and environment debate:

- *A national agenda.* The South needs to set its own agenda in this debate. Long-term support for and commitment to a national agenda are more likely once it is perceived as legitimate in its own right, because of its merits and its responsiveness to recognized concerns. Anything imposed from the outside will never be embraced with real enthusiasm.
- *Clarifying priorities.* Developing nations need to focus on what they want, instead of passively objecting to what they do not want. A national trade and environment agenda should be understood as a means for accomplishing desirable goals, not merely as a defensive tool.
- *Multi-sector dialogue.* A domestic trade and environment agenda requires participation by business, environmental authorities, and other representatives of civil society, not just government officials. The more feedback and constructive criticism the government receives and processes, the more solid and legitimate its proposals become. In other words, the process of defining an official trade and environment position should not be secretive. Secretive processes provoke nothing but suspicion and backlash. The more sectors that think about these issues, the more policy options can emerge, and the greater the degree of innovation that will be brought to bear.

A domestic discussion needs to address concrete proposals, followed by an analytically rigorous assessment of their advantages, disadvantages, and impacts on both trade and environmental policymaking. Without a constructive approach with clear and relevant goals, these issues are likely to have an early death, because the incentives to join the domestic forum will be rather low.

The impetus for a trade and environment debate in the South could be improved by focusing on unexplored opportunities for the country in general, and its exporters in particular. Governments need to provide more information and data not just on legal or institutional issues, but also on economic aspects (e.g. the costs and benefits for key sectors in their economies). What must be avoided is framing the national debate in terms of lose-all or win-all dilemmas, such as whether trade is good or bad for the environment and vice versa, or whether or not a trade and environment agenda is a means to Northern protectionism. Such all-or-nothing polarizations hardly ever arrive at credible conclusions.

Promoting a constructive dialogue on the trade and environment interface is also a key responsibility of industrialized nations. By shifting from a confrontational to a cooperative approach they could help to build common ground on trade and environmental issues, both domestically and in the multilateral system. First, avoiding a sanctions-based approach, while maintaining the commitment to make trade and environment mutually supportive, would go a long way to reducing developing countries' legitimate concerns about the risk of protectionist manipulation of environmental issues. Secondly, industrialized countries must acknowledge that the trade and environment interface is an extremely knowledge-intensive, state-of-the-art subject, and that the development and implementation of sophisticated regulations in this area demand institutional and human capacities that many developing countries simply lack. This underlines the importance of promoting institutional capacity-building in developing countries and providing related technical assistance. The difficulties in implementing international commitments in other regulatory and institutionally intensive areas demonstrate that writing a commitment in a trade agreement is not an automatic guarantee of compliance.

A new systematic and explicit approach to trade and environment

The core system of rules that the WTO inherited from the GATT was driven by the prevailing reasoning at the end of the 1940s, in a world that was very different from the world today. Back then, current critical issues such as global warming, biodiversity protection, or industrial pollution were totally absent from the international agenda.

After a 50-year process of strengthening the trading system and eight rounds of difficult negotiations, it is not surprising that the trade community should be uncomfortable with the idea of restructuring the current regime to better incorporate new concepts—sustainable development among them. But, as Renato Ruggiero rightly points out, the WTO "cannot operate in isolation from the world in which it exists."[48]

In the future, a new approach to trade and environment should incorporate environmental considerations in a way that is both explicit and systematic. There is a need to ensure that trade liberalization will go hand in hand with environmental policy-making. Even if fears about "the race to the bottom" in environmental regulation have been overstated, there is some evidence that the globalization process has inhibited a "race to the top," producing what some authors call a "regulatory chill."[49]

At least two specific trade and environment issues need to be explicitly addressed in the WTO (not just the CTE): one is the relationship of WTO agreements and multilateral environmental agreements (MEAs) with trade measures; the other is the use of process and production methods (PPMs) as the basis for product discrimination. Other issues such as the precautionary principle are important but could be addressed in a second stage.

Multilateral environmental agreements

The search for solutions to a set of global environmental problems (e.g. the threat of global climate change) has boosted international collective action to avoid overexploitation of the "global commons." Today, nearly 200 MEAs have been set up with membership ranging from a small group to 170 nations. Over 20 of these agreements incorporate trade measures regarding substances or products, either between parties to the agreement and/or between parties and non-parties.[50] As environmental problems become more global in scope, international efforts to address them are likely to increase, raising new questions about the relationship between global environmental treaties and the rules of the multilateral trading system.

The WTO–MEA relationship has received a great deal of attention in the CTE, yet little *rapprochement* has been accomplished. As noted above, the case for further accommodating trade measures pursuant to MEAs within the WTO rules has been strongly contested, especially by developing countries. Consequently, uncertainty regarding the hierarchy and compatibility between the two regimes still remains.[51]

Despite the fact that no trade measures pursuant to an MEA have been challenged in the WTO, there is no guarantee that such conflicts will not arise in the future. In fact, the interaction between both regimes is expected to increase. One recent and straightforward example of the trade and environment overlap was the Cartagena Protocol on Biosafety, which regulates some biotechnology-related issues.[52] One key lesson from the controversial process leading to the Protocol was that it was best to take an explicit approach to reconciling the rules of the environmental agreement and those of the trade regime, in spite of the strong resistance of the trade community and related business sectors.[53] Unfortunately, how to address the interaction between the climate change regime and the trading system still remains unsolved.[54]

The recommendation here is not that the regimes be united. Clearly, they address different issues and must keep a certain distance. What should be stressed, however, is that reducing the likelihood of future clashes is in the best interests of both the trade and the environmental communities. This could be achieved by developing an understanding, an interpretative decision, or a set of guidelines that explicitly set out how the WTO–MEA relationship should be worked out, thereby creating greater predictability and legal certainty.

Process and production methods

Process and production methods have become a central issue in the trade and environment debate. Although there is agreement among WTO members that PPMs that have an impact on the final product (known as product-related PPMs or incorporated PPMs) are allowed by the WTO Agreement on Technical Barriers to Trade (TBT), fierce disagreement remains over whether or not PPMs that do not affect the final product (unincorporated PPMs or non-product-related PPMs) are allowed. The position of most developing countries is that the TBT Agreement prohibits the use of standards based on non-product-related PPMs because its definition of standards does not include those that are based on such PPMs and product differentiation on these grounds is not allowed by GATT/WTO jurisprudence. They claim it is inadmissible for products to be differentiated on the basis of the environmental effects created in the exporting countries.[55]

However, this claim will be difficult to sustain in the long run. Environmental protection efforts are leading to environmentally friendlier products, consumers, and voters. The South sells its exports to markets where there is growing demand for information not only about the products themselves, but also about how these products were manufactured. Additionally, WTO case law has opened up a window supporting PPM-based discrimination in the Appellate Body's decision on the Shrimp–Turtle case mentioned above. These trends are unlikely to fade away, and ignoring the debate may have a high cost for the South.

Opposition from free-traders and some business sectors to the inclusion of PPM-based standards as a means for differentiating between products is based on a claim that their acceptance would increase the impetus for discriminatory and extra-territorial behaviour, thus overriding non-discrimination principles, which have been the cornerstone of the multilateral trading system.[56] The developing country argument, while similar, emphasizes the suspicion that PPM-based differentiation could become extremely vulnerable to protectionist abuse. In addition, they fear their systems of production will not be able to meet the high standards demanded by the industrialized countries. These fears are not groundless and should not be ignored. Explicitly addressing the concerns of the poorer nations is one of the biggest challenges ahead. A creative approach would be an international system that identifies the appropriate baseline standards and punishes unfair PPM-based discrimination.

Final remarks

The WTO needs to address environmental concerns in a way that strengthens the organization as a key and legitimate pillar of the global governance architecture. Global responsibility for promoting trade while advancing environmental policy should not be transferred entirely to the WTO but, especially in the absence of a global counterpart for environmental issues, the trade body cannot turn its back on this task. Developing countries should participate in this debate, not only to strengthen the WTO but also to ensure that their concerns are heard and addressed in the process.

Developing countries that engage in the kind of domestic trade and environment dialogue outlined in this chapter will be better able to define a sound and explicit position that maximizes the opportunities and minimizes the risks. It is then more likely that they will play a constructive role in the WTO context by contributing to the support of new trade rules that promote both free trade and environmental protection.

Given the vast North–South divide, one effective way to encourage the participation of developing countries could be a Northern commitment to avoid domestic pressures that favour unilateralism as well as protectionism. Additionally, Northern countries that are pushing for "greener" WTO rules should also create a momentum of their own for initiatives rewarding Southern efforts to address trade and environment issues proactively.

Identifying and rejecting cases where environmental claims are being used as a mask for trade protectionism is in the interests of the global trade community as a whole, not just the developing countries. This balance is essential. But most important of all, as deeper integration takes place, the transition to a new approach to the interface between trade and other legitimate global goals—such as environmental protection—has to be driven by a philosophy in which the WTO and its rules and procedures are seen not as an end in themselves, but as the means for maximizing the opportunities to improve the quality of life of the greatest number of people, and for the longest period of time.

Notes

1. For one of the early proposals, see Daniel Esty, *Greening the GATT*, Washington, DC: Institute for International Economics, 1994.

2. For example, in July 2000 the European Union established an informal working group to analyse the possibility of creating a World Environment Organization that "could unite the various multilateral treaties and conventions concerning the environment and serve as a counterweight to the [WTO]." "EU Working Group Formed to Examine Creation of World Environmental Organization," *International Environment Reporter*, 19 July 2000, p. 556. Renato Ruggiero also underscored the need for such an organization in his speech to the World Trade Organization's High Level Symposium on Trade and Environment, 15–16 March 1999, Geneva (online at http://www.wto.org/english/tratop_e/envir_e/dgenv.htm). Also see "Why Greens Should Love Trade: The Environment Does Need to Be Protected but Not from Trade," *The Economist*, 9–11 October 1999, p. 18.

3. The United Nations Conference on Trade and Development (UNCTAD) has from its very beginning stressed these three central ideas. See UNCTAD, *Address by Mr. Rubens Ricupero, Secretary-General of UNCTAD*, TD/L/363, February 2000.

4. Rubens Ricupero, "Trade and Environment: Strengthening Complementarities and Reducing Conflicts," in Gary Sampson and Bradnee Chambers, eds., *Trade, Environment, and the Millennium*, Tokyo: United Nations University Press, 1999, pp. 23–34.

5. In fact, many analysts agree that the spirit of goodwill and cooperation generated at Rio 1992 has already dissipated and may deteriorate further in the absence of a renewed commitment. See Gary Bryner, "Agenda 21: Myth or Reality?" in Norman J. Vig and Regina S. Axelrod, eds., *The Global Environment. Institutions, Law, and Policy*, Washington, DC: Congressional Quarterly, 1999, pp. 157–189.

6. The Multifibre Arrangement provided the basis for establishing quotas on imports of textiles and clothing from several developing countries. It was replaced by the WTO Agreement on Textiles and Clothing in 1995. World Trade Organization, *Annual Report 2000*, Geneva: World Trade Organization, 2000.

7. Data published by the Textile Exporters Association quoted in Rubens Ricupero, "The World Trading System. Seattle and Beyond," in Jeffrey Schott,

ed., *The WTO after Seattle,* Washington, DC: Institute for International Economics. 2000, pp. 65–70. Ernest Pregg, "The South Rises in Seattle," *Journal of International Law,* 3(1), 2000, pp. 183–185.

8. See Roger Porter and Pierre Sauvé, eds., *Seattle, the WTO, and the Future of the Multilateral Trading System,* Center for Business and Government, John F. Kennedy School of Government, Massachusetts: Harvard University, 2000. Also see Pregg, "The South Rises"; and Monica Araya, "Lessons from the Stalemate in Seattle," *Journal of Environment and Development,* 9(2), June 2000, pp. 183–189.

9. Jeffrey Schott, "The WTO after Seattle," in Schott, ed., *The WTO after Seattle,* pp. 3–40.

10. The meeting took place in Bangkok, Thailand, 12–29 February 2000. Although supporting globalization, the Bangkok Declaration on Global Dialogue and Dynamic Engagement highlighted some of the Southern disappointments about the process, in which "asymmetries and imbalances within and among countries in the international economy have intensified." More information is available online at http://www.unctad-10.org/index_en.htm.

11. For an example of this claim see A. V. Ganesan, "Seattle and Beyond: Developing-Country Perspectives," in Schott, ed., *The WTO after Seattle,* pp. 85–87. Magda Shahin, "Trade and Environment: How Real Is the Debate?" in Sampson and Chambers, eds., *Trade, Environment, and the Millennium,* pp. 35–64.

12. Schott, "The WTO after Seattle," p. 5.

13. For a summary of the history of the debate since the start of the 1970s in the GATT, see World Trade Organization, *Background Note: High Level Symposium on Trade and Environment,* Geneva: World Trade Organization, March 1999 (available online at http://www.wto.org/english/tratop_e/envir_e/tr_envbadoc.htm).

14. Its two-fold overarching goal is (a) to identify the link between trade measures and environmental measures in order to promote sustainable development; and (b) to recommend whether the multilateral trading regime provisions need to be modified, in a way that is compatible with the nature of the regime (non-discriminatory, open, and equitable). Ibid.

15. All the discussions of the CTE are summarized in the WTO Trade and Environment Bulletins (available online at http://www.wto.org/english/tratop_e/envir_e/bull_e.htm).

16. The World Conservation Union and the International Institute for Sustainable Development (IISD) issued a joint statement criticizing the work undertaken in the CTE for being unfocused and too narrow. "EU Official Calls for High-Level Meeting to Push on Trade, Environment Agenda," *International Environment Reporter,* 1 April 1998; "Environmental Groups Urge U.S. Administration to Press for Reforms at WTO Ministerial," *International Environment Reporter,* 13 October 1999, p. 837.

17. The Division currently has 10 members (World Trade Organization, *Annual Report 2000,* p. 110).

18. Other transparency measures include the creation of an NGO section on the WTO website (http://www.wto.org/wto/english/forums_e/ngo_e/ngo_e.htm) and a monthly list of NGO position papers received by the

Secretariat, which are available for the information of members upon request (World Trade Organization, *Background Note*).

19. "Developing Countries Resist Expansion of Environmental Role for World Trade Body," *International Environment*, 22, 17 March 1999. The High Level Symposium on Trade and Environment (15–16 March 1999, Geneva) brought together a large number of government officials, intergovernmental organizations, and people from academia, business, and the NGO community (online at http://www.wto.org/english/tratop_e/envir_e/hlmenv_e.htm).

20. The decision is still pending (World Trade Organization, *Annual Report 2000*, p. 88).

21. See Veena Jha, René Vossenaar, and Ulrich Hoffmann, "Trade and Environment: Issues Raised in Proposals Submitted to the WTO Council during the Seattle Process and Their Possible Implications for Developing Countries," in Peider Könz et al., eds., *Trade, Environment and Sustainable Development: Views from Sub-Saharan Africa and Latin America. A Reader,* Geneva: United Nations University Press and the International Center for Trade and Sustainable Development, 2000, pp. 375–404. Also see Daniel Esty, "Environmental Governance at the WTO: Outreach to Civil Society," in Sampson and Chambers, eds., *Trade, Environment, and the Millennium*, pp. 97–119, for a contrasting view.

22. A recent controversy emerged in the WTO after the Appellate Body issued a procedural on 10 May 2000 holding that it may accept an *amicus curiae* brief from the public in the WTO case against US countervailing duties on British steel. For an analysis see *New World Trade Organization Decision May Widen Opportunities for Amicus Briefs,* Washington, DC: Environmental Law Institute, July 2000, and see, generally, John Jackson, "Dispute Settlement and the WTO," in Porter and Sauvé, eds., *Seattle*.

23. Håkan Nordström and Scott Vaughan, *Trade and Environment,* Geneva: World Trade Organization, Special Studies 4, 1999 (available online at http://www.wto.org/english/tratop_e/envir_e/stud99_e.htm).

24. Ibid., p.11.

25. "Embracing Greenery," *The Economist,* 9–11 October 1999, pp. 89–90.

26. According to this principle, "in some cases—particularly where the costs of action are low and the risks of inaction are high—preventive action should be taken, even without full scientific certainty about the problem being addressed." Aaron Cosbey and Stas Burgiel, *The Cartagena Protocol on Biosafety: An Analysis of Results,* an IISD Briefing Note, Winnipeg: International Institute for Sustainable Development, 2000, p. 4.

27. See World Trade Organization, *Background Note.*

28. For a comprehensive analysis on developing countries' stakes, see Jha, Vossenaar, and Hoffmann, "Trade and Environment: Issues." Also see Shahin, "Trade and Environment."

29. During the July 2000 CTE meeting, China, Hong Kong, India, Brazil, Malaysia, and Pakistan expressed their views regarding the WTO–MEA relationship, highlighting that clarification in the area was not necessary and that "concerns in this area should not be exaggerated" (World Trade Organization, Trade and Environment Bulletin, No. 33 , p. 5).

30. See *Trade and Sustainable Development. Communication from the United States,* WT/GC/W/194, 1 June 1999. The US proposal on the elimination of subsidies that contribute to the fisheries overcapacity has created some convergence among WTO members. For example, Australia, Iceland, New Zealand, Norway, Peru, and the Philippines have also endorsed such initiatives (Jha, Vossenaar, and Hoffman, "Trade and Environment: Issues").

31. See proposals presented to the General Council: *European Commission Approach to Trade and Environment in the New WTO Round,* WT/GC/W/194, 1 June 1999; *Preparations for the 1999 Ministerial Conference. Trade and Environment. Communication from Norway,* WT/GC/W/176, 30 April 1999; *Canadian Approach to Trade and Environment in the New WTO Round,* WT/GC/W/358, 12 October 1999, and *Trade and Sustainable Development. Communication from the United States.*

32. India has stressed the need to address the potential conflicts between the goals of the TRIPS Agreement and the efforts to protect biodiversity and traditional knowledge. For a recent proposal see *Protection of Biodiversity and Traditional Knowledge. The Indian Experience. Submission by India,* WT/CTE/W/156 and WT/CTE/W/156Corr.1, 14 July 2000, suggesting the need to establish minimum multilateral standards to protect traditional knowledge. Such calls for international action have been endorsed by Brazil, Cuba, Malaysia, and Peru (World Trade Organization, Trade and Environment Bulletin, No. 33).

33. The GATT started to address this issue back in 1982, leading to the creation of a Working Group in 1989 for the analysis of trade-related aspects of the export of domestically prohibited goods and other hazardous substances. Between 1995 and 1998, Nigeria presented several proposals to the CTE and was particularly active in this area. World Trade Organization, *Background Note.* For a recent proposal, see *Trade in Domestically Prohibited Goods. Submission by Bangladesh,* WT/CTE/W/141, 15 July 2000.

34. Ricupero, "The World Trading System."

35. For an analysis of the situation of US trade policy and the emergence of "new issues" in the policy agenda, see I. M. Destler and Peter J. Balint, *The New Politics of American Trade: Trade, Labor, and the Environment,* Policy Analyses in International Economics, No. 58, Washington, DC: Institute for International Economics, 1999.

36. For example, in a poll on "Americans and Globalization" conducted by Harris Interactive in April 2000, even though 68 per cent of those interviewed thought globalization was good for consumers, 80 per cent considered that protecting the environment should become a major priority of US trade agreements. See Aaron Bernstein, "Backlash: Behind the Anxiety over Globalization," *Business Week,* 24 April 2000, pp. 38–44.

37. Prior to Seattle, several US environmental groups (National Wildlife Federation, Friends of the Earth, Sierra Club, Defenders of Wildlife, and the Center for International Environmental Law) pledged to oppose any request by President Clinton for fast-track authority if the administration failed to push for environmental reforms at the WTO ("Environmental Groups Urge U.S. Administration to Press for Reforms at WTO Ministerial"). Fast-track author-

ity allows the President to present draft legislation to Congress to implement a trade agreement that the government has negotiated. Congress approves or rejects the bill, without amendments. Fast-track authority lapsed in 1993 and a renewal has been blocked since. See, generally, Robert E. Baldwin and Christopher S. Magee, *Congressional Trade Votes: From NAFTA Approval to Fast-Track Defeat,* Policy Analyses in International Economics, No. 59, Washington, DC: Institute for International Economics, 1999.

38. Strong opposition was led by an international coalition of NGOs, which, especially in 1997 and 1998, organized a campaign—basically through the internet—to create domestic opposition in the capitals of the OECD countries, supported by members of the parliaments, especially in Canada, the United States, the United Kingdom, New Zealand, and Australia. For a perspective from key MAI opponents, see Maude Barlow and Tony Clarke, *MAI: The Multilateral Agreement on Investment and the Threat to American Freedom,* New York: Stoddart Publishing, 1998. For a look at both sides of the issue, see Stephen J. Kobrins, "The MAI and the Clash of Globalizations," *Foreign Policy,* Fall 1998.

39. "NGOs from 60 Countries Team up to Halt Next WTO Round on Environmental Grounds," *International Environment Reporter,* 26 May 1999, p. 446.

40. For a very illustrative example of the organizational skills of those leading the "battle" against globalization, see the interview with one of the leaders of the anti-WTO protests in Seattle, "Lory's War," *Foreign Policy,* 118, 2000, pp. 29–55.

41. "The Non-Governmental Order," *The Economist,* 11–17 December 1999, p. 22. However, it is also important to stress that most analysts agree that the Seattle talks were in fact derailed not by the activities of NGOs in the streets, but by a combination of major divisions among the WTO members on key issues, lack of adequate preparation before the meeting, and problems with the consultation and decision-making procedures.

42. David Schorr, "Fishery Subsidies and the WTO," in Sampson and Chambers, eds., *Trade, Environment, and the Millennium,* pp. 143–170.

43. An extensive analysis of ecolabelling schemes is found in Arthur Appleton, "Environmental Labelling Schemes: WTO Law and Developing Country Implications," in Sampson and Chambers, eds., *Trade, Environment, and the Millennium,* pp. 195–222.

44. "Agreement on Environmental Issues Not Likely for WTO Members, Experts Say," *International Environment Reporter,* 2 August 2000.

45. Ibid., p. 602.

46. *United States–Import Prohibition of Certain Shrimp and Shrimp Products,* Appellate Body Report, WT/DS58/AB/R, adopted 6 November 1998. One groundbreaking aspect of this decision was the Appellate Body's conclusion that all the WTO agreements needed to be interpreted in light of the WTO Preamble, which states that one objective of the organization is to support sustainable development and that no jurisdictional limitation exists that would prevent the Article XX provision on the environment from being used by a WTO member beyond its borders. Additionally, the Appellate Body established that a panel had the discretionary authority either to accept and consider or to reject information and advice submitted to it, whether requested by the

panel or not. This includes information from NGOs such as *amicus curiae* briefs. For reactions to the ruling see "WTO Upholds Ruling that U.S. Restrictions Linked to Sea Turtles Violate Trade Rules," *International Environment Reporter,* 28 October 1998.

47. The decision was expected to become public by the middle of September 2000. "WTO Panel Issues Ruling Upholding French Ban of Chrysotile Asbestos," *International Environment Reporter,* 2 August 2000. Asbestos is a known carcinogen and most forms of it are banned, at least in industrialized countries (chrysotile asbestos is the only one still allowed in the European Union and a ban is scheduled for 2005). "Asbestos Ban Is Justified under Health Exception," *Bridges* 4(5), 2000, p. 5.

48. Renato Ruggiero, "Reflections from Seattle," in Schott, ed., *The WTO after Seattle,* p. xv.

49. For an in-depth analysis on this issue, see Daniel Esty and Damien Geradin, "Environmental Protection and International Competitiveness: A Conceptual Framework," *Journal of World Trade,* 32, 1998, pp. 5–46.

50. Steve Charnovitz, "Multilateral Environmental Agreements and Trade Rules," *Environmental Policy and Law,* 26(4), 1996, p. 164.

51. For an in-depth analysis, see Duncan Brack, "Environmental Treaties and Trade: Multilateral Environmental Agreements and the Multilateral Trading System," in Sampson and Chambers, eds., *Trade, Environment, and the Millennium,* pp. 271–298.

52. Pursuant to Article 19 of the Convention on Biological Diversity, the Conference of the Parties had decided to negotiate the Protocol to set the appropriate procedures in the field of the safe transfer, handling, and use of any living modified organisms resulting from biotechnology that might have adverse effects on biodiversity. The Protocol was agreed in Montreal on 29 January 2000. More information about the process, the treaty, and the official decisions is available online at http://www.biodiv.org/biosafe/protocol. The Protocol is open for signature from May 2000 to June 2001.

53. The agreement came as a surprise indeed—especially to the environmental community. Many feared the Protocol would not survive the concerns about potential conflict with the multilateral trading system and that pressure from strong commercial interests would lead to a collapse of the talks in Montreal. For more information about the process see Cosbey and Burgiel, *The Cartagena Protocol on Biosafety.*

54. For recent discussions about trade–climate change linkages see Duncan Brack et al., *International Trade and Climate Change Policy,* London: Royal Institute for International Affairs, 2000.

55. Doaa Abdel Motaal, "The Agreement on Technical Barriers to Trade, the Committee on Trade and Environment, and Eco-labelling," in Sampson and Chambers, eds., *Trade, Environment, and the Millennium,* pp. 223–238.

56. "Better Integration of Environmental Issues May Create New Barriers, Industry Says," *International Environment Reporter,* 23 June 1999, p. 542.

9

What the world needs from the multilateral trading system

Martin Wolf
Associate Editor and Chief Economics
Commentator, *Financial Times*

The multilateral trading system at the beginning of the twenty-first century is the most remarkable achievement in institutionalized global economic cooperation that there has ever been. The emergence of the gold standard in the four decades leading up to the First World War was unplanned. The *système des traités* that governed trade within Europe from 1860 was inherently fragile and limited in geographical scope, above all because the United States remained outside it. The Bretton Woods system of fixed exchange rates lasted for a quarter of a century, before its collapse in the early 1970s. But the General Agreement on Tariffs and Trade (GATT) of 1948—throughout its history no more than the provisionally applied commercial policy remnants of the still-born International Trade Organization—has done more than survive huge challenges. It has thrived. Reborn as the World Trade Organization (WTO) in January 1995, this institution, long of interest only to a narrow group of specialists, has become the most prominent symbol of globalization. Once threatened by ignorant indifference, it now confronts often equally ignorant malevolence. The central question to be addressed below is what wise policy makers ought to do in response to the pressures now falling on the system.

Achievements of the trading system

How has it been possible for a tiny institution—with a staff of 530 and a paltry annual budget of SFr127 million (US$75m), no more than the US contribution to the United Nation's Food and Agriculture Organization—to become so important? The answer is that it is not the institution that matters; it is rather the agreements among its currently 138 member states (up from only 23 in 1947) that the institution oversees. Those agreements are the results of eight rounds of international trade negotiations among an everwidening circle of participants. The commitments that have been built up over more than half a century largely determine the conditions under which international trade is conducted. To the extent that this is not true today, it soon will be, with the forthcoming membership of the People's Republic of China. There can be little doubt that the institution will soon become global in membership.

The WTO itself argues that it brings as many as 10 benefits.[1] But these can be reduced to two: agreed liberalization and the rule of law.

Agreed liberalization

Trade has been liberalized progressively, at first almost exclusively among today's high-income economies but increasingly in the rest of the world. This has generated an unprecedented expansion in world trade and output. Over the post-war period as a whole, world population rose almost two and a half times and so did world average incomes per head.[2] Nothing like this has ever happened before—even in the half-century before 1914.

While the volume of world production rose more than 8 times between 1948 and 1998, world merchandise exports grew 18 times. Over the same period, the volume of world output of manufactures increased 10 times, while exports of manufactures, the area where trade liberalization concentrated, grew 43 times. Between 1950 and the mid-1990s, the share of trade in global output increased from about 7 per cent to over 20 per cent.[3] This expansion in trade, on which all other forms of international economic integration ultimately depend, has not just been huge. It has also been consistent:

the volume of world trade grew faster than output in virtually every year since the Second World War.

The consequent growth in specialization and international competition has, together with technological advance, been the principal driving force behind a half-century of unprecedented prosperity. It explains the triumph of the Western market economies over their socialist rivals. A wave of liberalization has, in consequence, broken over almost all the world over the past two decades. It has struck China, India, the rest of southern and eastern Asia, the remnants of the former Soviet empire, and, not least, Latin American countries, long seduced by dreams of import substitution and self-sufficiency. This worldwide move towards liberalization is the fruit not of theoretical fancies, but of practical experience. International economic integration through market-driven trade has worked. For this reason, one can say with confidence that those who argue against liberalization are condemning hundreds of millions of people to needlessly prolonged poverty.

The rule of law

If liberalization is the first great achievement of the trading system, the second is the entrenchment of a working system of international law that, by governing the behaviour of the most powerful states, protects the world economy from arbitrary political interference and governments from narrow sectional interests. The resulting security for trade is not only a spur to economic integration but also a basis for peaceful relations among—and within—states. Although rule-governed trade may not guarantee peace, it does remove a potent cause of conflict. It offers an alternative to reliance on unbridled force in the trading relations among states.

These rules are what makes the institutions of the trading system uniquely potent. The International Monetary Fund has, for two decades, had effective leverage only over developing counties and countries in transition. The World Bank has never enjoyed more than this, except in the brief era of post-war reconstruction. The Organisation for Economic Co-operation and Economic Development is a purely advisory body. But the WTO is an effective system of international economic law. As such, the trading system is, arguably, more than just the greatest achievement in institutionalized global economic cooperation; it is the greatest achievement in institution-alized global cooperation, *tout court.*

Dangers created by success

Success creates new dangers. The WTO is a very different institu-tion from the GATT of two or three decades ago and, as such, is exposed to new hazards.

First, the WTO now has an increasingly active membership of almost all the countries in the world. Its members vary hugely, how-ever, in their economic size, level of development, and capacity to engage actively in the institution, with such giants as the United States and the European Union at one end, and such small develop-ing countries as St. Kitts and Nevis and St. Lucia at the other. Yet the organization still works on the basis of consensus.

Secondly, with the addition of agriculture, services, trade-related investment (TRIMs), and trade-related intellectual property (TRIPS) in the course of the Uruguay Round, the system covers almost all trade, an astonishing total of US$6,800 billion in 1999 (US$5,460 billion in merchandise trade, with the remainder in commercial services).

Thirdly, as liberalization has advanced, the WTO has increasingly come to affect what were thought of as purely domestic regulatory de-cisions. Examples of such "deep integration" are the Uruguay Round's agreements on sanitary and phytosanitary standards, which accompa-nied liberalization of agriculture, and on technical barriers to trade.[4]

Fourthly, the WTO has also become a single undertaking with universal participation in all its disciplines. All members, including developing countries, have found themselves forced to make com-mitments, including onerous ones, salient examples being customs valuation procedures and protection of intellectual property.[5]

Fifthly, the dispute settlement system has become more potent and legalistic than ever before. No longer can a party to a dispute block the adoption of a panel finding. On the contrary, it is unable to halt the inexorable progress of cases. The result has been far more active use of the dispute settlement process since the establishment of the WTO in January 1995 than in the old GATT, with consultation requests running at a rate of 40–50 a year.[6]

This extension and strengthening of the trading system happened for the best of motives: to spread liberalization into areas previously immune to it, notably agriculture; to reduce the capacity of governments to employ domestic regulations for protectionist ends; to bring in new economic interests in favour of trade liberalization, notably those of the service sector and of companies seeking protection of intellectual property; to include more countries in the circle of mutual obligations and reciprocal liberalization; to eliminate the grey areas that had grown up in the system, including voluntary export restraints and the Multifibre Arrangement (MFA), which governs restrictions on trade in textiles; and, above all, to put the structure on more secure foundations.

Behind this was at least partly the view that history had confirmed the success of the internationally open market economy, restored after the calamities that befell the world between 1914 and 1945. Now, at last, there was a chance for the world as a whole, not just part of it, to move forward on this basis. It is to the credit of the world's principal policy makers that they saw both the need and the opportunity, particularly after the fall of the Berlin Wall in 1989 and the subsequent collapse of the Soviet Union in 1991. The much-postponed completion of the Uruguay Round in 1994 may be seen as a fitting coda to that drama.

Although the leaders were right to take the step of creating the WTO, they did not anticipate the resistance that this would create. What is evident is that their new creation is indeed far more visible, intrusive, and potent than the system it replaced. As important, trade itself has also become more visible, intrusive, and potent as it has grown. These new realities have created a corresponding increase in the pressures upon the trading system.

Pressures from outside the WTO

Who are the sources of this pressure? The answer is that they vary from fanatical opponents of globalization to those who accept the basic logic of the system but want it to change in often mutually inconsistent directions.

The more extreme of those forces became visible at the disastrous Ministerial Meeting of the WTO in Seattle at the end of 1999.[7] Many of those who demonstrated in Seattle were cranks: "anarchists" who believe that the power of the states they supposedly despise should be used to halt trade; "friends of the poor" who argue that the world's destitute would benefit from being driven back into self-sufficiency; and "consumer advocates" who want to deprive their fellow citizens of access to cheap goods.

Attitudes that had foundered in the shipwreck of twentieth-century nationalism and totalitarianism were bubbling up again, like flotsam, to the surface of political life. Old desires for the comforts of community over individual striving, for traditional ways over rapid change, for the beneficence of the state over the cold logic of the market, for collectivism over freedom, and for the nation over the global economy were re-born. However, if the first time had been tragedy, now—with the clowns prancing around in their turtle suits—it was farce. Marxist, nationalist, and fascist opponents of liberal capitalism had aspired to tribalism in a post-enlightenment guise. Today's demands are more atavistic. The guiding spirits are not Karl Marx, but Jean-Jacques Rousseau and William Blake—the former for his myth of the noble savage, the latter for his contempt for science and industry.

It is because of the WTO's successes that those who hate the modern world view it as the totemic symbol of globalization. "Stop the world, we want to push you all off" is their motto. It is one of the nicer ironies that the Internet—the foremost contemporary example of an integrating technology—is bringing these anti-globalizers together. The WTO should consider their attacks an honour. They show that it is presiding over something important and vital. But such opponents will never be assuaged. People who believe that "production should be for people, not for profit," who regard the multinational corporation as intrinsically evil, or who see the historic high points of human culture as the Palaeolithic hunter-gatherer band or the self-sufficient manorial economy of the European dark ages will never be persuaded of the merits of a dynamic, market-based international economy.

Yet, behind such nonsense, it is possible to identify more rational forces. One is traditional protectionist interests. The labour movement of the United States has, for example, become strongly opposed to liberal trade. In this, it reflects the interests of its members, many of whom work in import-threatened industries, such as steel and textiles and clothing. The fact that unions represent only 9 per cent of US private sector workers, almost entirely in the "old economy," means that they are bound to be a voice against liberal trade. As the late Mancur Olson pointed out, only an "encompassing organization," namely, one that represents most of the economic interests in society, is likely to campaign for policies that raise overall incomes rather than increase the incomes of their members at the expense of others.[8] It is not surprising therefore that Scandinavian trades unions are more sensible in their views on trade than their US counterparts are, since they represent a far wider spectrum of the workforce. But labour is, of course, not the only interest often opposed to liberal trade. Farmers in high-income countries are still more effective.

Meanwhile, environmentalists and trades unions in high-income countries make the fundamental complaint that the WTO is subservient to the demands of multinational business (as voiced by such bodies as the International Chamber of Commerce) and places a higher priority on trade than on other objectives, above all protection of the environment and social welfare. They argue that the combination of liberalization with the absence of effectively enforced global minimum standards is generating a regulatory race to the bottom, at the expense of painfully acquired standards in their countries.

This race to the regulatory bottom is, it is argued, exacerbated by three specific defects of the trading system. First, it does not permit countries to restrict what may turn out to be harmful imports, particularly in the areas of food and farming, if scientific support for such restrictions cannot be found. In particular, the Agreement on the Application of Sanitary and Phytosanitary Measures (SPS) gives insufficient weight to the "precautionary principle."[9]

Secondly, the WTO does not permit importing countries to distinguish between products on the basis of how they are made, so-called "process and production methods" (PPMs), unless those differences affect the nature of the product. If a PPM cannot be identified in the product it becomes a "non-product-related PPM"

(NPR-PPM), against which countries are not allowed to act. This prohibition makes it difficult for countries to use trade policy as a way to influence how goods and services they import are produced. This issue has been central to several important disputes within the WTO, notably Tuna–Dolphin and Shrimp–Turtle, both of which pitched the extra-territorial impact of US environmental law against the interests of developing country exporters. It is also central to the question of whether environmental labelling schemes are consistent with the WTO.[10]

The same issue of NPR-PPMs arises in the context of labour standards. It is the aim of protagonists of such standards to use trade measures to enforce what they consider to be minimum standards on exporting developing countries.[11] Here, too, then there would be a distinction among products on the basis of how they are produced, this time not on the basis of their environmental impact but rather on the basis of how workers are treated. However, labour standards are even further from incorporation in the WTO than are those for the environment. There already is a Committee on Trade and Environment. But developing countries have resisted any comparable committee on trade and labour standards, insisting, instead, that all such matters should be dealt with inside the International Labour Organization.

Thirdly, the WTO does not adequately accommodate the growing number of multilateral environmental agreements (MEAs), many of which directly control trade in harmful products or use trade sanctions as an enforcement device. Although no MEA has been challenged within the WTO, there is potential for conflict where a trade measure is authorized for use against a non-member by the MEA but is over-ruled by the WTO.[12]

Finally, these groups argue that decision-making in the WTO is undemocratic: it removes sovereignty from legislatures, putting in its place the rule of unaccountable bureaucrats in Geneva. To this is added the objection that this decision-making is not transparent. The combination of lack of democracy with lack of transparency does, it is argued, exclude the voices of "civil society," above all those of non-governmental campaigning organizations, from proper participation in decision-making.[13]

Meanwhile, business in aggregate has remained the strongest out-side supporter of liberalization and of the global trading system, though this does not preclude strong protectionist lobbying by par-ticular businesses or sectors. The International Chamber of Commerce (ICC), for example, which has more than 7,000 member companies and business associations in 132 countries, has consistently called for an ambitious new round of trade negotiations.[14] It is also concerned by "the large number of high-profile trade disputes among members of the group of seven leading high-income countries that are currently being allowed to sour international trade relations and that are weak-ening the authority and effectiveness of the WTO and its disputes set-tlement system." The ICC recommends an ambitious agenda for a new trade round.[15] At the same time, it "believes that governments should be vigilant not to undermine the rules of the multilateral trading sys-tem when designing policies intended to achieve environmental objectives, and in particular to ensure that such policies are not misused for protectionist purposes."[16] Furthermore, "we believe that trade sanctions are neither an appropriate nor an effective means to improve labor standards. Indeed, ultimately, labor standards will be most rapidly and securely advanced by sound economic development based on all countries' full participation in the multilateral trading system."[17] Business then strongly resists the efforts to bring the envi-ronment and labour standards within the trading system.

Response of member governments

The governments of the high-income countries are, in different ways, trying to balance the opposing ideas of business, on the one hand, and the various breeds of policy activist, on the other. They are also, for the most part, trying to achieve further liberalization in the interests of their economies. Where precisely they come out tends to depend on the political complexions of their countries and of themselves.

President Clinton, for example, has made much of the need to give globalization a "human face." His comment, at the time of the Seattle Ministerial Meeting, that the United States would seek to enforce minimum labour standards with the use of sanctions destroyed any lingering chances of launching a new round of multilateral trade negotiations at that time. He remains an unrepentant supporter of this idea.[18] The European Union also wants to incorporate labour standards within the WTO, but does not propose trade sanctions. However, the European Union is even more determined than the United States to modify the WTO, to give greater room for policies allegedly aimed at the environment and health. This is partly because of opposition within the European Union both to the import of beef that has been given growth-promoting hormones and to the use of genetically modified organisms.

Current pressures from the high-income countries in the area of the environment centre on three aims:

1. A review or reinterpretation of GATT Article XX, to provide further accommodation of trade measures (including discriminatory trade measures against non-parties) pursuant to multilateral environmental agreements (MEAs). This may have implications for the use of unilateral measures.

2. Accommodation of trade measures based on non-product-related PPMs on environmental grounds, particularly in the context of eco-labelling.

3. Greater scope for the use of the precautionary principle.[19]

In all these respects, the governments of the high-income countries, particularly the European Union, are responding to pressures arising from "civil society."

Differences between the United States and the European Union show up, however, over how far the agenda of any new round should go beyond the negotiations on agriculture and services that have already begun, in accordance with the "built-in agenda" created by the Uruguay Round. The European Union, with its proposal for a "Millennium Round," wishes to include competition and investment and to pursue the social clause, environmental policy, cultural diversity, and animal welfare. The United States, too, is interested in labour standards and the environment, but not in competition, investment, and culture (which is code for a desire for protection from US popular culture). Many in the United States (and elsewhere) believe that the European Union is interested in this wide and intractable agenda in order to reduce the pressure to liberalize its extremely protectionist agricultural policies.[20]

Meanwhile, governments of the developing countries find themselves in opposition to the policy activists and governments of the North over the links between the environment and labour standards and trade. They are understandably concerned over the implied assault on their always fragile sovereignty—a sensitivity that even casual acquaintance with history adequately explains.

Yet developing countries have wider concerns. Their most important worry remains lack of market access: the MFA is supposed to be liberalized by 2005, but little progress has been made so far; barriers to exports of agricultural products remain an important obstacle to some developing countries, while others are worried by the possible impact of agricultural liberalization on the price of food imports; tariff peaks and tariff escalation remain impediments to exports of labour-intensive and processed agricultural commodities; and so-called "contingent protection," notably anti-dumping duties, remains a costly obstacle to developing country exports to the markets of high-income countries, not just because of the duties but because of the uncertainty they create and the costs of fighting legal cases.

Also significant for developing countries are the standards they have had imposed upon them in the course of the Uruguay Round. J. Michael Finger of the World Bank notes, convincingly, that obligations in such areas as intellectual property, industrial standards, customs valuation, and sanitary and phytosanitary standards are costly for many developing countries. He states that "implementing these obligations would require the least developed countries to invest in buildings, equipment, training, and so forth that would cost each of them $150m—for many of the least developed countries this represents a full year's development budget."[21]

Demands for change assessed

The pressures on the WTO have therefore become truly formidable in their diversity. It has become too important an institution for anyone to ignore, but there is also no consensus on where it should go. Its fiercest critics want it closed down. Others want a host of mutually inconsistent things. The risk then is that the failure of governments to agree will first deprive the institution of hope of progress and then generate an increasingly universal and corrosive dissatisfaction, leading ultimately to collapse.

What is to be done? The approach taken below is not to deal with the detailed issues now under discussion, but to go back to first principles instead. If progress is to be made, indeed if what has been achieved is to be preserved, it is essential to understand what the trading system can be and also what it cannot be. In the rest of this chapter, six issues are analysed: (1) how the system works; (2) why it does not subvert national sovereignty; (3) why it should be more open, but does not subvert democracy; (4) why agreements to liberalize trade do not require enforceable rules on minimum standards; (5) why the scope of the trading system should be circumscribed; and (6) how its remit can be reconciled with the pursuit of other legitimate objectives.

How the global trading system works

The global trading system provides an international public good.[22] In practice, this good has largely been provided by economies that offer the biggest markets, foremost among them the United States and the European Union, which provide roughly 40 per cent of the world's total markets for imports (excluding intra-EU trade). Such large players have entered into reciprocal commitments to liberalize trade whose benefits have been spread worldwide through the principle of non-discrimination. As Douglas Irwin of Dartmouth College argues, "the WTO is useful because it changes the political economy of trade policy in a way that tends to facilitate trade liberalization as an outcome."[23] The combination of reciprocity with non-discrimination has created a liberal, law-governed trading system on the basis of co-operation among sovereign states, each acting in its own perceived self-interest. Economists are right to argue that the calculus underlying the WTO is mercantilist. But they also must agree that this disarmament treaty for mercantilists has worked.

Within these agreements, the sanction against violations is withdrawal of a concession. The aim is to restore the situation before the agreement was disturbed by one of the parties. Thus it is wrong, strictly speaking, to view a trade measure taken in response to a violation as a "sanction." It is better to think of such action as rebalancing the agreement, subsequent to a violation. This system evidently needs a body to determine whether or not a country's rights have been violated. This is the logic of the dispute settlement system. It is a way for sovereign nations to secure protection from the arbitrary actions of others, by accepting that their freedom to retaliate should be governed by an impartial procedure.

The inequality in the power of nations is not removed by the WTO. It remains the case that countries with big markets have greater ability to secure market access and deter actions against their exporters than countries with small markets have. This reflects the fact that the WTO is not a system of global government, but rather a way of organizing and disciplining the intrinsically unequal capacity for self-help of member states. However, to the extent that countries abide by non-discrimination, this capacity for action is in effect at the disposal of all.

For all its great merits, the WTO has limits as a tool for liberalizing trade. The first such limit is that the WTO is not the only way to liberalize. On the contrary, both high-income and developing countries have liberalized extensively, both unilaterally and in the context of preferential trading arrangements. The second limit is that international rule-making is not always and necessarily liberalizing. Anti-dumping is an egregious example of bad trade policy that is enshrined in the WTO. The balance of payments exemption for import restrictions is another. The third limit is that the WTO's clout has become attractive to those who have no interest in liberalization. The extension of the trading system beyond the explicit goal of trade liberalization began, in the Uruguay Round, with TRIPs. Nowadays, however, commercial interests are no longer alone in recognizing what they can gain by employing WTO-authorized sanctions against imports. A rich assortment of activists have realized the potential value of the WTO's enforcement mechanisms for their own varied purposes. Yet a WTO that raises regulatory barriers worldwide and eliminates both valid diversity among regulatory regimes and competition among them could even be worse than no WTO at all.

Why international agreements do not subvert sovereignty

The WTO system has provided a brilliant answer to the question of how to provide the benefits of a global trading system to a world of close to 200 sovereign states. But many argue that the result has been a huge infringement of national sovereignty. This charge is false. It is true that member countries have voluntarily chosen to limit the exercise of their untrammelled discretion in the interests of securing agreement with other states. Yet, in so doing they secure more opportunities for their citizens than would be possible if each state did whatever it pleased.

In making such deals, sovereignty is not lost. The WTO "wields no power of enforcement. It has no authority or power to levy fines, impose sanctions, change tariff rates, or modify domestic laws . . . If a member refuses to comply with rules it previously agreed to follow, all the WTO can do is approve a request by the complaining member to impose sanctions—a power that member governments have always been able to wield."[24] Indeed, any country can even withdraw from the WTO and renounce the agreements it has reached within it. But it will then lose the benefits of membership. It may have the advantage of unlimited sovereignty, but it will have to accept the equally unlimited sovereignty of other countries. An extremely powerful country, such as the United States, might be able to obtain everything it now has, even in those circumstances. Yet experience suggests that it would be unwise for even so powerful an actor to take that for granted.

Why the trading system does not undermine democracy

The bedrock of the trading system is enforceable agreements among states, most of them embodied in domestic law. Only governments, with their monopoly of legislation and law enforcement, can make law. For this reason, the system is unavoidably intergovernmental. The WTO is merely a secretariat servicing a structure of intergovernmental agreements. It is not a government.

It follows that the place for democratic accountability is the legislatures of each of its members. This is where the governments engaged in the trading system need to explain what they are doing and why. It also follows that each individual legislature can no longer determine its own country's trade policy, on a day-to-day basis, even though it continues to set the negotiating authority of its government and retains the ultimate (and decisive) power of ratification of any results. This limitation on the discretion of legislatures was accepted partly because trade policy cannot be sensibly made, at least by those who refuse to accept unilateral liberalization, without consideration of the trade policies of others. It also happened because legislatures have, historically, tended to make dreadful trade policy.

This self-imposed constraint on the freedom of legislatures does not subvert democracy. All modern democracies are constitutional. That is, they recognize that limits can properly be imposed on the discretion of a temporary majority (or plurality) within a legislature. This is for two reasons. The first is that the interests of citizens should not be at the mercy of the legislative majority. Such a state would be a form of tyranny. The second is that no legislature represents the interests of the people as a whole.[25] In general, two kinds of interests tend to be overrepresented, at the expense of the public at large: concentrated producer interests (producer lobbies); and groups with strong emotional commitments to particular policy goals (notably non-governmental organizations). As Professor Robert Hudec of Minnesota University has noted, reliance on international negotiations to "circumvent" a legislative process dominated by such groups may be a rational and desirable way to secure a better outcome for the public at large than is likely to emerge from the domestic legislative process.[26]

Those who find their ability to determine domestic legislation reduced resent the international process that has this result. The question, however, is how far the WTO should accommodate their

desire to influence the processes of negotiation and dispute settlement more directly, under the general rubric of democracy—or, as
Professor Daniel Esty of Yale University puts it, in the interests of
the system's "legitimacy, authoritativeness, and a commitment to
fairness."[27] He argues that "public support cannot be founded on
government authority. Individual acceptance is what matters. The
organization must therefore demonstrate that it has genuine con-
nections to the citizens of the world and that its decisions reflect the
will of the people across the planet. Non-governmental organizations represent an important mechanism by which the WTO can
reach out to citizens and build the requisite bridge to global civil
society."[28]

Yet how is the "will of the people across the planet" to be defined
and assessed, other than as expressed by elected governments? There
is surely no reason to accept that a ragbag collection of NGOs, dominated by the relatively well-resourced institutions of the North,
represents the "will of the people across the planet." The governments of developing countries may reasonably respond that the
North's sudden concern for labour standards and environmental protection reflects a hypocritical form of protectionism or, in the case of
the environment, a desire to preserve the comforts of its resource-
intensive way of life at the expense of the South's chance of development. It is little wonder that they view the demands for opening the
WTO to the NGOs as leaving themselves, grossly under-resourced,
to face both powerful Northern governments and their NGOs.

If there is to be more democracy at the global level, it needs to be far
better thought out than this. In truth, the principles on which a global
democracy should be established are not obvious. At present, the WTO
works on the basis of a consensus among states, with the biggest and
most economically significant having, informally, the greatest influence. This seems a reasonable accommodation to the realities of a world
in which public goods are provided by a collection of governments.
What, after all, is the alternative? One-person-one-vote would give
India and China close to 40 per cent of the votes. It is difficult to imagine that this is what activists in the North have in mind.

The conclusion, then, is that demands for popular democracy
within the WTO are misplaced and misguided. Almost as problem-

atic is the desire to open up the dispute settlement system to the voices of non-governmental actors. There can be no objection to any wish of panels to obtain the views of qualified experts, including those working for, or funded by, NGOs and private business. But if such voices are to be heard, as of right, a number of important theoretical and practical concerns must be addressed. The first is that the non-governmental voices that have a right to be heard must not be limited in some arbitrary way. The second is that members of the WTO and private corporations, neither of which have this right at present, must also be heard. The third is that some way must then be found to fund the involvement of governments and private organizations based in developing countries. The fourth is that a way must also be found to increase funding of the dispute settlement process, to ensure that it is not utterly overwhelmed.[29]

This leaves only the wider issue of transparency to the public at large. Here the way ahead should be relatively uncontroversial. The WTO needs to take forward its programme of symposia and seminars with non-governmental actors. It also needs to improve further the dissemination of documents. The website is an extremely important step in this direction. More of the WTO's activities could also be opened to the press. But, for these things to happen, and particularly for voices from developing countries to be heard, the WTO must be better funded.

Why further liberalization does not require enforceable labour and environmental standards

There is now strong pressure to attach a range of minimum standards, particularly on the environment and labour, to trade. These demands emanate from the high-income countries and are viewed by developing countries with grave suspicion. They are right to do so.[30]

The first objection is that the high-income countries are pursuing an internally inconsistent set of objectives. After the Seattle débâcle, Lori Wallach of Public Citizen, a US consumer organization dedicated to curbing trade, argued that "we have succeeded in turning back the invasion of the WTO into domestic policy decisions."[31]

Yet, both governments of high-income countries and their pressure groups want to use their trade clout to alter the way developing countries run their economies. Their motto is that "we shall do what we want and you will also do what we want."

The second objection is that this approach is possible only for countries with clout. In practice, this means the United States and the European Union. But the trading system then becomes a vehicle by which two particular players extend their preferences to the rest of the world. It ceases to be just another way to impose conditionality on developing countries. In the long run, as a number of very large developing countries—notably India and China—achieve more influence in world trade, such a one-way approach will be unsustainable. It will almost certainly fail to achieve its aims even now.

The third objection is that the high-income countries are not in a good moral position to make such demands. The poor treatment of labour, including child labour, reflects poverty. The challenge concerns development (or rather the lack of it), not trade. Yet, some of the countries most insistent on turning labour standards into a trade issue have been among the most niggardly in providing assistance for development. Similarly, it ill behoves countries that have cut down most of their own forests and, most important, have been—and still are—the world's biggest producers of greenhouse gases, both absolutely and per head, to lecture developing countries on the environment. Since global warming is, arguably, the most important worldwide environmental problem, it is hypocritical for the countries that have created this danger to approach the question of the environment in trade as if they held the moral high ground.

The fourth objection is to the assumption that it would be easy to agree on and enforce minimum standards in a non-protectionist way. Finding out how the labour employed in producing an export that has gone through many stages of production has been treated would be immensely hard (and costly for exporters). The same is true, to a still greater extent, for the environmental impact of production methods that cannot be identified in the final product.

The fifth objection is that there is no compelling reason for common minimum standards on labour and the environment. Countries with different resources, levels of development, administrative capacity, and preferences should employ different methods of production. To allow importers to set such policies for exporters, unilaterally, not only would be an intolerable intrusion, but would prove a serious obstacle to the efficient use of resources. The fact that the desired standards would diverge among the importing countries could only make a bad situation worse. Some argue that low standards represent a form of dumping or subsidization. But there is no evidence that lower labour or environmental standards provide a large competitive advantage to exporters. It is also certain that quantifying any such advantage would be practically impossible.

The sixth objection is that acceptance of the right of importing countries to use trade sanctions as a means of changing the practices of exporting countries would transform the trading system. It can be argued that the incorporation of intellectual property rights is already a step towards using trade policy instruments for non-trade ends. But to take this process further would turn the WTO from an international agreement on trade to a system that uses trade measures to transform the policies of members across a growing array of policies and practices. This would risk overloading the system to the point of fracture.

The seventh objection is that regulatory competition among states is desirable, except where global public bads are concerned. But there have to be global agreements to deal with such bads. The genuinely worldwide problems of global warming, species extinction, or mass poverty cannot be resolved within the WTO.

For these reasons, incorporation within the WTO of minimum standards that do not have much to do with trade is a perilous undertaking. It could too easily destroy the fundamental attributes of the trading system—its restricted focus on trade itself and its reliance on consensus. It would take the WTO another step towards becoming an enforcer of universal norms by the powerful on the weak—and on the cheap.

Why the scope of the trading system should remain limited

The WTO is not a system of world government. Maybe a century or so from now such a system will emerge. But at present the world does best by constructing regimes designed to achieve specific and limited ends. This raises the question of how far any arrangement should stretch. Since the Uruguay Round, the WTO covers virtually all trade and a vast range of domestic regulations. Now, it is suggested, it should stretch further, to cover foreign direct investment and competition policy. This aim is shared by a number of high-income countries and business organizations. Yet stretching the agreement in this way is risky and probably unnecessary.

It is risky because, the wider the WTO stretches and the more it seems subservient to the goals of business, the greater the danger that other activists will want to load it with their own goals. For this reason alone, the decision to add intellectual property to the agreement was almost certainly an error. It is unnecessary because, in many of the new areas of activity, international agreement is needed to achieve liberalization. Thus, in the case of foreign direct investment, it is quite unclear why there needs to be global agreement. Similarly, competition policy hardly creates a serious obstacle to economic integration. Thus, by asking whether a particular extension of the trading system is necessary, some of its apparently irresistible tendency to spread can be curtailed.

The case for being cautious about extending the scope of the trading system has been underlined by experience with the agreements on Technical Barriers to Trade, SPS, and TRIPS and other regulatory agreements within the Uruguay Round. The desire to minimize the extent to which regulations are used as a protectionist trade barrier is understandable. But, however irrational they may appear, regulations often reflect the democratic will of a particular country. It is dangerous for countries to use the WTO to try to force others to change such policies. It would help if countries had sounder and better-based systems for establishing risk. But it must be accepted that the risks societies are prepared to run may differ. There is no one right scientific answer. It may be that the best solution is to try to establish an international norm, but to accept that financial compensation will frequently be the best way of handling the situation that arises when a particular country is not prepared, for whatever reason, to abide by it.

Difficulties have also occurred where agreements on regulatory standards impose heavy costs on developing countries. It should become an accepted part of the negotiating process that exporting developing countries should be directly recompensed for such costs. If this had been part of the Uruguay Round, some of the demands might never have been made. This would have been entirely desirable.

How to relate trade to other objectives

Finally, as the WTO has spread, it has created the potential for overlap with other legitimate areas of interest, such as the environment. There is no doubt both that there are genuine international environmental spillovers and that a system of international agreements is needed to manage the consequences. There can be no doubt, too, that, in the absence of international agreements, such risks as global warming, ozone depletion, and species extinction may not be successfully managed. It follows that the overlaps between the WTO and MEAs need to be handled. There is, however, no neat way of doing so. Where an MEA contains a trade provision—and particularly a trade sanction—that may be imposed on non-parties that are parties to the WTO, conflict is possible, even though this has as yet not happened. There have already been disputes when countries have unilaterally adopted measures in violation of the WTO. Conflict between the WTO and MEAs should not happen, however, when the parties are members of both.[32]

A part of the answer is to minimize reliance on trade measures within MEAs. Although they are sometimes necessary and even desirable, there will often be more effective and equitable alternatives, including direct assistance or positive inducements to adopt the desired change in policy. Where a trade measure is necessary and needs to be imposed on non-members of the MEA in order to eliminate the incentive for free-riding, two solutions suggest themselves. One would be to offer compensation in some other area of trade to a non-member of the MEA whose WTO rights are being violated. However, this approach would have the disadvantage of encouraging free-riding. The second alternative would be to exempt from WTO disciplines measures taken in accordance with an MEA that has a membership of a sufficiently large size—say, half the membership of the WTO.

Conclusion

The trading system has been an extraordinary success. But its very success has made it more visible, more intrusive, and more powerful than ever before. It has, accordingly, more enemies, as was shown on the streets of Seattle. Nor are these activists the only source of pressure upon the system. Business wants more liberalization, while other important pressure groups want the WTO to recognize their own specific concerns, particularly over the environment and labour standards. As a result, quite big gaps have emerged between the demands of the high-income countries, on the one hand, and those of the developing countries, on the other.

If these pressures are to be managed, more is needed than the usual horse-trading. It is necessary to consider what the WTO can and cannot do. The trading system provides an increasingly integrated world economy with the underlying predictability and liberalism that it needs. In this role it protects the economy from the arbitrary interventions of governments and protects governments from political pressures arising in the economy. This system has brought the world economy back to the liberal and mutually advantageous trade that was so brutally and foolishly cut short in the era of economic nationalism that dominated the first half of the twentieth century.

This system is no threat to national sovereignty, properly understood. Equally, calls to make it more democratic are mistaken. It is, unavoidably, intergovernmental, but the WTO does need to be more transparent. Much pressure is being put on developing countries to accept minimum standards for the environment and labour, backed by trade sanctions. But they are right to resist. Much pressure is also being placed on members to accept further increases in the scope and intrusiveness of the system. This idea, too, is dangerous. Finally, messy overlaps between the WTO and environmental agreements are unavoidable. Solutions will never be neat. But, with common sense, they can be found.

The only way forward is to protect the fundamental principles of the system, while being as cautious as possible about its extension into new areas of activity and the domestic regulatory regimes of its members. High-income countries, in particular, should forgo the pleasures of using trade weapons to force others to behave in ways they desire, while insisting on their freedom to do as they please. However, a way must be found to reconcile the legitimate aims and functions of the trading system with the achievement of other objectives, particularly environmental protection. With good sense and circumspection, this can be done. There is no sane alternative.

Notes

1. See "10 benefits of the WTO trading system," online at http://www.wto.org/english/thewto_e/whatis_e/10ben_e/10b00_e.htm, accessed 26 September 2000.
2. Peter Jay, *Road to Riches or the Wealth of Man,* London: Weidenfeld & Nicolson, 2000, pp. 270–271.
3. Data on the growth of world output and trade are from the WTO Secretariat. The extent to which international economic integration exceeds that of the period before the First World War is controversial. The evidence suggests that trade is now far more liberalized and has grown faster, for longer, than ever before. This is also true for short-term capital flows. But this is not yet true for long-term capital flows and is certainly untrue for movement of people. See, on this, Vincent Cable, *Globalisation and Global Governance,* London: Royal Institute of International Affairs, 1999, and Paul Hirst and Grahame Thompson, *Globalization in Question: The International Economy and the Possibilities of Governance,* 2nd edn., Oxford: Polity Press, 1999. See also Richard Baldwin and Philippe Martin, "Two Waves of Globalization: Superficial Similarities, Fundamental Differences," National Bureau of Economic Research Working Paper 6904, 1999; Michael Bordo, Barry Eichengreen, and Jongwoo Kim, "Was There Really an Earlier Period of International Financial Integration Comparable to Today's?" National Bureau of Economic Research Working Paper 6738, 1998; and Michael Bordo, Barry Eichengreen, and Douglas Irwin, "Is Globalization Today Really Different Than Globalization a Hundred Years Ago?" National Bureau of Economic Research Working Paper 7195, 1999.
4. The idea of deep integration is discussed at length by Nancy Birdsall and Robert Z. Lawrence, "Deep Integration and Trade Agreements: Good for Developing Countries?" in Inge Kaul, Isabelle Grunberg, and Marc A. Stern, eds., *Global Public Goods: International Cooperation in the 21ˢᵗ Century,* New York: Oxford University Press, for the United Nations Development Programme, 1999, pp. 128–151.
5. On the costly consequences of parts of the WTO for developing countries, see J. Michael Finger, "The WTO's Special Burden on Less Developed Countries," *Cato Journal,* 19(3), Winter 2000, pp. 425–437.

6. On the WTO's dispute settlement system, see Robert E. Hudec, "The New WTO Dispute Settlement Procedure: Overview of the First Three Years," *Minnesota Journal of Global Trade,* Winter 1999, pp. 1–53, and William J. Davey, "The WTO Dispute Settlement System," in Gary P. Sampson and W. Bradnee Chambers, eds., *Trade, Environment, and the Millennium,* Tokyo: United Nations University Press, 1999, pp. 119–142.

7. An important analysis of the Seattle débâcle is contained in "What *Really* Happened in Seattle," by Professor Jagdish N. Bhagwati, online at http://www.columbia.edu/~jb38/really.pdf, accessed 28 September 2000. An earlier abbreviated version appeared in the *Financial Times,* 21 December 1999.

8. Mancur Olson, *The Rise and Decline of Nation: Economic Growth, Stagflation, and Social Rigidities,* New Haven, CT: Yale University Press, 1982.

9. On SPS, see Steve Charnowitz, "Improving the Agreement on Sanitary and Phytosanitary Standards," in Sampson and Chambers, eds., *Trade, Environment, and the Millennium,* pp. 171–194. On the precautionary principle, see James Cameron, "The Precautionary Principle," in ibid., pp. 239–269. A comprehensive discussion of the debate on trade and the environment is contained in Gary P. Sampson, *Trade, Environment and the WTO: The Post-Seattle Agenda,* Policy Essay No. 27, Washington, DC: Overseas Development Council, 2000.

10. On ecolabelling, see Arthur E. Appleton, "Environmental Labelling Schemes: WTO Law and Developing Country Implications," in Sampson and Chambers, eds., *Trade, Environment, and the Millennium,* pp. 195–221.

11. The core standards under discussion are: freedom of association, the right to form organizations, the right to collective bargaining, suppression of forced labour, non-discrimination, equal pay for men and women, and rules restricting child labour. See Birdsall and Lawrence, "Deep Integration and Trade Agreements," p. 143. See also http://www.ilo.org.

12. There are almost 200 MEAs today, with membership ranging from a small group to about 170 countries. The main global MEAs are, however, the 1973 Convention on International Trade in Endangered Species (CITES), the 1987 Montreal Protocol on Substances that Deplete the Ozone Layer, the 1989 Basel Convention on the Control of Transboundary Movements of Hazardous Wastes and Their Disposal, the 1992 Rio agreements (the Framework Convention on Climate Change, the Convention on Biological Diversity, and the Convention to Combat Desertification), the 1997 Kyoto Protocol on climate change, the 1998 Rotterdam Convention on hazardous chemicals in international trade, and draft MEAs, under negotiation, including a Convention on the control of persistent organic pollutants and the Biosafety Protocol to the Biodiversity Convention. See Duncan Brack, "Environmental Treaties and Trade: Multilateral Environmental Agreements and the Multilateral Trading System," in Sampson and Chambers, eds., *Trade, Environment, and the Millennium,* pp. 271–296.

13. An excellent statement of the complaints about the WTO's lack of transparency and failure to incorporate the voice of "civil society" is by Daniel C. Esty, "Non-Governmental Organizations at the World Trade Organization: Cooperation, Competition or Exclusion," *Journal of International Economic Law* 1, 1998, pp. 123–147. See also Esty, "Environmental Governance at the WTO: Outreach to Civil Society," in Sampson and Chambers, eds., *Trade, Environment, and the Millennium,* pp. 97–117.

14. International Chamber of Commerce, "World Business Priorities for a New Round of Multilateral Trade Negotiations," Document 103/213, 21 June 1999, online at http://www.iccwbo.org/home/statements_rules/statements/1999/multilateral_trade_negociations_june1999.asp, and "Business Wants G7 Leaders to Make New Trade Round Their Top Priority," 10 July 2000, online at http://www.iccwbo.org/home/news_archives/2000/summit_trade.asp, both accessed 28 September 2000.

15. ICC, "Business Wants G7 leaders."

16. ICC, "World Business Priorities."

17. Ibid.

18. The Democratic Party in the United States is committed to the labour standards agenda largely because of its heavy dependence on the trades unions for supplies of both money and personnel.

19. Veena Jha and René Vossenaar, "Breaking the Deadlock: A Positive Agenda on Trade, Environment, and Development," in Sampson and Chambers, eds., *Trade, Environment, and the Millennium*, p. 69.

20. These are the relatively controversial areas for negotiation. There is greater consensus on such areas as e-commerce, transparency in public procurement, trade facilitation, and market access, particularly tariffs.

21. Finger, "The WTO's Special Burden," p. 435.

22. A pure public good has two characteristics: first, nobody can be prevented from consuming it; second, it can be consumed without being depleted. The first quality makes the good "non-excludable"; the second makes it "non-rival." Such goods cannot normally be provided adequately by the market. A global compact to liberalize trade has strong public good elements. Many of these take the form of network effects. Thus, every member country (and often non-members as well) gains from a trade agreement between the United States and the European Union on the basis of non-discrimination.

23. Douglas A. Irwin, "Do We Need the WTO?" *Cato Journal*, Winter 2000, p. 353.

24. William Lash and Daniel Griswold, "WTO Report Card II: An Exercise or Surrender of U.S. Sovereignty?" Cato Institute's Center for Trade Policy Studies, Trade Briefing Paper No. 9, 4 May 2000; online at http://www.freetrade.org/pubs/briefs/tbp-009es.html, accessed 28 September 2000.

25. See on this Mancur Olson, *The Logic of Collective Action: Public Goods and the Theory of Groups,* Cambridge, MA: Harvard University Press, 1965; and Anthony Downs, *An Economic Theory of Democracy,* New York: Harper, 1957.

26. Robert Hudec, "'Circumventing Democracy': The Political Morality of Trade Negotiations," *New York University Journal of International Law and Politics,* 1993, pp. 311–322, reprinted in Hudec, *Essays on the Nature of International Trade Law,* London: Cameron May, 1999, chapter 7.

27. Esty, "Environmental Governance at the WTO," p. 98.

28. Ibid., p. 99.

29. On this issue, see Sampson, *Trade, Environment and the WTO*, especially pp. 116–117.

30. Magda Shahin presents a compelling statement of the suspicions of the developing countries over efforts to incorporate environmental issues within

the WTO. See "Trade and Environment: How Real Is the Debate?" in Sampson and Chambers, eds., *Trade, Environment, and the Millennium,* pp. 35–64. See also "Third World Intellectuals and NGOs Statement against Linkage (TWIN-SAL)," 1999, online at http://www.columbia.edu/~jb38/twin-sal12.pdf, accessed 28 September 2000.

31. Quoted by me in my column "In Defense of Global Capitalism," *Financial Times,* 8 December 1999.

32. See, on this issue, Brack, "Environmental Treaties and Trade," pp. 271–298.

10

Making the global economy work for human rights

Mary Robinson
UN High Commissioner for Human Rights

Coming to grips with the impact of an increasingly global economy on the enjoyment of human rights is no easy task. There has been too little research to assist our understanding of the role of globalization generally, and trade liberalization specifically, for good or ill, in the implementation of human rights standards.

Despite the lack of data, the links between trade, development, and human rights are increasingly plain to see—from the impact of open markets on jobs in developed countries to the implementation of labour and environmental standards in developing countries, from the question of trade-restrictive measures to protect public health to barriers to full participation by developing countries in the international economic system. These are just some of the difficult issues that must be addressed if we are to ensure that the global economy contributes to the realization of all human rights for all people.

Our point of departure should be that trade and economic growth are not ends in themselves. As the Director-General of the World Trade Organization, Mike Moore, has pointed out, the international trading system must contribute to better living standards and a safer world and the WTO should reflect the needs of all its members. The 1994 WTO Agreement incorporates the objectives of higher standards of living, steady growth of real income, full employment, and economic growth patterns compatible with sustainable development. The Agreement's Preamble proclaims that even the least developed countries will share the benefits of global production and trade in goods.

The theme I want to develop in this chapter is that human rights are, indeed, inextricably linked with the international economic system. Human rights provide the common moral and legal underpinnings for the global economy. By integrating human rights standards into all aspects of economic policy-making, we will help ensure that markets are not only open and efficient, but also fair and just.

It should be recognized that human rights norms and standards are as relevant to the fields of international trade, finance, and investment as to any other area of human activity. The pursuit of equitable development and fair trade are legitimate human rights concerns. In this respect it is important to note that two trends happening in the world are of crucial importance because they both bring a new degree of urgency to addressing the need for the formulation of effective policies in the area of human rights, trade, and development. The first is the growing determination of the international community that human rights can and should play a central role in the lives of all people and that the mechanisms to deliver a strengthened set of human rights standards should work effectively. The second is the emerging interest that is being taken in improving international financial, trade, and development instruments so that they meet the needs of all of the people on the planet, including the poorest. Recognition of the link between human rights and the international economic system is indeed timely.

Human rights and a rules-based society

The legal regimes of trade and human rights have developed more or less independently from one another. The same can be said of international development strategies. What has not been fully appreciated is that their goals are mutually reinforcing. Many of the principles enunciated in the Universal Declaration of Human Rights and the body of international legal instruments that have been developed over the past 50 years involve the creation of a stable, rule-based society necessary for economic growth. Applying human rights principles thoroughly and consistently contributes to the development of legal systems in which contracts are enforced fairly, bribery and corruption are less prevalent, and all business entities have equal access to legal process and equal protection under law.

The WTO establishes the legally binding rules for international commerce in goods, services, and intellectual property rights at both the national and international level.[1] Indeed, one of the frequently stated objectives of WTO member governments is for the rules-based trading system to bring stability and predictability to world commerce, as well as to improve access to markets through the progressive liberalization of world trade. Few would argue with the proposition that the WTO—and the General Agreement on Tariffs and Trade before it—have been remarkably successful in this area. However, here too there is a mutuality of interests to be served.[2]

From both an economic and a social perspective, stable and rules-based societies constitute a necessary condition for sustainable development, a well-functioning world economy, and an international trading system. There is certainly a mutuality of interests between the international trading community and those of us whose primary concern is ensuring the implementation of international human rights law. Yet the reality is that, whereas the rules that favour the expansion of the global economy have become stronger and more enforceable, equally important rules relating to human rights as well as environmental and labour standards have not kept pace in terms of their implementation. This has been at the heart of the "backlash against globalization" that UN Secretary-General Kofi Annan has described so compellingly in chapter 1 of this volume. The question for us now to answer is how the right balance can be struck. How can we make the globalization of human rights central to the global economy? By looking back, we may find a way forward.

Human rights and the international economic system

A vital impetus for the strengthening of human rights came out of the horrors of the conflict of the Second World War. It was a determination that a better way must be found to protect the individual and to forestall a repetition of the terrible violations that had taken place. The great achievement of that post-war period was the Universal Declaration of Human Rights, a seminal document, adopted by the UN General Assembly in 1948. Starting from the powerful statement that all human beings are born free and equal in dignity and rights, the Universal Declaration sets out in its 30 Articles the fundamental freedoms to which all of us are entitled, simply by virtue of being human.[3]

During the past decade the emphasis has shifted from standard-setting to improving the implementation of human rights. A strong push to the effort was given with the holding of the World Conference on Human Rights in Vienna in 1993. One of the decisions of that Conference was to create the position that I now hold, that of High Commissioner for Human Rights, as part of moves to strengthen human rights mechanisms within the United Nations system.[4] The mandate of the High Commissioner includes coordinating all of the United Nations' human rights activities and improving their impact and overall efficiency.

Since being appointed High Commissioner I have sought to focus greater attention on economic, social, and cultural rights because I believe that the achievement of these rights is every bit as important as securing civil and political rights. The cornerstone of economic, social, and cultural rights is Article 22 of the Universal Declaration, which states that, as a member of society, everyone is entitled to the realization of the economic, social, and cultural rights that are indispensable for his or her dignity and free and full personal development. The five Articles that follow elaborate economic rights related to work, fair remuneration, and leisure, an adequate standard of living, health, well-being, and education, and the right to participate in the cultural life of the community. It should be emphasized that the intention was there from the start that these rights would be secured. It was not by accident that the drafters of the Universal Declaration incorporated economic, social, and cultural rights in their deliberations and in their final text.

The post-war efforts to build a better international architecture were not confined to human rights and world government but also foresaw the need to set up regulatory mechanisms to bring order to the international economic system. That was the rationale behind the establishment of the Bretton Woods institutions, which were designed to provide stability in international finances and to assist the poorest countries to put their economies on a par with those in the developed world.

The design of the post-war international economic system was based on the idea (which Peter Sutherland et al. refer to in chapter 5 as the "logic of 1945") that, in return for economic liberalization at the international level, national governments would provide for the social welfare needs of their citizens. The rules of the General Agreement on Tariffs and Trade (GATT) were to facilitate countries in their trade and economic endeavours, thereby "raising standards of living, ensuring full employment and a large and steadily growing volume of real income and effective demand, developing the full use of the resources of the world and expanding production and exchange of goods . . . . [through] mutually advantageous arrangements directed to the substantial reduction of tariffs and other barriers to trade and the elimination of discriminatory treatment in international commerce."[5] Whereas these rules were to deal with the economic aspects of the process of development through multilateral cooperation in trade, the responsibilities for the social order were seen to be elsewhere.

For a long time this separation of the rules for international economic transactions, whether financial or in the area of trade, from the welfare of the individual was carefully maintained. The richer countries have certainly benefited over the past 50 years from the role played by the International Monetary Fund (IMF), the World Bank, and the GATT/WTO. Increases in trade and capital flows have led to very significant growth in productivity and jobs in Western countries. This has been accompanied by strong improvements in the indicators of human well-being such as life expectancy, education, and nutrition. At the same time, some middle-income countries have seen their wealth and human development indicators draw closer to those of industrialized countries, as have a small number of developing countries.

Then there are the rest. The marginalized developing countries, far from sharing in the growth of wealth, have been bypassed along the way. The growth in real per capita income in the countries of sub-Saharan Africa from 1960 to 1995 was only US$28. The overall gap between the richest 20 per cent of humanity and the poorest 20 per cent doubled between 1940 and 1990. To give just one example: in 1976 Switzerland was 52 times richer than Mozambique; in 1997, it was 508 times richer. In our modern world, 3 billion people live on less than US$2 a day, 1.3 billion do not have clean water, and 40,000 children die every day because of hunger-related diseases. Although some of these statistics can be attributed to problems of governance, including corruption and mismanagement, it is clear that structural adjustment programmes, loan conditions, and external debt repayment schemes have not sufficiently considered the impacts of such programmes on the need to protect human rights. There are signs that this is now changing.

A new world: Global markets and global concern for human rights

In recent years, thanks in large part to one of the main features of globalization—the information and communications technology revolution—global concern for human rights has led to global concern at the negative human impact of some economic policies. The historic separation between the economic and the social has been brought into question. These developments have led many to urge that the human impact of policies and actions be considered as an integral part of policy formulation and implementation.

As Joseph Stiglitz, former Vice President of the World Bank, has noted, past development strategies failed because they focused on only one part of the problem and failed to take into account the broader context. Most focused narrowly on economics, aiming at increasing GDP per capita—perhaps through trade liberalization negotiated in the context of GATT and WTO negotiations—and confusing means with ends and cause with effect. They dealt with technical problems and proposed technical solutions: better planning, better trade and pricing polices, better macroeconomic frameworks. They dealt with "means"—in other words, low inflation—but did not focus on "ends"—that is, the human welfare of those concerned.

It is heartening that the World Bank—one of the most influential international organizations—is today looking objectively at its development experience in this way. I believe that this careful scrutiny is fully justified, given that 50 years of expenditure on development have, in many cases, failed to produce the desired results, and for reasons that cannot be simply attributed to external factors such as natural or human-caused disasters or economic mismanagement.

The IMF has earned respect for maintaining orderly exchange rates over the years, but it has also been criticized for lack of openness and, perhaps more important, for not paying sufficient attention to the disadvantage at which very poor countries are placed in the world economy. As with the World Bank, there are encouraging signs of a greater readiness on the part of the Fund to think hard about its own role—to "examine its conscience" as it were. The IMF should listen to civil society, and to the non-governmental organizations in particular, which have valid arguments to make about the human impact of strict fiscal policies on poor countries. It should be noted that the former Managing Director of the IMF, Michel Camdessus, urged that more must be done to develop policies that will promote growth, sustainable development, and poverty reduction. He called as well for a reduction in military spending, for higher spending on social welfare, and for increased aid flows. The proof will be when organizations such as the World Bank implement on the ground policies that are really designed in such a way as to secure economic, social, and cultural rights and the right to development.

Where does the work of the WTO come into this picture? How can it ensure that human rights are taken into account? The UN Committee on Economic, Social and Cultural Rights, in its task of monitoring compliance by States Parties with their obligations under the International Covenant on Economic, Social and Cultural Rights, has become increasingly aware of the extent to which international economic policies and practices affect the ability of states to fulfil their treaty obligations. In a message to the WTO Ministerial Meeting in 1999, the Committee endorsed the call from the United Nations Sub-Commission on the Promotion and Protection of Human Rights in its resolution 1999/30 of 26 August 1999 for steps to be taken "to ensure that human rights principles and obligations are fully integrated in future negotiations in the World Trade Organization," and for proper study to be undertaken of the "human rights and social impacts of economic liberalization programmes, policies and laws."

GATT Article XX is often referred to when the links between trade and human rights law are made. Article XX provides that nothing in GATT should prevent the adoption or enforcement of measures "to protect human, animal or plant life or health" or the "conservation of exhaustible natural resources." In fact, for the first time in its six-year history, a WTO panel recently upheld trade-restrictive measures in the interest of protecting health in a case involving the import of asbestos. This case has shown that concerns related to human rights can be addressed within the WTO.

The WTO has also advanced its Comprehensive and Integrated Plan of Action for Least Developed Countries, which includes duty-free access to the markets for the exports of least developed countries (LDCs) to a number of developed trading partners. That 47 LDCs account for less than 0.3 per cent of world trade (and that percentage is falling) should be considered as unacceptable to all members of the international community. In more general terms, the negotiations under the auspices of the WTO must work on effectively integrating developing countries into the world trading system so that they may enjoy the benefits of a liberal and rules-based multilateral trading system.[6] There is need, too, for the WTO, as an instrument designed to improve the lives of people, to listen carefully to the concerns of civil society.

A rights-based approach to development

Human rights bring to the development and trade discussion a unifying set of standards—a common reference for setting objectives and assessing the impact of actions taken. The 1986 United Nations Declaration on the Right to Development was a major step forward in defining development from a human rights perspective. The Declaration states that "the human being is the central subject of development and should be the active participant and beneficiary of the right to development." It also recognizes that "development is a comprehensive economic, social, cultural and political process which aims at the constant improvement of the well-being of the entire population and of all individuals on the basis of their active, free and meaningful participation in development and in the fair distribution of benefits resulting therefrom."

In my Office we are approaching development issues within the context of the Declaration. We are working towards this end with our partner agencies in the UN system. The United Nations Development Assistance Framework has been established to overcome fragmentation and overlap in development efforts at the country level. We are also working with our partners at the United Nations Development Programme on a new joint initiative known as HURIST (Human Rights Strengthening programme). This initiative is intended to identify best practices and learning opportunities in the development of national capacity for the promotion and protection of human rights and to apply a human rights approach to development programming at the country level.

Some continue to argue that development is technical in nature and that the effectiveness of policies would be weakened if supposedly outside considerations were to be introduced. But economic policies, such as those relating to budget deficits, inflation, unemployment, and trade liberalization through the adoption of outward-oriented trade policies, have real and measurable impacts on the enjoyment of human rights, and those impacts must be taken into account.

A good illustration is the effect on children. In 1999 we commemorated the tenth anniversary of the adoption of the Convention on the Rights of the Child. Studies on the relationship between macroeconomic policies and the enjoyment by children of their rights show that economic growth is important for child rights, but it is not enough. The policies behind that growth are just as important.

In the case of developing countries, a comparison of GDP per capita with measures of child welfare such as child mortality, education, and nutrition shows that countries with similar income levels are producing very different results in these areas. Those countries that achieve little in relation to their per capita GDP are generally characterized by inequalities in the distribution of income and very likely unequal access to resources.

The human rights vision of the United Nations is that all spheres of activity, international, regional, national, and local, should be inspired and influenced by the human rights norms elaborated at the United Nations. Development, as well as peace, should have in view the dignity of the individual and his or her rights. The International Covenant on Economic, Social and Cultural Rights requires states to pursue policies and strategies aimed at the realization, for every person on the planet, of the right to food, health, shelter, education, work, and social security. A globalizing world must never lose sight of these imperatives. A globalizing world that results in any departure from these human rights precepts is a world that is anti-people. We must never tolerate this.

The way forward

What can be done towards tangible progress in making the global economy help rather than hinder human rights? It is not beyond the capacity of the international community to devise strategies to help to secure economic, social, and cultural rights for all and to honour the often repeated pledges to support the right to development. The following suggestions provide an outline for how progress can be made if there is willingness and open-mindedness on the part of the international community.

- *A commitment is needed to a rights-based approach to development* that integrates the norms, standards, and principles of international human rights law into the plans, policies, and processes of development efforts at all levels. This means defining the objectives of development and aid in terms of particular rights, as legally enforceable entitlements, and creating express normative links to international, regional, and national human rights instruments. It requires raising the levels of accountability in the development process by identifying claim-holders (and their entitlements) and corresponding duty-holders (and their obligations). Thanks to the work of our partners within the UN family such as the UN Development Programme, we are taking important steps in this direction, but we need governments and other international organizations to take the lead.

- *Human rights should permeate macroeconomic policies,* embracing fiscal policies, monetary policies, exchange rate policies, and trade policies. To take the example of children again, one economist has noted that "[t]rade and exchange rate policies may have a larger impact on children's development than the relative size of the budget allocated to health and education. An incompetent Central Bank can be more harmful to children than an incompetent Ministry of Education."[7] The international economic institutions should lead the way. They must take greater account of the human dimension of their activities and the huge impact that economic policies can have on local economies, especially in our increasingly globalized world.

- *Debt relief should be a top priority.* More and more attention is focused these days on the crushing burden of debt faced by the poorest countries, a huge obstacle to their meeting economic challenges and, hence, strengthening the human rights of their citizens. Initiatives to date aimed at providing relief to highly indebted poor countries have been painfully slow. That is in spite of the clear evidence that public opinion supports debt relief, as manifested by the activities of the many religious and humanitarian groups that have come together in the Jubilee 2000 Coalition.

The IMF/World Bank HIPC (Heavily Indebted Poor Country) initiative offers important assistance for certain heavily indebted poor countries in reducing to more sustainable levels the external debt burden of these countries. Its human rights promise comes from its focus on ensuring additional finance for social sector programmes, primarily basic health and education, themselves basic human rights. In 1999, the G-8 nations agreed to "the Cologne Initiative," a package of measures designed to reduce the debt burden of the 33 poorest countries of the world. These countries collectively owe US$127 billion to industrialized countries and institutions such as the IMF and the World Bank. Sceptics of debt relief have argued that previous measures did not filter through to ordinary citizens because the savings made were often diverted to wasteful or corrupt purposes. The Cologne Initiative requires debtor nations to show that they are using the benefits primarily for expenditure on education and health. But one year later, the promise of the Cologne Initiative has not been fulfilled. Debt relief for the most heavily indebted countries should be given the renewed political priority it deserves.

- *The private sector must take a more active role in promoting and protecting human rights.* Undoubtedly, the most powerful player in international economic relations is the business community. In fact, a great deal of international activity, be it via the World Trade Organization or the International Monetary Fund, is aimed at providing a stable environment for international economic exchanges. On an international level, corporations are indeed important. The largest 100 companies have combined annual revenues that exceed the GDP of half of the world's nations.

Big corporations have the power to bring great benefits to poor communities, but they can cause great damage too—through degradation of the environment, exploitation of economically weak communities, or the use of child labour. In recent years there has been an increasing awareness on the part of business that it must face up to its responsibilities in the human rights field. The launch of the UN Secretary-General's Global Compact initiative has the potential to make a significant impact on the international business community. By adopting good practices in the areas of human rights, labour, and environmental standards and by advocating effective global governance mechanisms, corporations will be doing their part to ensure that the global economic system meets the needs of all people. The positive business response to this challenge should be welcomed, as should the willingness of trade unions and civil society organizations to engage directly with the United Nations in this new form of partnership and accountability.

Conclusion

The tide is running in favour of embedding a strong culture of human rights in the world. Making the global economy part of that culture will not happen without considerable effort and goodwill on the part of all of the actors involved. Although the role of international economic actors has been stressed here, we must not forget the responsibilities that governments are called on to discharge. There is a particular onus on governments to lead by example. The developed states should halt the downward slide in funding devoted to Official Development Assistance and make genuine moves to allow free access to their markets. The developing countries, for their part, should make sure that funds are not squandered on unproductive or wasteful projects.

Denial of the right to development puts all human rights at risk. Seeking to achieve economic, social, and cultural rights for all the peoples of the world, as well as their civil and political rights, is first and foremost our moral and legal obligation. But making human rights a reality is also our best hope for achieving the UN Charter's goal of "social progress and better standards of living in larger freedom."

Notes

1. Countries now frequently trade more than one-third of their national production. With close to 140 member governments, the WTO is approaching the status of a truly global institution. This means one-third of world production is traded according to legally enforceable WTO rules.
2. For further discussion of this issue, see chapter 4 in this volume by Clare Short.
3. Those who drew up the Declaration knew that it was only the first step and that the process of defending human rights throughout the world would be long and difficult. The work was carried forward through the adoption of two

International Covenants, one on Civil and Political Rights, the other on Economic, Social and Cultural Rights. These two Covenants spell out in greater detail what the fundamental rights mean and how they are to be applied. A whole body of human rights law flowed from these basic texts—over 60 treaties addressing such issues as slavery, genocide, humanitarian law, the administration of justice, religious tolerance, discrimination, violence against women, and the status of refugees and minorities.

4. A good deal of progress has been made in improving human rights mechanisms. Implementation of the core human rights treaties is carried out by committees, or "treaty monitoring bodies," which monitor the performance of governments on a regular basis, identify shortcomings, and recommend improvements. Special Rapporteurs are appointed to investigate human rights situations in particular countries. There are also Special Rapporteurs who pursue thematic mandates such as torture, religious intolerance, summary executions, and violence against women.

5. See Preamble to the General Agreement on Tariffs and Trade in *The Results of the Uruguay Round of Multilateral Trade Negotiations: the Legal Texts,* Geneva: WTO Secretariat, 1995, p. 486.

6. See chapter 3 in this volume by Rubens Ricupero.

7. Stefan de Vylder, "Macro Economic Rights Policies and Children's Rights," Sweden: Ljungbergs Klippan for Save the Children, 2000.

11

Health, equity, and trade:
A failure in global governance

James Orbinski
President, International Council of Médecins sans Frontières

The mission of Médecins sans Frontières (MSF) is to relieve suffering, to seek to restore dignity, to reveal injustice, and to locate political responsibility. Why is the MSF movement—a medical humanitarian organization—now concerned with trade and the WTO? Quite simply, because our patients are dying. This is the problem. It is wholly unacceptable from any perspective that millions of people are dying and will die because trade is privileged over their dignity as human beings and over their right to access health care. Our diagnosis and recommended treatment demand that a balance be struck between private and public interests—a balance that gives priority to equitable access to essential medicines as a right over the rules governing their trade and, in effect, the research and development (R&D) process for new innovative drugs. Finding a solution will involve not only the World Trade Organization (WTO), but also the World Health Organization (WHO), national governments and their intergovernmental institutions, and the pharmaceutical industry. Ultimately it is a question of global health and governance, and not simply a matter of rules made by trade specialists. But first, let us define the problem.

In MSF's 400 projects around the world, equitable access to essential life-saving medicines is not improving, but getting worse. We are witnessing not an improvement in health access, but a deterioration. We see not better health for the poor and the marginalized, but only an increase in the political rhetoric that promises it. We consistently hear of the positive effects of economic trade liberalization, but we also consistently witness its negative effects. The majority of the world's population (4 billion people), having been added to a global market economy, have less and less chance of access to the apparent benefits of trade liberalization.

Today, 1.2 billion people—20 per cent more than in 1995—live on less than US$1 per day. Real per capita income has not risen, but fallen in 30 countries over the past 35 years.[1] In addition, existing debt servicing and payment costs, and the growing privatization of public health care delivery capacity under the World Bank's and the International Monetary Fund's structural adjustment programmes, are preventing a solid and effective public infrastructural approach to public health needs. This in turn sustains irrational drug use, encouraging the emergence of drug-resistant micro-organisms. Resistant strains spread within communities and across the globe with the movement of people and goods, as is now the case with malaria and tuberculosis. These factors, at their most basic level, translate into people dying because they cannot afford access to health care. These effects are particularly evident in access to essential and innovative medicines, where the world is divided into two groups—those who have access, and those who do not. At a minimum, 2 billion people belong to the second group. And their numbers are growing as a free market system now dominates virtually every aspect of the formal global social, political, and economic space.

Each year, 17 million people die of infectious diseases, more than 90 per cent of whom are in poor countries. The causes are indeed complex, but they must be faced. Access to essential and innovative medicines is affected by a number of factors such as a lack of public health infrastructure and logistical capacity, a lack of good-quality drug production in the South, and irrational drug choice and use. The availability of medicines is not the only aspect of access to quality health care. But it is essential. To prioritize either availability of medicines or infrastructure delivery capacity is to engage in a fools' game that never ends, leading to inaction. Yet infrastructure will never expand if the possibility of affordable medicines is not realized. Most immediately, access to essential drugs is in effect denied because drugs are too expensive as a result of patent protection (as with anti-retrovirals for the treatment of HIV/AIDS) or are no longer produced because their sale does not guarantee a significant return on investment for the manufacturer (e.g. DFMO for African sleeping sickness) or because there is no new research and development of new and innovative drugs for old and high-prevalence problems such as tuberculosis. These three factors are linked to a disengagement of national and international authorities from ensuring access to health care, the abdication of the problem to the pharmaceutical industry, and the weakness of the WHO mandate. What does this mean concretely?

Overcoming barriers to existing medicine: HIV/AIDS

An estimated 34 million people worldwide live with HIV—24 million in Africa alone; 19 million have died of AIDS, and 5.4 million are newly infected every year.[2] And yet, only a fraction of these—approximately 400,000 people living mainly in Europe and North America—have access to patented anti-retroviral therapy and have therefore seen their AIDS mortality rates drop by more than 70 per cent.[3] Some estimates suggest that half a billion people will be infected with HIV by the year 2020. Other predictions are worse.[4] Entire African nations are on the verge of collapse because teachers, military personnel, doctors, health care professionals, and civil servants are dying of AIDS.

HIV should be a treatable chronic disease, but is it really when treatment with patented anti-retroviral therapy costs about US$10,000 per year for the drugs alone, never mind treatment for opportunistic infections, or the public cost of health infrastructure and trained staff to monitor therapy. Must we simply accept, for example, that maternal–child transmission of HIV, which can be interrupted with prenatal anti-retroviral therapy, goes untreated among the poor because patent protection keeps the drugs prohibi-

tively expensive? Must we accept that the interdependency of treatment and prevention is broken because of monopoly protection on
patented anti-retrovirals?[5] Must we also accept that nearly 34 million people alive today, and untold millions tomorrow, will die of a
treatable infectious disease, largely because patent protection makes
drugs unaffordable? From a humanitarian, political, or moral perspective, the answer is an unequivocal "no."

The majority of anti-retrovirals whose patents are now exclusively
exercised by big pharmaceutical companies were the result of
research that was largely publicly funded.[6] Public money in Europe
and the United States developed the drugs, huge profits go to private
companies that now exercise those patents exclusively, and virtually
none of the people with HIV worldwide have access to their patent-
protected products. Something is wrong with this outcome.

In June 2000, under growing international public pressure, five
large pharmaceutical companies announced their intention of reducing prices of their patent-protected anti-retrovirals for sub-Saharan
Africa to an average US$2,000 per patient per year.[7] In July 2000,
the United States offered loans at 7 per cent interest to 24 already
heavily indebted sub-Saharan African countries to buy these patent-
protected drug products. South Africa and Namibia rejected the
proposal, and other African nations will likely do the same.[8] What
is needed is not apparent solutions that consolidate and protect
existing monopoly commercial interests. Affordable and sustainable
access to essential medicines is required, and not more national debt
that will further impede, among other things, public health infrastructure development.

For anti-retrovirals, generic production and competition in the
developing world are part of a real and viable solution. Fully legal
production exists in the developing world and must be expanded.
Least developed countries that are part of the WTO have until 2006
to adopt intellectual property laws that guarantee 20 years of patent
protection for medicines. Because this is not a retroactive agreement, there are generic sources of anti-retrovirals in countries that
did not respect patents before entering the WTO. In these countries, as is always the case when there is market competition rather
than monopoly, the price has fallen. Our private discussions with

generic industry producers have revealed that it is now possible to produce a year's worth of full anti-viral therapy for between US$800 and US$1,000 per year. Further, with competition, the price could be reduced and still be profitable to the generic industry at about US$250 per year. That is a far cry from the average cost today of US$10,000, or from the recent "concessionary" price of US$2,000.

However, even a commercially viable price as low as US$250 per year will still not guarantee access for the poorest of the poor living and dying with HIV/AIDS. Theirs is a plight that fundamentally questions the responsibility of government to include, or to ensure that market forces include rather than exclude, the poorest of the poor in a social and economic order. Practically speaking, governments need to take measures to address this question of equity for all people, even the poorest of the poor. International institutions and donor governments need to support such measures actively, not remain blind to the needs of the excluded, or oppose or obstruct measures taken to address them.

Governments in developing countries will more and more need to ensure an adequate and affordable supply of anti-retrovirals by issuing compulsory licences to generic producers, or by using parallel importing as a safeguard. Compulsory licences that allow governments to seek generic drug production while paying a reasonable royalty fee to the patent holder are fully legal under the provisions of the Agreement on Trade-Related Intellectual Property Rights (TRIPS) when, for example, a public health emergency such as HIV/AIDS is at hand. Recent efforts by governments to issue such licences, for example by South Africa and Thailand, came under intense political pressure from the United States and the European Union, which threatened trade sanctions if such licences were issued. Despite the pressure and in the face of overwhelming need, South Africa has adopted laws allowing the issuing of TRIPS-compliant compulsory licences. In Thailand, MSF and people infected with HIV are legally challenging Bristol-Myers Squibb's 20-year monopoly patent on the sale of the anti-retroviral DDI so that generic production will be possible.

Why is it that large pharmaceutical companies do not want governments to encourage generic production or to use TRIPS provisions that allow nation states to issue compulsory licences for life-saving essential medicines? Because this would likely reveal the true cost of production and the true profit margins for patented drugs. This would stimulate consumer demand for cheaper drugs and drive down profits from lucrative patent-protected markets, and apparently too the capacity of large pharmaceutical companies to do R&D for new innovative drugs.

Unless large pharmaceutical companies make drugs available at genuinely affordable prices in poorer countries, then generic production and compulsory licensing are the only options for governments faced with a public health catastrophe. These are legal and existing provisions of TRIPS, and must be exercised by nation states whose responsibility is to protect, promote, and ensure people's right to access to health care. The large pharmaceutical companies cannot have it both ways—for, in doing so, millions of people will die of treatable disease. By any political, moral, or philosophical standard, this is not acceptable.

MSF is not "anti-globalization" or "anti-free trade." However, MSF will not remain silent in the face of trade practices that mean inequity and ultimately unnecessary suffering and death for the people we work with on a daily basis. We are taking active measures to ensure access to essential medicines. Because, for example, East Africans sometimes pay more than twice what Europeans pay for essential medicines, MSF is investigating the cost of high-quality generic and patented drugs, including anti-retrovirals, and making this information freely available on the World Wide Web to nation states; in so doing, it is encouraging competition that will bring prices down even further.[9] We are working with other non-governmental organizations (NGOs), the UNAIDS programme, the WHO, and UNICEF to pool this information on prices, manufacturers, and the status of patents in each country as well as quality control data. We also firmly oppose any measure that gives any more patent protection than is already afforded by the TRIPS agreement. So-called "TRIPS-plus" measures have been promoted by the United States and the European Union. These may be appropriate for protecting intellectual property rights in industrialized countries, but they will stifle if not kill pharmaceutical manufacturing capacity and generic drug availability in developing countries. TRIPS itself already has this potential and unacceptable risk. To this end, MSF is actively urging countries not to sign agreements such as the Bangui agreement.[10]

From our perspective, a solution to overcoming barriers to access to anti-retrovirals and other existing drugs lies in differential pricing. This means establishing a real differential pricing policy, so that patients in poor countries pay much less for essential medicines. Here state intervention is necessary. It will require a political process and decision at the global governance level, and could well involve the WTO. Differential pricing should include the granting of voluntary licences for limited use in poor countries and active support of governments seeking a compulsory licence when required. These measures have already successfully increased access to vaccines and oral contraceptives (with prices 100 times cheaper in poorer countries). These measures must also include technology transfers to allow the development of national and regional industries capable of producing quality generic drugs. Differential pricing, however, will affect access only to existing high-price and high-demand medicines. It will do nothing for essential drugs whose production has been in effect abandoned.

Obtaining access to abandoned drugs: African sleeping sickness

Many common and fatal diseases in, for example, Africa are neglected to the point that the production of existing life-saving medicines has been abandoned. Even when need and therapy exist, the drugs are not produced because there is no viable commercial market for them. Those with a treatable disease simply die. This is the case with leishmaniasis and certain forms of meningitis. It is also the case with African sleeping sickness, a fatal neurological disease carried by the tsetse fly that now infects 300,000 people in Africa a year. Sixty million people are at risk. Resistance to melarsoprol, the first-line treatment, is as high as 25 per cent in some areas, and is growing.[11] For these people, DFMO (eflornithine) is the only effective treatment for this disease. DFMO was developed in the mid-1980s as an anti-cancer agent and received US government approval for the treatment of sleeping sickness, but production was abandoned in 1994 because sales did not guarantee an adequate return on investment for the manufacturer. At the special request of MSF, Aventis Pharmaceuticals agreed to produce a final batch of DFMO, and in 1999 transferred the licence to the WHO.

It is the same problem again: poor people have a need but no purchasing power, and therefore their need does not represent a viable market for the private sector. This market failure has yet to be overcome. MSF is leading the search for a manufacturer that will produce DFMO on a long-term basis. To reduce commercial risk, MSF and WHO, with the support of funders, are ready to guarantee the purchase of a significant supply of the drug. At present, more than 25 companies have expressed an interest in producing the drug. Of these, six companies have been identified as potential producers.

In our view, it is imperative to restart production of abandoned medicines and protect essential medicines at risk of being abandoned. In the absence of a viable market, demand should be guaranteed to producers by alliances of public and private purchasers, and maintained by public funds where necessary.

Stimulating R&D for new and innovative drugs: Tuberculosis

Similar issues can be raised about tuberculosis (TB), elucidating different kinds of failures. Over 2 billion people carry *Mycobacterium tuberculosis* as a latent infection, 16 million live with active tuberculosis disease (half of whom are contagious), 2 million die annually, and there are over 8 million new cases of TB a year. By the year 2020 the number of new cases of active tuberculosis per year may be as high as 11 million, and 70 million people may have died of the disease.[12] The TB epidemic is fed by the HIV epidemic. Because HIV reduces immunity, latent TB infection is activated, leading to disease and further spread. Again, not surprisingly, the majority of people with active TB are the poorest of the poor: 95 per cent of cases occur in the developing world, where profound need exists but where a "market" for new TB drugs does not.

There have been no new drugs for the treatment of TB since the development of rifampicin in 1967. The BCG vaccine was developed in 1909 and first used in 1921, and gives only limited protection by primarily preventing serious forms of tuberculosis in children. In adults, its efficacy is widely contested. There is no other vaccine. An explosion of scientific knowledge and techniques in the past 10 years has not yet led to new drugs or vaccines for TB. The question "Is the market for anti-TB medications large enough to interest the pharmaceutical industry?" was posed at a conference in February 2000 on TB drug development in Cape Town, South Africa. That this question can be entertained as the only reasonable hope for new TB drug development at the start of the twenty-first century—a time of unprecedented global wealth and scientific innovation, and of unprecedented government reluctance to intervene in the market—is little short of obscene.

The recent genome sequencing of *M. tuberculosis* suggests new possibilities for vaccine and drug target identification, but has not been followed by commercial interest. The tools for drug development exist, but the commercial will does not. Even when potentially viable drug targets do exist, as with P824, there is a paucity of investment to take drug development further because the potential market is not lucrative enough. Among the new quinolone antibiotics, testing for TB indications has stopped because of the feared pricing impact on more lucrative therapeutic indications in Western markets. The absence of TB drug development since the late 1960s is an irrefutable example of market and government failure.

In practice, existing standard TB therapy is effective, but it is not efficient and access is not equitable. Only one in six people with active tuberculosis worldwide has access to treatment.[13] Although the drug cost of standard therapy is US$20–40 per full treatment, treatment takes too long (six–eight months) and is too complicated, with on average six different drugs taken several times every day. People cannot afford to stay away from work—work that earns them on average US$1–2 per day. For them, it is a question of practicality and usually the immediate survival of the family, nothing else.

Shorter, simpler drug therapy is urgently needed, but little if any public or private research to this end is taking place. Equitable access to treatment must be broadened beyond existing clinics and programmes to include currently excluded groups or persons. Measures such as these would increase equity of access and would reduce labour costs for governments as well as wage and social costs for patients undergoing standard therapy.

The inefficiency and inequity in access have consequences beyond the individual patient suffering with TB. When patients interrupt standard therapy to, for example, go back to work, drug resistance develops and therefore multi-drug-resistant TB (MDRTB). Though TB is curable today, it may not be for long. MDRTB has emerged in over 100 countries around the world as a result of poor compliance with and implementation of standard therapy for TB. In some settings, the situation is extreme. For example, in some prison populations both TB and MDRTB are rampant, increasing exposure to civilian populations on prisoner release. Today the medications alone for the treatment of MDRTB cost US$8,000–15,000 per patient. At this cost, realistically, how many will start treatment, how many will stop treatment, how many more will be infected with MDRTB, and how many people will die?

Both TB and MDRTB are currently curable. Yet 79 per cent of people with TB do not have access to treatment, and only hundreds of the estimated 100,000 people with MDRTB today have access to treatment—the majority live and suffer with a death sentence. Sourcing and encouraging local generic production of quality second-line drugs can reduce drug costs; and MSF is working with the WHO to achieve this. However, second-line drugs for MDRTB offer a lengthy and often painful therapy, and the high mutagenicity of *M. tuberculosis* means that resistance to second-line drugs will inevitably develop. In fact, several cases of fully drug-resistant TB have already been identified, so that what was once a risk of a totally untreatable form of TB is now a reality.[14] New innovative therapy for TB is, without question, a global public health priority.

To confront this public health challenge, the role of governments is either to intervene in the market or to establish their own public capacity to address R&D for new drugs. To date, governments have failed, the pharmaceutical industry has failed, and market forces alone will continue to fail to address the need for shorter-course, more efficient standard therapy and the need for a truly innovative new therapy for TB. TB is a global priority disease, and, as with HIV/AIDS, nothing short of a concrete global political commitment to equity of access to treatment and to R&D will contain and control this pandemic.

R&D for priority diseases: Whose responsibility?

The same lack of innovative drug R&D is true for tropical diseases, most of which have been all but neglected. Of 1,223 new medicines brought to market between 1975 and 1997, only 13 were for the treatment of tropical diseases, and half of these resulted from veterinary research.[15] There is a need for broader debate on worldwide R&D and marketing for tropical diseases. The present profit-driven system is unable to keep pace with current and evolving needs, and thus far the public sector has not provided the optimum environment for such activities.[16] Although opportunities exist, basic academic research generates drug leads that are not exploited and candidates are not developed.[17] MSF has convened a global working group to examine how to stimulate R&D. Academic and industry researchers are working together to help set priorities and create drug development partnerships, and to convince the European Union, US international organizations, and foundation decision makers to increase funding and to define a new infrastructure to set the clinical research agenda.

Although interaction between the public and private sectors could break new ground, R&D priorities are currently virtually defined by private industry alone. They are in effect regulated by market forces and patent protection, which grants private industry a monopoly on patented drug sales, ostensibly to promote R&D for new drug innovations. If patent protection meant appropriate levels of R&D for priority global diseases, then the argument that patent protection is needed to ensure R&D could be accepted. Yet, only 0.2 per cent of the

US$60 billion annual global pharmaceutical R&D budget goes toward tuberculosis, malaria, and acute respiratory infections, which account for 18 per cent of global mortality from all diseases.

Research and development spending by large pharmaceutical industries is largely on lifestyle diseases and diseases of the affluent, for which there is a "blockbuster" return on investment.[18] Moreover, income generated from pharmaceutical sales—which, globally, reached US$337 billion in 1999[19]—is spent mostly on marketing in viable markets and not on R&D. The core competency of big pharmaceutical companies is increasingly not drug R&D, but marketing. At Pfizer Inc. for instance, marketing and administration make up 39 per cent of expenses, compared with 17 per cent for R&D.[20] Today, the question is: "What exactly are patents protecting—R&D for global priority diseases or a growing capacity to market limited blockbuster drugs in limited affluent markets?" Although patent protection is necessary to stimulate innovation, it must be balanced with public goods such as access to essential medicines and innovative R&D for global priority diseases.

With or without a viable commercial market for truly innovative R&D for new drugs, governments individually and collectively have a political responsibility to promote, protect, and ensure people's right to health care. The current solutions advocated by most for new drug development are public–private partnerships, or adding "push" (public investment in drug development) and "pull" (pooled funding to buy new drugs) mechanisms to "market forces." These solutions must include transfer of manufacturing technology from the North to the South (at least to the emerging countries that already have a drug production capacity). Further, equity of access must be a defining parameter of any public–private partnership for new innovative drug development. Such new drugs must be public goods so that they are affordable, and issues of intellectual property rights must not impede this necessary defining parameter in these ventures. It must be remembered, however, that public–private partnerships are new and experimental solutions to this challenge and, whether effective or not, the state is still responsible and accountable for ensuring public goods such as access to health care and to essential medicines and innovative drug R&D.

Increasing research and development of new medicines that respond to priority global diseases—such as TB and tropical diseases—cannot happen without government commitment and intervention. Several public measures must be considered: the definition of priorities for international research; the allocation of public funds for R&D and for establishing new markets; the creation of a regulatory and fiscal framework that encourages R&D; the creation of a fully public drug R&D capacity; and the expansion of the idea that new medicines are "public goods" that cannot be subject only to market forces.

Global health and governance

There is no question that WTO decisions have wide-ranging implications for health.[21] With the exception of a recent ruling on trade in asbestos, WTO dispute settlements have to date placed trade above public health.[22] There is a clear lack of firm leadership on global public health issues, particularly as they affect access to essential medicines and innovations in drug R&D. The WHO's limited mandate, limited resources, and limited institutional capacity have prevented it from playing this essential role in a fully effective way. The WHO should be the most vocal and powerful global public health advocate. This should not be left to other private or intergovernmental actors whose skills, interests, and values are not overtly consistent with those of an institution whose primary mandate should be to protect, promote, and ensure health internationally. Although the WHO now has a World Health Assembly mandate to make public health paramount in trade agreements and to monitor the health effects of trade agreements, the WHO has essentially been relegated to the background in the WTO decision-making process.[23]

To address some of the issues raised in this chapter, and others, Health Action International, Médecins sans Frontières, and the Consumer Project on Technology organized a conference on "Increasing Access to Essential Drugs in a Globalised Economy Working Towards Solutions" in Amsterdam, the Netherlands, in November 1999.[24] Participants called for health to be made a priority at the

WTO Seattle negotiations and demanded a balance between the rights of patent holders and the rights of citizens in intellectual property rights regulations. These views were shared by representatives of the UN Development Programme, the WHO, the WTO, the Dutch and Thai governments, and NGOs that attended the Amsterdam conference. Conference organizers called for the WTO to create a "Standing Working Group on Access to Medicines." This working group would work with the Council for TRIPS and other WTO bodies to review a number of issues concerning intellectual property rules as they relate to access to medicines. It should work within the WTO to consider the impact of trade policies on people in developing and least developed countries, and provide a public health framework for the interpretation of key features of WTO agreements. The WHO and other relevant international organizations should actively support the activities of the working group.

The TRIPS Agreement is meant to protect intellectual property rights while also protecting and advancing various public interest objectives. The balance must be addressed to ensure that people have access to essential and life-saving medicines. As countries implement the TRIPS Agreement, the WTO will be asked to resolve disputes in areas that are subject to numerous different interpretations. The WTO is also constantly evaluating proposals for changing the TRIPS Agreement. The Standing Working Group on Access to Medicines would provide a forum for considering public health issues and the rights of people in both of these processes. The working group would examine a number of important issues in the implementation of the existing TRIPS Agreement, such as:

- compulsory licensing of patents, as permitted under Article 31 of the TRIPS Agreement—the working group should look for ways to best operationalize this article;
- allowing for exceptions to patent rights (under Article 30 of TRIPS) for the production of medicines for export markets when the medicine is exported to a country with a compulsory licence—this would ensure that countries with small domestic markets can benefit from compulsory licensing;

- allowing for exceptions to patent rights (under Article 30 of TRIPS) for medical research, so that patents are not used to stop research and hamper the introduction of generic medicines;
- avoiding overly restrictive and anti-competitive interpretations of TRIPS rules regarding the protection of health registration data or other unnecessary regulatory barriers to competition;
- avoiding restrictive interpretations of trademark rights on issues such as generic labelling and prescribing practices;
- assessing the impact of inadequate reviews of patentability standards (novelty and usefulness) on access to medicines;
- recommending differential rules for essential medicines, such as simplified and fast-track compulsory licensing procedures;
- examining new paradigms for intellectual property rights and health care, including "burden-sharing" approaches for R&D that permit countries to consider a wider range of policy instruments to promote R&D;
- assessing the practical burdens on poor countries of administrating patent systems and resolving disputes over rights.

With the failure of the WTO Ministerial Meeting in December 1999, no state, no institution, and no member state of the WTO has yet formally taken up this initiative. We believe it to be a practical beginning to the issues we and others have raised. In our view, essential medicines and the capacity to create new innovations in medicines cannot be treated simply like a commodity. A life-saving medicine is not the same as a new compact disc. One fulfils a need, the other a want.

MSF is not against patents and patent legislation. True innovative capacity needs to be protected and appropriately compensated. It also needs to be encouraged. To this end, national governments and intergovernmental actors need to develop new approaches to ensure funding for R&D for neglected diseases. These should include:

- increased public and donor funding of health care research;
- compulsory research obligations, such as requirements that companies reinvest a percentage of pharmaceutical sales into R&D, either directly or through public or private sector R&D programmes;

- development of a "Neglected Disease Act" that could be used to stimulate private investment in communicable disease vaccines and medicines.

We advocate a balanced intellectual property protection system that fully accounts for the specific needs and priorities of developing countries, and that follows all the principles outlined in the TRIPS Agreement, including the use of compulsory licensing. In sum, patents should benefit the innovator and those who need access to the innovation. Should it not be possible to achieve this balance under the present international agreements, it will be necessary in the TRIPS review process to strengthen the public interest further by providing explicit exemptions for key health care technologies—an "*exception sanitaire.*" It may also be necessary to consider a tax on global pharmaceutical sales, to be redirected into publicly mandated R&D for innovative treatments for global priority diseases.

Concluding comments

The proposals outlined here are concrete, practical, and viable. MSF exists not in the abstract world of the balance of power and trade relations, but in the daily living reality of its 400 projects around the world. As I said at the opening of this chapter, our patients are dying. Access to essential and innovative medicines is much more than a technical medical issue. It is a social, economic, moral, and ultimately political issue. The balance between private and public interests and between patent rights and patient rights, and the question of what constitutes a public good, are fundamentally issues of human equity.

If all human beings are equal in worth and dignity and access to health care is a human right—and not simply modern-day political rhetoric—then access to essential medicines and to meaningful R&D for innovative drug therapies must be a political and practical priority. Most immediately, rapacious patent protection that makes drugs unaffordable for the poor, a failure to produce existing and effective treatments, and a failure to research and develop innovative treatment for priority global diseases are three of the principal causes behind a dearth of access to essential medicines. The failure of market forces, the failure of governments to regulate these or substitute for them, and the lack of a clear global public health policy have caused the current inhumane, mostly silent, and wholly unacceptable human catastrophe that lack of access to health care and essential medicines represents. The WTO, by design or by default, is at the heart of this issue.

The WTO is now an integral part of an emerging global governance architecture. It ostensibly uses an evidence-based system for adjudicating trade disputes within a defined rules-based system (including TRIPS) that governs trade between nations. This system is not designed to acknowledge evidence beyond what its own rules permit. Within this system, the trade in medicines can be managed without recognition of its life and death implications for millions if not billions of people. Neither the United Nations nor the WHO is yet an institutional counterweight to the WTO, and they have no formal role or seat in the adjudication process, unless, of course, they are invited. The process operates as a closed system, immune to the evidence of human suffering and to the social, labour, environmental, political, and public health consequences of its decisions. These, it is said, are not the responsibility of a trade organization. Perhaps this is true, but it is then also true that the WTO is regulating the global economic market in a global governance vacuum.

There is a deep paradoxical inconsistency in state obligations under international treaties, most notably expressed in the polarity between obligations to protect human life and dignity and obligations to protect patents. Ideally, intellectual property protection can be seen as a part of a social contract between private interests and actors and the state that provides a means of both protecting private interests and prioritizing and pursuing public goods. For essential medicines and innovative drug R&D capacity, this may be appropriate where a given society has been able to create such medicines and capacity, and where it can legally enforce the regulation of private actors and market forces. However, as a stand-alone measure on a global level, intellectual property protection exists in a governance vacuum where there are as yet no such capacity and legal enforcement and regulation mechanisms to ensure that public interests and public goods are given priority over private interests.

Because its decisions are enforceable (unlike other international agreements on the environment, human rights, and social welfare), the WTO is now, in effect, the world's most powerful international institution. Its regulation of trade reaches into the very structure of a national economy and, in so doing, it regulates the lifeblood of any nation. Its rules-based system evaluates according to considerations of economic efficiency, which dominate most modern economic analyses. It does not evaluate with respect to general social consequences. The result is a de facto global social policy as technocracy rather than as vision.

The emerging global governance architecture has failed to date to balance private and collective interests, to ensure equity, and, from our perspective, to ensure the right to access health care and essential medicines. In practical terms, for millions with disease and for billions without access to health care, this is a question of life or death, not of self-referential trade rules. There is nothing anti-liberal or anti-trade about seeking and demanding that the right to access health care be respected, protected, and promoted. There is no liberty without life and, for one-third of the world's people, this is their demand today, and not simply a trickle-down issue to be considered tomorrow.

Notes

1. World Bank, *A Better World for All,* 2000.
2. See UNAIDS website, http://www.unaids.org, accessed 28 June 2000.
3. F. J. Palalla, K. M. Delaney, A. C. Moorman et al., "Declining Morbidity and Mortality among Patients with Advanced Human Immunodeficiency Virus Infection," *New England Journal of Medicine* 279, 1999, pp. 853–860.
4. Laurie Garrett, *The Betrayal of Trust: The Collapse of Global Public Health,* New York: Hyperion, 2000, p. 574.
5. P. Chirac, T. von Schoen-Angerer, T. Kasper, N. Ford, "AIDS: Patient Rights versus Patent Rights," *The Lancet,* 356, 2000, p. 502.
6. See http://fda.gov/cder/ob/default.htm and http://www.patents.ibm.com.
7. J. Kahn, "U.S. Offers Africa Billions to Fight Aids," *New York Times,* 19 July 2000.
8. R. Swarns, "South Africa Rejects AIDS Drug Loans," *International Herald Tribune,* 23 August 2000.
9. See Campaign for Access to Essential Medicines, press release, "Act Up, Health Action International (HAI), Medecins Sans Frontieres (MSF)—Public Health Advocates Call for Transparency on Global Medicine Pricing Information,"

Geneva, 17 May 2000; online at http://www.accessmed-msf.org/msf/accessmed/accessmed.nsf/html/4DTSR2?OpenDocument, accessed 4 October 2000.

10. See Campaign for Access to Essential Medicines, press release, "New Agreement on Patents for Medicines in Francophone Africa Threaten Health of Populations: Médecins Sans Frontières Calls upon the Francophone Countries of Africa Not to Sign the New Patent Agreements," Abidjan, 11 May 2000; online at http://www.accessmed-msf.org/msf/accessmed/accessmed.nsf/html/4DTSR2?OpenDocument, accessed 4 October 2000.

11. See Campaign for Access to Essential Medicines, "Physicians Left with Archaic Drugs to Treat Rising Epidemic," 23 November 1999; online at http://www.accessmed-msf.org/msf/accessmed/accessmed.nsf/html/4FUG9L?OpenDocument, accessed 4 October 2000.

12. Chris Dye, Chief Epidemiologist, the WHO, "Stopping TB: Weighing the Alternatives," paper delivered at Rockefeller Foundation Conference on TB Drug Development, Cape Town, South Africa, 6–8 February 2000.

13. C. Holme, L. Cranberg, J. Owen-Drife, "Tuberculosis: Story of Medical Failure," *British Medical Journal,* 317, 1998, p. 1260.

14. Personal communication, Professor Jim Kim, PHRI, Harvard Social Sciences and Infectious Diseases Program, 20 February 2000.

15. B. Pecoul, P. Chirac, P. Trouiller, and J. Pinel, "Access to Essential Medicines in Poor Countries: A Lost Battle?" *Journal of the American Medical Association,* 281, 1999, pp. 361–367.

16. P. Trouiller, C. Battistella, J. Pinel, and B. Pecoul, "Is Orphan Drug Status Beneficial to Tropical Diseases Control? Comparison of the American and Future European Orphan Drug Acts," *Tropical Medicine and International Health* (in press).

17. P. Trouiller and P. Olliaro, "Drug Development Output: What Proportion Tropical Diseases?" *The Lancet,* 354, 10 July 1999.

18. For a lighter example, see S. Avery, "Compulsive Shoppers Can Take a Pill for Quick Relief," *National Post* (Canada), 5 August 2000, p. 1.

19. See http://www.ims-global.com/insight/report/market_growth/report0600.htm, accessed 4 October 2000.

20. G. Harris, "Drug Industry Seeks Cure through Marketing," *Globe and Mail* (Canada), 7 July 2000.

21. N. Drager, "Making Trade Work for Public Health," *British Medical Journal,* 319, 1999, p. 1214.

22. M. Koivusalo, *World Trade Organization and Trade-creep in Health and Social Policies,* Occasional Paper No. 4, Helsinki: STAKES, 1999; online at http://www.stakes.fi/gaspp/occasional%20papers/GASPP4-1999.pdf.

23. L. Aventin, "Trade Agreements and Public Health: Role of WHO," *The Lancet,* 355, 2000, p. 580.

24. The meeting brought together 350 participants from 50 developing and developed countries, from both the private and the public sectors. The "Amsterdam Statement to WTO Member States on Access to Medicine" was developed at the conference; online at http://www.accessmed-msf.org/msf/accessmed/accessmed.nsf/html/4DTSR2?OpenDocument, accessed 4 October 2000.

12

Building a WTO that can contribute effectively to economic and social development worldwide

Bill Jordan
General Secretary, International Confederation
of Free Trade Unions

Since the collapse of efforts to launch a new round of trade negotiations at the third Ministerial Meeting of the World Trade Organization (WTO) in Seattle (30 November—3 December 1999), public confidence in the multilateral trading system has fallen extremely low in both the developing and the industrialized countries. Most developing countries remain apprehensive about the international trading system, concerned that areas such as intellectual property, investment, market access, and transparency of WTO decision-making stand to work against their interests. Worldwide, there is concern that the WTO dispute settlement mechanism undermines domestic sovereignty, particularly in areas where trade can have a socially and environmentally damaging impact. The WTO's trade disputes system places enormous pressure on its members' ability to maintain a domestic consensus in support of trade liberalization. Further trade disputes conducted under existing WTO rules risk to result in a continued series of rulings (in disputes such as bananas and hormones, and potentially in areas such as genetically modified organisms) that will be socially and environmentally damaging and cause increasing opposition to the WTO among the general public in many countries.

Taken all together, these developments must be of serious concern to the WTO and its member governments. Not only is there little sign of consensus on the main elements of possible new trade negotiations, but questions are being raised about the future of the WTO system that go beyond the issue of a new WTO trade round. Countries might even stop implementing WTO rulings. In such a case, the trade disputes system could break down, particularly if there were a fall in world economic growth prospects that weakened support for trade governed by the WTO.

"Trade . . . should be conducted with a view to raising standards of living"

The Preamble to the General Agreement on Tariffs and Trade (GATT)—also written into the founding articles of the WTO—states that "relations in the field of trade and economic endeavour should be conducted with a view to raising standards of living, ensuring full employment and a large and steadily growing volume of real income and effective demand, developing the full use of the resources of the world and expanding the production and exchange of goods." For the trade unions from 143 countries that constitute the International Confederation of Free Trade Unions (ICFTU), representing a total of 123 million workers, this quotation sums up the *raison d'être* of the WTO. The WTO exists as a means to an end. That end is to enhance the welfare and living conditions of all, both within and across countries—developed and developing alike. This requires policy coherence between trade policy and other public policy goals. It means putting trade policy into a context of overall national and international objectives, which include social, environmental, and other developmental priorities.

During the process of the Uruguay Round negotiations and the first years of the WTO, the multilateral community lost sight of this need for policy coherence. As external barriers to trade have come down and product, capital, and labour markets have become increasingly integrated, the agenda of the GATT and the WTO has begun to have a more direct effect on national policies and regulations. Although the WTO's rules now affect many areas that are not purely commercial and had previously been considered to be of primarily national concern, the WTO has not been given a mandate adequately to address the social and environmental repercussions of globalization in cooperation with other international bodies. As a result, it is unable to go beyond certain purely economic factors lying behind trade disputes, national trade policies, and other issues on its agenda. This leaves the WTO vulnerable to the widespread and growing public concern about the course of globalization, including the liberalization of trade.

In these circumstances, the best and perhaps only way for the WTO to make headway is for it to put trade policy into a wider perspective of international action to shape and balance globalization so that it takes into account broader issues, including questions such as respect for internationally agreed fundamental workers' rights. This is a major challenge that the ICFTU does not underestimate. However it is a challenge that cannot be avoided.

The need for rules in the multilateral trading system

The ICFTU, itself one of the main non-governmental actors in the global economy, does not share the view of the more extreme non-governmental organizations (NGOs) that oppose the globalization process through the WTO in its entirety. The ICFTU supports open, fair, and transparent world trade and, over the past 50 years, has backed the removal of barriers to trade at the WTO and its predecessor, the GATT.

In the eyes of the ICFTU, a strong multilateral rules-based trade regime, attained through the WTO, is essential to developing a comprehensive system of world governance of the global market. But, at the same time, it is no longer possible to separate trade policy from issues such as progress on international workers' rights, economic development, and social progress.

With rising inequalities between and within countries, support for the removal of further barriers to trade is fragile, particularly in developing countries—as was demonstrated by some of the difficulties faced in reaching an agreement at Seattle. In order to support development more effectively and gain public credibility, it is vital that the WTO not only opens up trade but does so in a way that responds to social and development concerns and works to reduce inequalities. *These concerns will not go away.* They are growing and they must be addressed. That must be done sooner rather than later, because in addressing these challenges the WTO can help to ensure that trade liberalization does what it is supposed to do—help make people's lives better.

Development priorities and the WTO

To rebuild confidence in the WTO ahead of the next WTO Ministerial Conference, the WTO's member governments must now give the WTO a mandate to take development goals and social and environmental issues fully into account. Among a range of measures that should be taken to address vital issues, first and foremost the WTO and its member governments need to develop a comprehensive development agenda to ensure that people in developing countries benefit from world trade. This must include:

- agreement on deep and sustained debt relief, translated into action at national and international levels, and far-reaching reforms to IMF/World Bank structural adjustment policies so they promote social and economic development;
- a substantial increase in development assistance, including the strengthening of trading capacities;
- acceptance of the need for special and differential treatment to allow developing countries increased flexibility, including taking tariff-freezing, tariff-raising, or import-limiting measures when necessary;
- early moves to provide improved market access, particularly for least developed countries, including positive incentives such as

preferential market access (including tariff and quota reductions and extensions of market access to sectors presently excluded) linked to the respect of human rights at work;

- the incorporation of development objectives into the built-in review of the Agreement on Trade-Related Aspects of Intellectual Property Rights;
- multilateral agreement to extend the Uruguay Round implementation deadlines for developing countries;
- a commitment by the industrialized countries to keep on schedule for their own implementation requirements under the Uruguay Round;
- opening up world trade in agricultural products to benefit the exports of developing countries;
- a commitment not to use the GATS (General Agreement on Trade in Services) negotiations as a tool to undermine developing countries' public education, health, and water systems; and
- a commitment to respect core labour standards, so that developing countries do not face unchecked competition from trading partners that, in many cases, violate core labour standards extensively.

The links between globalization and basic workers' rights

It may be instructive to review the evidence for the negative links so often seen between globalization and the violation of basic workers' rights. Over the past 20 years, the global competition for trade and investment has put increasing downward pressure on fundamental workers' rights. Rather than trade being the wellspring for improving living and working conditions through the resources provided by higher exports, it has all too often been a source of misery as governments actually reduce workers' rights in order to minimize labour costs.

Although freer trade has brought prosperity for some, it has also brought poverty for many, notably the weakest members of our societies. Unscrupulous companies or governments are able to gain short-term competitive advantage by abusing fundamental workers' freedoms. This has been seen most clearly in countries such as

Malaysia, where workers in the electronics export sector are denied the opportunity of joining trade unions, Mexico, where a failure to apply the law in the "maquiladora" free trade zones deprives over 1 million workers (mainly young women) of freedom of association, Turkey, where workers in free trade zones are denied the right to strike, Lesotho, where the mainly women workers in export estates producing goods such as textiles and garments face violation of basic working conditions, police violence, and even shooting, and Egypt, where child labour is extensively employed in export sectors such as commercial agriculture, textiles, leather, and carpet-making. A myriad other examples from export sectors around the world have been extensively documented in the 50 reports the ICFTU has produced over the past two years on respect for core labour standards in many countries of the world.[1]

Some countries will not tolerate free trade unions at all. China is becoming a powerful player on the global economic stage, with many experts predicting it will have the biggest economy in the world within the next 25 years. In southern China alone, there are 153 million manufacturing workers powering an economy unencumbered (as that dictatorship would see it) by any kind of independent voice demanding higher standards or fair wages. Many factories in China are run by the army, and the country has an extensive forced system of labour camps where the labour is unpaid. It is difficult to see how any other government could compete with that.

Yet that is what many governments seem to be trying to do, especially those that are competing for foreign investment. All over the world, governments are investing heavily in export processing zones and touting them as sources of cheap labour where unions are suppressed. On average, 80 per cent of the workers in these zones are women. To keep up with international competition, the average wage paid to these women can be half of what men get. Some countries even boast about the fact that they employ women workers in advertising aimed at attracting foreign investment, pointing out that not only are the women cheap, but they are more docile and less likely to become trade union activists. Many multinational companies, keen to escape high wages, stricter laws, and stronger unions in the industrialized world, have been only too happy to take advantage.

At least 15 million children are working in export production. These children are to be found in sectors such as mining, garments and textiles, shoe production, agriculture, carpet-making, footballs, and even the production of surgical instruments. A minority of countries are prepared to tolerate child labour in the belief that it will give them a competitive edge. But any short-term gain those countries obtain will easily be outweighed by the long-term damage being done to a country's skills base by putting its children in factories rather than in classrooms. In other words, today's child labourers are tomorrow's unskilled and unemployed young workers.

Forced labour is often described nowadays, quite accurately, as a contemporary form of slavery. Forced labour exists in 15–20 countries around the world. In Burma, at least 160,000 indigenous people are working on railways and pipelines linking huge natural gas deposits to customers. The workers are supervised by armed guards. Foreign companies involved include the French-based oil giant TOTAL, and the US-based UNOCAL. Burma is an extreme case, but it is not the only offender. Forced labour exists in Latin America, Africa, the - Middle East, and elsewhere in Asia. In Peru, forced labour is to be found in the gold mines. In Brazil, it is in the vast rural estates. In Pakistan, several million people are enslaved in different forms of forced labour. Typical working conditions involve incredibly long hours of work, seven days a week, 52 weeks a year; serious neglect of basic occupational health and safety standards; steadily accumulating debt; and a predominantly child workforce in many sectors.

Globalization promises a great deal, but is delivering insecurity and cruelty to millions. The ICFTU believes the world cannot tolerate an economic system that depends on repression for profit, that exploits children and young women, and that makes slavery a sound business option. The challenge for the WTO is to secure measures to ensure a fair division of the benefits from world trade both between and within countries. At present, developing countries that wish to improve working and living conditions are undercut in world markets by countries whose governments suppress workers' rights. Those countries, failing to live up to the commitments they have made on core labour standards, threaten the legitimacy of the world trading system by undermining the basic rights of working people.

Achieving respect for basic workers' rights through the WTO would create the potential for a different world trading system, one that achieves economic development and growth on the basis of respect for human rights and improvement in living and working conditions for all world citizens.

The way forward on core labour standards at the WTO

In order to build popular support for the multilateral trading system, one of the key issues is to prevent the worsening repression of basic workers' rights in developing countries.

The international community already agrees that the global economy needs global regulation. That is the whole basis for the World Trade Organization, for international standard-setting, for laws banning the manufacture and sale of counterfeit goods and protecting intellectual copyright, and for the environmental initiatives following on from the Earth Summit. Many of the mechanisms set up to enforce these regulations operate across the jurisdiction of nation states. There seems no justification for allowing all this but claiming that the same type of international regulation cannot operate to protect basic human and trade union rights.

The challenge before the international trading community now is to devise effective and enforceable procedures to pressure the minority of countries that violate core labour standards to live up to their commitments. Core labour standards are fundamental human rights for all workers, irrespective of their level of development. These standards, endorsed by the UN Copenhagen and Beijing Summits and by the Declaration on Fundamental Principles and Rights at Work of the International Labour Organization (ILO), are defined by the following eight ILO instruments:

- Conventions 87 and 98 on the rights to freedom of association and to bargain collectively;
- Conventions 29 and 105 on the abolition of forced labour;
- Conventions 111 and 100 on the prevention of discrimination in employment and on equal pay for work of equal value; and

- Conventions 138 on the minimum age for employment (prohibition of child labour) and 182 on the elimination of the worst forms of child labour.

What is urgently needed is a series of practical steps to incorporate enforceable core labour standards into concrete actions by the WTO to reinforce the weight of the ILO's internationally recognized standards. (Minimum wages have never been part of the ICFTU proposal.)

Many developing country governments have argued that developed countries simply want to impose standards on them in order to remove their comparative advantage of cheap labour costs. But the ICFTU proposal to include core labour standards at the WTO is aimed not at protecting markets but at protecting the rights of all workers worldwide. Indeed, it should be recalled that two-thirds of the ICFTU's affiliates are from developing countries.

The ICFTU sees agreement on international rules that prevent the exacerbation of the negative aspects of the relationship between trade and respect for core labour standards as being part and parcel of a process of reinforcing the credibility of the WTO. A system-wide effort is needed to prevent nineteenth-century living and working conditions surviving into the twenty-first century.

The WTO needs to seize the opportunity by starting a process of discussions about how to make the world trading system start to reinforce, and not undermine, respect for basic workers' rights. The WTO General Council needs to agree on some form of working or study group or similar body, with the participation of the ILO, that would constitute the first effective follow-up to the commitment on core labour standards enshrined in the Singapore Declaration of the first WTO Ministerial Conference in December 1996. That body should be asked to undertake analysis and to make recommendations about WTO statutes and procedures in order to ensure consistency of trade negotiations and agreements with respect for core labour standards within the work of the WTO. It should also examine the social impact of trade more generally, including the impact of trade policies on women. The analysis would include examination of the best way to implement a scheme of positive incentives, the consideration of measures to be taken where trade liberalization was associated with violations of core labour standards, and a review of the mechanisms of the WTO (including trade policy reviews and dispute settlement) in order to help to work towards increased openness and transparency.

At the same time, all industrialized country governments should actively demonstrate their commitment to improving core labour standards through enhanced trade incentives and increased development assistance in this area.

Reforming the WTO's decision-making structures

The WTO's decision-making structures were shown to be painfully deficient in Seattle. The WTO needs to work equally for all its members and be seen to do so. Concerted and sustained financial assistance by all industrialized countries is needed to ensure that all developing countries (particularly the least developed) are able to take part fully in all WTO activities and procedures, including its dispute settlement mechanisms.

At both national and international levels, there is a need for much closer interaction between trade policy and labour and social policy, the environment, women's rights, foreign direct investment, and business practices. The WTO therefore must increase its transparency and openness and collaboration with other agencies.

The WTO Singapore Declaration stated that "the WTO and ILO Secretariats will continue their existing collaboration," yet this collaboration has failed to occur. In view of the relevance of their work to the WTO, the ILO and all other UN agencies, in particular the UN Environment Programme, the World Health Organization, the UN Development Programme, and the UN Development Fund for Women (UNIFEM), should be granted observer status in the WTO and play a full role in all the different aspects of the WTO's structure through its various committees and mechanisms. Such observer status should be granted prior to the next WTO Conference, so that these agencies can attend the fourth Ministerial Meeting and address it on their particular concerns.

A formal consultative process should be established to ensure that international union, business, and other non-governmental organizations can present their views to WTO committees and discuss issues of mutual concern with trade ministers, on occasions such as WTO Ministerial Meetings. The WTO General Council should furthermore take immediate measures to improve public access to information emanating from the WTO. This should entail automatic derestriction of documents except in exceptional circumstances.

The WTO's current dispute settlement procedure provides little access for non-governmental actors even to submit documents for consideration, let alone to discuss their submissions with the expert panels or the litigating parties. In view of its unprecedented powers, the dispute settlement procedure needs to be opened up for public information and involvement. In relevant cases, such as those with health, labour, and environmental implications, the WTO should involve the UN agencies competent in the areas concerned. Civil society groups concerned by any dispute settlement process should be able to participate directly in the procedures. The experts judging a case should not just be trade specialists but should include people with varied backgrounds representing labour, environment, and development organizations. There should be a swift public release of the findings and conclusions of dispute settlement procedures. Making the procedures open would contribute to strengthening the WTO by reducing the scope for governments to misrepresent the processes and results of the procedures to suit their purposes.

The WTO's Trade Policy Review Mechanism (TPRM) is potentially a powerful tool to ensure that member states follow WTO rules, and it is gradually developing its methods of exercising pressure on WTO members. Its scope should be expanded to include trade-related environmental, social, and gender concerns, including core labour standards. The UN's specialized agencies should provide input to the TPRM process as part of the increased collaboration of the WTO with the broader family of UN institutions.

The fourth UN World Women's Conference stated that all multilateral organizations must disaggregate data and take the gender impact into account in all their activities. Accordingly, as part of a process of incorporating workers' rights into the WTO's mechanisms, the WTO, in conjunction with the ILO, should undertake an assessment of the impact of trade policy on women workers and collect gender-disaggregated data as a statistical baseline to follow in future years.

Ensuring the WTO does not undermine environmental or social protection

Environment- and health-related trade questions

The WTO will continue to arouse hostility and suspicion if its trade disputes mechanism encourages governments to undermine multilateral environmental agreements (MEAs). There are currently about 180 MEAs, including the UN Conventions on Ozone and on Climate Change. However, where they stand in relation to the WTO rules is unclear. Despite the fact that these multilateral agreements have been agreed on, and decisions taken that will protect the environment, if trade rules take legal precedence the MEAs are meaningless. WTO members must accept that an amendment to GATT Article XX, or a quasi-judicial statement of understanding, is required that would specify that the most universally endorsed MEAs are legitimate exceptions to trade rules. Although trade is vital it must not be at the expense of the environment.

In environmental disputes the burden of proof should be reversed so that the complaining country would have to prove that there was a case to answer. Formal recognition is needed in the WTO of the precedence of the precautionary principle in environment and health-related trade questions, including preventing hazards at work.

The WTO agreed in the Uruguay Round that, although states can control the import of final products that are damaging to health and environment, they cannot restrict the import of goods on the grounds that they have been produced using harmful process and production methods (PPMs). This has major implications not only for the environment but also for health and safety standards at work. The WTO should agree that it is legitimate to prevent the import of goods that are made using harmful PPMs. Legitimate standards should be achievable without this measure degenerating into protectionism. The WTO Technical Barriers to Trade Agreement should be amended to allow for the ecolabelling of goods that use harmful PPMs.

The WTO General Council should further agree that a global environmental and social impact assessment should be undertaken to monitor the impact of globalization and of any proposed future WTO trade liberalization on environmental and social protection.

GATS negotiations

The current negotiations under the General Agreement on Trade in Services have serious potential social implications, particularly in the health, education, and water sectors, relating to existing national regulations, to public services and the public/private sector balance, to standards, and to the capacity for continuing state support. The WTO General Council should include explicit reference to social and environmental concerns in the WTO negotiations on trade in services in order to anticipate and prevent the conclusion of any agreements that undermine vital and socially beneficial service sector activities. Countries must be able to retain the right to exempt public services from any agreement covering the service sector, and to take a future decision to increase the public sector role in their services sectors (for example following a change of government) without facing penalties under WTO rules.

Competition policy

The ICFTU supports the principle of extending authority to an international level over areas such as mergers and market abuses of different sorts, particularly by multinational companies (MNCs). Cross-border mergers and acquisitions are a major driving force in the globalization of the world economy and a purely national approach to the scrutiny of business consolidation is no longer sufficient. The institutional form of a new international regime for competition policy (which should not prevent existing competition authorities from continuing to regulate competition at the national and regional level) will necessarily have to include the WTO, with its overall mandate to promote competition in world markets. A particularly important aspect of this should be an inspection of the serious problems for developing countries caused by restrictive business practices, including corruption and transfer pricing by MNCs.

At the same time, any discussion of competition will have to take into account social and environmental goals. The aim of competition policy must be the efficient supply of goods and services to all sections of society and regions. Publicly provided services and appropriately regulated public ownership are in many cases the best means of achieving these goals. Any new international procedures should therefore respect the value of public services and state ownership and should not become a means to pressure governments to privatize sectors where state provision has been chosen as the best available option.

Government procurement

The ICFTU believes that any effort to develop a multilateral agreement that builds on the plurilateral (voluntary) Government Procurement Agreement (GPA), signed in 1996, must start by recognizing the legitimacy of the economic, social, and environmental factors that enter into much government purchasing policy. The ICFTU welcomes efforts to promote transparency of government procurement practices and emphasizes in this context the role of respect for core labour standards in providing necessary protections to workers employed on government contracts, particularly migrant workers who are especially vulnerable to labour rights abuses. Any WTO agreement should furthermore remedy some flaws in the GPA by authorizing public authorities to engage in ethical purchasing policies, so enabling public authorities to refuse to do business with companies engaged in violations of basic human rights.

Conclusions

An effective multilateral trading system that can produce social and economic improvements is in everyone's interest. Yet, until people's social, developmental, and environmental concerns are properly addressed within the WTO system, its lack of credibility can only grow. Accordingly, WTO member governments must find ways to ensure that world trade and investment do not lead to violation of fundamental workers' rights, a lowering of health and environmental standards, or a worsening of the prospects for development.

Preventing a repetition of Seattle will require progress through the WTO General Council on all fronts simultaneously: to tackle the concerns of developing countries about fair treatment in the multilateral trading system, to protect basic labour standards during globalization, and to make the trading system environmentally sustainable. A new consensus needs to be built so that the WTO can gain the public support it badly needs and begin to achieve the goals in the WTO statutes of increasing living standards, raising employment, and achieving sustainable growth.

Note

1. All these reports are available on the ICFTU's website: http://www.icftu.org.

13

Trade rules after Seattle:
A business perspective

Maria Livanos Cattaui
Secretary-General, International Chamber of Commerce

Despite the damaging setback at Seattle in 1999, world business continues to urge that the launch of a new broad-based round of multilateral trade negotiations under the aegis of the World Trade Organization (WTO) must be a top priority on the international economic agenda. A start has already been made with new negotiations on trade in services and agriculture, as mandated by the Uruguay Round. These must be advanced expeditiously, and expanded at an early date to cover a significantly broader trade agenda to improve the prospects of achieving a balanced result that all WTO members can subscribe to. It is the responsibility of the powerful countries to give leadership and impetus to this task, and to communicate more effectively to their general publics the benefits of trade and investment liberalization.

Globalization is presenting great challenges as well as great opportunities to societies the world over. Sound multilateral rules for the worldwide marketplace are vital to ensure the smooth functioning and good management of globalization. Markets, like freedom, work well only within a suitable framework of rules. It is the task of governments, with the help of business, to cooperate closely to find the balance between freedom and rules that maximizes the scope for business to create wealth and employment.

In Seattle in 1999, governments were unable to reach consensus even on the agenda for a new trade round. After all the hype and despite all the expectations, ministers floundered in a sea of division and indecision. Of course, we knew before Seattle that different governments—and different groups of governments—placed more emphasis on some issues than others did. And we knew that some governments were more ambitious than others in the scope they foresaw for the new round. It was these differences that ministers were supposed to reconcile in Seattle in a spirit of compromise and determination to strengthen the WTO and the rules-based multilateral trading system.

In June 1999, the International Chamber of Commerce (ICC) published its strategic objectives for a new round in the name of world business.[1] We opted for a broad-based agenda because we believe that the more opportunities there are for negotiators to give and take, the better the chances of success of achieving a balanced result. We suggested that new trade negotiations should embrace a much broader concept of market access than in previous trade rounds, with the focus on multilateral rules that enable companies to compete freely and on equal terms in a global marketplace.

The ICC statement recommended that governments should:

- implement all Uruguay Round commitments in full and on schedule;
- improve market access, especially for developing countries, by further reducing tariffs and introducing effective restraints on non-tariff barriers;
- prevent abusive resort to anti-dumping measures;
- push forward the process of creating high-standard multilateral rules within the WTO to protect and liberalize foreign investment;
- expand and improve commitments on trade in services reached during and since the Uruguay Round, including trade in basic telecommunications, financial services, and the movement of natural persons;
- make a start in the WTO on liberalizing maritime transport, air cargo, and postal and express delivery services;

- speed up the reduction of substantial protectionist barriers that impede and distort trade in agricultural products—barriers that are particularly damaging to the export capability of many developing countries; and
- develop comprehensive and effective multilateral rules to simplify and modernize trade procedures, and in particular slow and bureaucratic customs procedures.

Even after the Seattle failure, we still think that this agenda is realistic, provided that the political will can be forged among WTO members to carry it forward.

Although Seattle was a setback and the dust has still to settle, we do not see it as a halt to trade liberalization. As business people, we are convinced that the achievements of half a century of trade liberalization provide the example, and it is unthinkable that the process will not continue.

That said, the ICC remains gravely concerned at the large number of high-profile trade disputes among members of the G-7 that are currently being allowed to sour international trade relations further and that are weakening the authority and effectiveness of the WTO and its dispute settlement system. Our concern at what happened in Seattle, however, extends beyond disagreements among governments over substance. The WTO seems to have become the scapegoat for everyone with a grievance about the modern world, and that—at the very least—is an unhealthy trend.

In an atmosphere of massive and sometimes violent protest in Seattle, much false information about the WTO, about business, about globalization, and about international trade was endlessly repeated. The WTO itself was depicted as a secretive and undemocratic institution controlled by the multinationals. Some protesters seemed to regard trade itself as a curse to be lifted from the brow of humankind; as the cause of lost jobs and the exploitation of workers, and the source of environmental pollution. But if the WTO were undermined, that would be a threat to the rule of law in world trade. If we go back to the law of the jungle, and the WTO's effective dispute settlement machinery is disregarded, the principal nations to suffer will be the poor and the weak. The WTO is the best guarantee there is of a level playing field for all countries, at whatever stage of development.

In the interests of establishing a stable and predictable trading environment, it is important to understand the conditions that have given rise to this vocal opposition. In fact, the WTO has become the victim of its own success. Because it has a dispute settlement mechanism with teeth and its rules actually work, special interest groups are attempting to saddle it with issues that are not directly related to trade liberalization—and many of them want to sink it in the process. The WTO should be allowed to get on with its job of supervising the international trading system without being burdened with excess baggage. Its task is already dauntingly complex and difficult.

The protesters who would have the WTO abolished claim to represent the interests of the world's poor and disadvantaged. Those groups need reminding that, far from favouring the rich and powerful countries, international trade rules and WTO disciplines give the poorer countries the chance to defend themselves against pressures from powerful trading partners. The WTO is based on non-discrimination. Rich and poor countries alike can be challenged if they violate an agreement, and they have an equal right to challenge others through the WTO's dispute settlement procedures.

The claim that international trade is a negative rather than a positive force is difficult to understand. Look at the record of the twentieth century. As the United Nations Secretary-General, Kofi Annan, has remarked: the first half saw the world almost destroyed by war, partly as a result of its division into rival trade blocs. But the second half saw an unprecedented expansion of world trade, which also brought unprecedented economic growth. Since 1948, annual economic statistics have invariably shown growth in world trade outstripping economic growth. In other words, trade has been the engine of economic growth. This means that economic activity is more and more dependent upon trade as the years go by.

In 1998, world merchandise exports were worth over US$5 trillion, and in volume terms that represents an 18-fold increase over 1948. Although the world's population has more than doubled, to reach 6 billion in 1999, exports per capita are eight times as high in real terms as in 1948. The figures are so enormous it is difficult to take them in. Behind them is the reality that trade contributed enormously to world growth and prosperity over the half-century, bringing better jobs and more resources for education, health, and other social spending. Despite the poverty that still exists in too many countries, the fact is that the world is far more prosperous now than it has ever been.

In April 2000, A.T. Kearney, the management consulting unit of Electronic Data Systems Corp., released the results of its 18-month study on globalization.[2] It traced the effects on 34 countries of integration into the world economy. The accompanying "globalization index" showed that nations that opened up their markets to free trade had not only faster economic growth but also striking improvement in social indicators, education, life expectancy, and infant mortality—even cleaner water. Kearney conceded that inequality—that is, the rich–poor income gap—has also widened and that in this game there are losers as well as winners, but the statistics weigh heavily on the plus side.

The challenge therefore is for developing countries to make the necessary reforms to their economies to ensure that they are in a position to reap the economic rewards of globalization and to create the fundamental conditions for prosperity to take root. The chief failure of the past two decades was not that global economic integration went too far, but that it has not as yet gone far enough. Too many countries and regions have remained marginalized. If the critics now persuade governments to turn their economies inwards, they will have thrown away the world's best hope of a sustained reduction in poverty and global inequality.

Former Mexican President Ernesto Zedillo analysed the current state of play best at the World Economic Forum annual meeting in Davos in 1999, where he identified a peculiar alliance of anti-globalization forces. As he saw it, activists from the extreme left and the extreme right, environmental groups, trade unions of developed countries, and some self-appointed representatives of civil society have gathered around a common endeavour: to save the people of developing countries from development. He said that no one would claim that access to free trade and investment is sufficient to achieve sustained development and overcome poverty. Much more is needed in terms of sound macroeconomic policies, domestic liberalization, permanently increasing investment in education, health, and human capital in general (especially for the poorest), as well as the strengthening of democratic institutions, including those that guarantee the rule of law.

However, what is now clear from the historical evidence of the twentieth century is that, in every case where a poor nation has significantly overcome its poverty, this has been achieved while engaging in production for export markets and opening itself to the influx of foreign goods, investment, and technology; that is, by participating in globalization. Indeed, I travelled extensively in Asia in 1999, visiting the many ICC national committees spread throughout the continent. In Taipei, Singapore, Hong Kong, and Bangkok, the story was always the same. All the business people and government officials in these economies feel betrayed and abandoned by the most developed countries, which, it seems to them, want to restrain their chances. They feel betrayed by protectionist special groups in Europe and Asia. All too often, the anti-trade lobbies blame economic disruption and job losses on international competition when the cause is inevitable technological change. And they fail to see that, as old jobs in dying industries disappear, new ones—higher paid and of better quality—are created in the new industries.

Nobody seriously wants to put the clock back on human progress. Technological change is inevitably accompanied by the transformation of whole industries. Think what the advent of the motor car and the demise of the horsedrawn carriage meant for the job market in the early years of the twentieth century. More recently, consider the impact of the word processor on typewriter manufacturers, of radio on newspapers, of television on radio. They all had to adjust.

Business enterprise thrives on change, on seizing new opportunities, and on creating new products to satisfy new markets. Moreover, because we live in a global economy, it does not matter if those markets are at the uttermost ends of the earth.

We also have to admit, however, that business as a whole has not succeeded in convincing public opinion of the merits of trade liberalization or in making the case for the global economy. It is incumbent upon world business, together with governments, to explain to the greater world community the benefits and opportunities that flow from a readiness to embrace the world economy. The fears and misconceptions must be dispelled.

Furthermore, we should be very concerned with one particular aspect of the activities of anti-globalization special interest groups. An idea made popular at Seattle, and which is potentially damaging to multilateralism, is that democratically elected governments do not represent the will of their citizens. The corollary of this idea is that, since international organizations are composed of member governments, they similarly do not represent the will of citizens worldwide. This is a growing trend, which could have far-reaching systemic implications. However, no one elected the protesters to represent them. Democratically, the activists have no right to the "seat at the table" that they demand. But that does not mean that their views should not be heard. The protesting non-governmental organizations (NGOs) need to be reminded that, in democratic societies, the way to advance a cause is to submit it to the scrutiny of the voters, not to intimidate officials doing their best to implement the policies of elected governments.

The ICC is convinced that the emergence of a global market economy, a process that has only just begun, will bring unprecedented prosperity to millions. This is why, through its website and other means, the ICC is intensifying its efforts to better communicate this message on behalf of world business.

As in the build-up to Seattle, debate will continue to rage about whether or not trade should be linked with labour and environmental standards. All along, the ICC has maintained that governments must avoid saddling the multilateral world trading system with wider objectives, however laudable they may be. The ICC agrees with those who fear that labour and environmental issues could be a pretext for protectionism. Those fears received credence from suggestions in Seattle that trade sanctions should be used to punish countries deemed to be breaching core labour standards.

Any right-minded person believes that core labour standards should be established and maintained. But it is poverty that creates bad labour conditions, where such practices as abuse of child labour can flourish. The cure for poverty is economic growth and job creation. To quote the Secretary-General of the United Nations, Kofi Annan: "Practical experience has shown that trade and investment not only bring economic development but often bring higher standards of human rights and environmental protection as well. . . . Indeed, a developing civil society will generally insist on higher standards as soon as it is given the chance to do so."[3]

Trade sanctions would have the opposite effect, for they deny markets to an offending country, weaken its economy, and lower its living standards. Desperately poor rural workers in developing countries will certainly not benefit from such measures. Trade sanctions can only obstruct development and increase poverty.

The movement to keep trade negotiations separate from environmental or labour policies is not confined to business but is supported by the overwhelming majority of the 139 WTO member governments. Similar views are also held by the United Nations, as was made clear in July 1999, when an ICC delegation conferred with Mr. Annan and the heads of UN agencies on relations between business and the United Nations. In a joint statement, we agreed that the WTO-based multilateral trading system should not be called upon to deal with such non-trade issues as human rights, labour standards, and environmental protection.[4] To do so would expose the trading system to even greater strain and the risk of increased protectionism while failing to produce the required results. The right place for addressing these issues is the United Nations and its appropriate specialized agencies.

Business recognizes that the implementation of the rules and disciplines of the multilateral trading system can sometimes have a significant impact on other policy areas. We would therefore welcome a more coordinated collaboration between the WTO and other intergovernmental organizations with different but related policy responsibilities, especially in the fields of development and environmental policies. Currently, too much duplication and inadequate coordination are preventing intergovernmental bodies from taking effective global action to ensure the protection and conservation of international "public goods" in such areas as the oceans, the atmosphere, water, biodiversity, and public health.

Business looks to the United Nations to give a lead in tackling such global problems as cannot be resolved by isolated national or regional initiatives. There is a particular need for the United Nations to provide a strong single focal point on environmental issues, which have important linkages to the work of a host of other inter-governmental organizations. World business recognizes the need for the United Nations to have sufficient resources and authority to tackle effectively the complex and often interrelated global problems of today, while urging further streamlining as part of the institutional reforms being undertaken by the UN system to tackle bureaucracy and the duplication of tasks. The United Nations should be prepared to assume responsibility for coordinating international decision-making more efficiently.

The last year of the twentieth century saw a constructive new relationship develop between the United Nations and business, with each side recognizing that their respective goals are mutually supporting. Peace, development, the rule of law, and harmonious and constructive relations between nations are fundamental goals of the United Nations. Achievement of these goals enables business to expand and prosper. By creating wealth and jobs, by stimulating scientific and technical progress, and by constantly improving products under the stimulus of competition, companies help to defeat poverty and improve the quality of life. And poverty is the enemy of the humanitarian values espoused by the United Nations.

These complementary goals led the UN Secretary-General, Kofi Annan, to propose a Global Compact between the United Nations and business to uphold a set of core values in the areas of human rights, labour standards, and environmental practice. Business has now formally accepted Kofi Annan's challenge, and the ICC has started to use its website to demonstrate how the private sector is fulfilling the compact through corporate examples.

To succeed in business, you have to be an optimist and you have to be persistent. The WTO system has come through some fairly bruising recent conflicts involving its most powerful members and its dispute settlement mechanism is intact. The system works and its members are respecting it. The WTO evidently does have its attractions. Some 30 countries are lining up to join, so it must be doing something right. The turmoil in emerging markets in 1998 did not provoke the protectionist reaction that many experts predicted. The lesson that markets must be kept open despite temporary difficulties appears to have been well learned.

For almost half a century, the ICC gave strong support to the several successive rounds of negotiations to liberalize world trade carried out under the aegis of the General Agreement on Tariffs and Trade. We were particularly supportive of the ambitious Uruguay Round negotiations, which resulted in unprecedentedly wide-ranging agreements further to reduce tariff and non-tariff barriers to trade, and which initiated a process of extending multilateral rules to new trade-related policy areas of major importance to world business. We believe that, without the WTO and without the rules-based international system it is striving to establish, we will revert to bully economics.

From the point of view of world business, the following actions are surely needed now:

- The new balance of power within the WTO means that industrialized countries can no longer expect to impose their views on developing countries. A recent update of a survey on investment conditions in developing countries undertaken by the European Roundtable of Industrialists—with the assistance of the ICC—showed clearly that unilateral liberalization and market-opening reforms were taking place in developing countries irrespective of the WTO process.[5] This trend now seems firmly entrenched. However, the management of the global economy will require the development of effective global rules and the WTO must play a central role in this process.
- Efforts need to be intensified to devise a combination of measures to assist the least developed countries, including greater market access for their exports, and help in building up their institutional and human capacity and their infrastructure.
- Debt relief for the least developed is on the international agenda, but it makes no sense to spend extra billions of dollars on enhanced debt relief if the ability of poorer countries to reduce their debt burden is impeded by export barriers.

- We at the ICC intend to improve developing country participation in our policy work, and to work harder to mobilize the business communities in these nations.
- The ICC called for the establishment of more effective intergovernmental organizations in its recommendations for the Millennium Assembly of the United Nations in September 2000. Serious thinking is taking place at a high level within the United Nations as regards the creation of a world environmental organization, bringing together activities such as those of the UN Environment Programme and the UN Commission on Sustainable Development.
- Efforts should be made to advance trade and investment issues in other intergovernmental organizations in addition to the WTO. For example, the Organisation for Economic Co-operation and Development has undertaken analytical work on the liberalization of air cargo. The World Customs Organization has revised its Kyoto Convention on the Simplification and Harmonization of Customs Procedures, and might require business support from ICC national committees to encourage governments to ratify the revised convention.
- The ICC should seek to better explain to the general public the benefits of the WTO's work, and encourage WTO members to undertake the necessary preparatory work to launch mandated negotiations. Although business will not be able to convince the more vocal and extreme NGOs, it should continue to articulate its views through legitimate democratic consultative processes and work harder to convince parliamentary majorities in individual countries.
- The ICC should focus on the major difficulties to be addressed before multilateral trade negotiations resume, make further recommendations on specific issues, and encourage a more effective division of responsibilities among intergovernmental organizations.
- Liberalizing trade in services is a relatively new and complex area of WTO work, which entails changes in domestic regulatory frameworks rather than the more traditional disciplines on measures at the border involved in trade in goods. Further measures to liberalize investment are important to ensure successful further

liberalization of trade in services. Countries should be encouraged unilaterally to open their markets and to liberalize their investment regimes.

- An important feature of the global economy is the growing importance of intra-firm trade in goods and services, which accounts for between one-third and one-half of world trade. Governments must keep up with the needs of global business, for example in the area of the simplification of trade procedures.

We know that liberal trade conducted under a system of multilateral rules agreed among nations is the best hope of future prosperity for everybody, whether rich or poor. It is also a powerful force for peace in the world. This is a lesson we should all take with us as we step into the twenty-first century.

Notes

1. "World Business Priorities for a New Round of Multilateral Trade Negotiations," Commission on Trade and Investment, 21 June 1999, Document 103/213; online at http://www.iccwbo.org/home/statements_rules/statements/1999/multilateral_trade_negotiations_june1999.asp.
2. A. T. Kearney, "Globalisation Ledger," Global Business Policy Council, April 2000.
3. See chapter 1 in this volume.
4. "Joint Statement on the Global Compact Proposed by the Secretary-General of the United Nations," Geneva, 5 July 1999; online at http://www.iccwbo.org/home/statements_rules/statements/1999/joint_statement_on_global_compact.asp.
5. "Improved Investment Conditions: Third Survey on Improvements in Conditions for Investment in the Developing World," Report to the European Round Table of Industrialists in Cooperation with UN and ICC, 10 July 1999. See http://www.ert.be/pb/pbb/enbb_frame.htm for details.

Contributors

Kofi Annan of Ghana is the seventh Secretary-General of the United Nations and the first to be elected from the ranks of United Nations staff. In more than 35 years with the Organization, his career has encompassed refugee protection, management, budget, personnel, peacekeeping, and various special assignments. Mr. Annan's priorities as Secretary-General have been to revitalize the United Nations through a comprehensive programme of reform; to strengthen the Organization's traditional work in the areas of development and peace and security; to advocate human rights and the rule of law; to exercise his "good offices" where appropriate; and to restore public confidence in the Organization by, in his words, "bringing the United Nations closer to the people."

Mónica Araya is the Director of the Sustainable Americas Project at the Yale Center for Environmental Law and Policy. She is a Research Associate and Co-ordinator of Programs at the Global Environment and Trade Study (GETS). Her research focuses on the trade and environment debate and its North–South interface. Previously she worked as an adviser to the Department of International Negotiations at the Ministry of Foreign Trade in Costa Rica. She holds a Master's degree in Economic Policy (Universidad Nacional) and a Master's degree in Environmental Management (Yale University).

Maria Livanos Cattaui was appointed Secretary-General of the International Chamber of Commerce (ICC) in 1996. As chief executive of the world business organization, she is responsible for overseeing global policy formulation and representing the interests of world business to governments and international organizations. Prior to joining the ICC, Mrs. Cattaui was the Managing Director of the World Economic Forum (WEF) and responsible for its annual meeting in Davos, Switzerland. She was educated in the United States and is an Honours graduate of Harvard University.

José María Figueres Olsen graduated in Industrial Engineering from the United States Military Academy (West Point), and completed his Master's degree in Public Administration at Harvard's JFK School of Government. He served as Minister of Foreign Trade and Agriculture in Costa Rica. He became the youngest elected President of Costa Rica in the twentieth century in 1994. He made sustainable development the centre-piece of his administration, undertaking important transformations to achieve macroeconomic balances, strengthen human development, and construct a strong alliance with nature. He also led Costa Rica's achievements in moving into the digital era. He lectures worldwide on technology and sustainability issues and is a board member of several international organizations. He founded the Costa Rica Foundation for Sustainable Development. He is appointed director of MIT's Digital Nations Consortium and Managing Director of the World Economic Forum.

Bill Jordan, CBE, became General Secretary of the International Confederation of Free Trade Unions in December 1994. He has been active in the trade union movement all his working life, starting as a shop steward in the engineering union. In 1986, he was elected as National President of the Amalgamated Engineering Union (AEU). Mr. Jordan was a member of the General Council of the British Trade Union Confederation, and served on all its major committees. He served on the National Economic Development Council and chaired its Engineering Industry Committee, was on the ACAS Council, and was a member of the Foundation for Manufacturing and Industry. He was President of the European Metalworkers' Federation and was an executive member of the International Metalworkers' Federation and the European Trade Union Confederation.

Frank E. Loy is the Under Secretary of State for Global Affairs in the United States of America. He has served in the federal government four times, three of those in the Department of State. He has previously served as a senior business executive with Pan American World Airways and Penn Central Transportation Company. He has been active in the non-profit community, serving as President of the German Marshall Fund of the United States and chairman of numerous boards of non-governmental organizations, including the Environmental Defense Fund and the League of Conservation Voters. In 1996, he was a Visiting Lecturer at the Yale Law School, teaching a course in international environmental law and policy.

Claude Martin was appointed Director General of WWF International in October 1993. Prior to this, he served as Deputy Director General from 1990 to 1993. Before joining WWF International, Claude Martin was Director and Chief Executive of WWF-Switzerland from 1980 to 1990. Under his leadership, WWF-Switzerland emerged as one of the strongest of the national organizations within the WWF network. His career with WWF started in the early 1970s, when he lived in central India, studying the ecology of the threatened Barasingha deer in Kanha National Park. From 1975 to 1978 Claude Martin served as Director of protected areas in the Western Region of Ghana. He is the author of *The Rainforests of West Africa* (Birkhäuser Verlag, Basel, 1991), a comprehensive study examining the ecology, utilization, and conservation of these forest areas. Claude Martin is a member of the China Council for International Co-operation on Environment and Development—a high-level advisory body to the Chinese government—as well as a board member of numerous other conservation bodies.

James Orbinski is President of the International Council of Médecins sans Frontières (MSF). He has worked with MSF since 1991, being Medical Co-ordinator in Somalia in 1992–1993 and in Afghanistan in 1994, and Head of Mission in Rwanda during the genocide of 1994. He also worked in Goma Zaire in 1996 as Head of Mission. Dr. Orbinski received his MD degree from McMaster University in 1990, and held an IDRC research fellowship in 1989 to study paediatric HIV in sub-Saharan Africa. Dr. Orbinski was a founding member of MSF Canada in 1990, and its Vice President until 1995. He has been President of the MSF International Council since June 1998.

Rubens Ricupero was appointed as UNCTAD's fifth Secretary-General in September 1995. In the course of a long Brazilian government career, he was Minister of Environment and Amazonian Affairs in 1993 and then Minister of Finance in 1994. Mr. Ricupero has held several diplomatic and academic posts, including Ambassador, Permanent Representative to the United Nations and GATT in Geneva (1987–1991), Ambassador to the United States of America (1991–1993), and professorships at the University of Brasilia and at the Rio Branco Institute. He is the author of several books and essays on international relations, problems of economic development, and international trade and diplomatic history.

Mary Robinson took up her duties as United Nations High Commissioner for Human Rights on 12 September 1997. As a lawyer, activist, Senator and President of Ireland, she has displayed a lifetime commitment to human rights both in her country and throughout the world. Mrs. Robinson has served as a member of the International Commission of Jurists and of the Advisory Commission of Inter-Rights. She was the first Head of State to visit Rwanda in the aftermath of the genocide, and Somalia following the crisis there in 1992. As High Commissioner, she has been responsible for implementing UN Secretary-General Kofi Annan's reforms to integrate human rights throughout the work of the Organization and has consistently called for action to extend the full range of human rights—civil, cultural, economic, political, and social—to all people.

José Manuel Salazar-Xirinachs assumed his current position as Chief Trade Advisor and Director of the Trade Unit at the Organization of American States (OAS) in Washington in June 1998. Prior to that he served as Minister of Foreign Trade of Costa Rica. He has also served as Executive Director of the Business Network for

Hemispheric Integration (1996–1997), Vice President of the Board of the Central Bank of Costa Rica (1995–1996), and Executive Director and Chief Economist of the Federation of Private Entities of Central America and Panama (FEDEPRICAP, 1991–1995). Dr. Salazar-Xirinachs is an economist, with Master's and Doctorate degrees in Economics from the University of Cambridge, England. He has published extensively on issues related to economic integration, trade theory and policy, technology, and competitiveness.

Gary P. Sampson worked at UNCTAD from 1975 to 1983. From 1984 to 1986 he was Senior Fellow in Economic Policy at the Reserve Bank of Australia and Professorial Fellow at the Centre of Policy Studies at Monash University. In 1987, he was appointed Director at the GATT and in 1995 Director at the WTO. He is currently on leave from the WTO. He holds the posts of Professor of International Economic Governance at the Institute of Advanced Studies at the United Nations University and Visiting Academic at the London School of Economics. He teaches on a regular basis at the Melbourne Business School and INSEAD in France. He has written extensively on areas relating to international economic governance and his most recent book is entitled *Trade, Environment and the WTO: the Post Seattle Agenda.*

John W. Sewell has been President of the Overseas Development Council (ODC) since 1980. Under his leadership, ODC has compiled a distinguished record of policy research and analysis on US development interests and policies. ODC has recently transformed itself into an international policy research institution that seeks to improve multilateral decision-making in order to promote more effective development and the better management of related global problems. Mr. Sewell has written extensively on globalization, governance, and the reform of American development programmes. Mr. Sewell's current policy and research interests focus on how the forces of globalization have affected the relationships between the old industrial countries, the new emerging economic powers in Asia and Latin America, and the poorer countries that risk marginalization. A graduate of the University of Rochester and New York

University, Mr. Sewell was a member of the Foreign Service and was with the Brookings Institution prior to joining ODC.

Clare Short is Secretary of State for International Development of the United Kingdom. Ms. Short graduated as a Bachelor of Arts with Honours in Political Science. A former civil servant at the Home Office, she entered the House of Commons in 1983. In her long career as a Member of Parliament for the Opposition, she focused on policy areas such as overseas development, women, transport, environment protection, social security, employment, home affairs, and race relations. She has been a member of the National Executive Committee (NEC) of the Labour Party and Chair of the NEC Women's Committee and the International Committee. She is also Chair of the Human Rights Committee of the Socialist International. Since 1997 she has headed the newly created Department for International Development. Ms. Short's main political interests are overseas development and employment quality.

Supachai Panitchpakdi is Deputy Prime Minister and Minister of Commerce for Thailand. He received his doctorate at the Netherlands School of Economics (now Erasmus University) and subsequently engaged in extensive research at the University of Cambridge and the International Labour Office. He then commenced a long and distinguished career at the Bank of Thailand. Dr. Supachai has been a staunch advocate of liberalism in Thailand and has been an initiator and active supporter of numerous trade and investment facilitating forums. He is a firm believer in the multilateral trading system and was Thailand's chief negotiator in the final phase of the Uruguay Round. He played a decisive role in Thailand's becoming a founding member of the WTO. Dr. Supachai will take up new responsibilities as Director-General of the WTO in 2002.

Peter Sutherland is Chairman of Goldman Sachs International and non-executive Chairman of BP Amoco plc. Mr. Sutherland joined Goldman Sachs in 1995 after serving as Director-General of the World Trade Organization (formerly the GATT) from 1993 to 1995. Prior to this role Mr. Sutherland served as Chairman of Allied

Irish Banks (1989–1993), EC Commissioner responsible for Competition Policy (1985–1989), and Attorney General of Ireland (1981–1984). Of Irish nationality, he was educated at Gonzaga College, University College Dublin, and the King's Inns. Mr. Sutherland graduated in Civil Law. He was also admitted to practice before the Supreme Court of the United States of America. From 1969 to 1981 he practised at the bar. Mr. Sutherland has received numerous awards and has eleven honorary doctorates from universities in Europe and America.

David Weiner is a Senior Fellow at the Overseas Development Council (ODC). Prior to joining ODC in 1998, Mr. Weiner served for five years as the international economic policy specialist on the Democratic staff of the International Relations Committee of the US House of Representatives. From 1988 to 1993, he was a member of the staff of the Subcommittee on Europe and the Middle East of the House International Relations Committee. Mr. Weiner has also served as Editor at the Institute for International Economics. He has degrees from Princeton University and Amherst College.

Martin Wolf, CBE, is Associate Editor and Chief Economics Commentator at the *Financial Times,* London. He was awarded the CBE (Commander of the British Empire) in 2000 for services to financial journalism. He is a visiting fellow of Nuffield College, Oxford University, and a special professor at the University of Nottingham. Mr. Wolf was joint winner of the Wincott Foundation senior prize for excellence in financial journalism in 1989 and again in 1997 and won the RTZ David Watt memorial prize in 1994, a prize granted annually "to a writer judged to have made an outstanding contribution in the English language towards the clarification of national, international and political issues and the promotion of their greater understanding." Mr. Wolf obtained an M.Phil. in Economics from Oxford University in 1971. He joined the World Bank as a Young Professional in 1971. In 1981, he became Director of Studies at the Trade Policy Research Centre, London. He joined the *Financial Times* as Chief Economics Leader Writer in 1987. He was promoted to Associate Editor in 1990 and Chief Economics Commentator in 1996.

Index

Note: Page numbers followed by letter *n* indicate material presented in endnotes.

on exports from, 21–22, 24; and trade and environment debate, 164–69, 170–71; trade liberalization and benefits to, 60, 65–67, 79*n;* and trade rules, implementation difficulties, 71–74; and trade rules, objectives on, 67–69; transitional periods for, inadequacy of, 51; in Uruguay Round, 6, 21, 30, 62–63, 64; and WTO decision-making, 6, 97; dissatisfaction with, 5–6

Development: and environment, analysis of interface between, 146; vs. environment, developing country position on, 159; export-oriented, WTO and, 21; globalization and, 20; rights-based approach to, 217–19; trade and, 20, 60–61; in WTO agenda, 246–47

Development round: agenda for, positions on, 60; and implementation difficulties, opportunities to address, 56, 73–74; minimum results needed from, 55–56; new agenda items in, support for, 69–71; opportunities for developing countries in, 65–69; preparing for, 78–79; prospect for, 59–60, 64–65; steps toward, 54–55

DFMO (eflornithine), 229–30

Differential pricing and access to medicines, 229

Dispute prevention, 143

Dispute settlement mechanism, WTO, 2, 127, 143; *amicus curiae* briefs in, proposals for, 129, 130, 162, 178*n;* developing

countries and, 32; environmentalists' position on, 143–44; imaginative proposals regarding, 11; importance of, 115; logic of, 195; vs. national sovereignty, 243; need for transparency in, 127–30, 199, 253; opening up, conditions required for, 199; performance of, 85; public observers in, 128, 130; strength of, 186–87; trade and environment debate and pressure on, 168–69

Documents, WTO calls for de-restriction of, 125–26, 253

Dumping, of surplus food, 22

Dunkel, Arthur, 34

ECJ. *See* European Court of Justice

Ecolabelling, 147; win–win potential of, 167

Economic growth, trade and, 262

Economic integration, environmental impact of, 162

Egypt, violation of workers' rights in, 248

EIAs. *See* Environmental impact assessments

Electronic Data Systems Corp., 263

Energy, subsidies in, proposals for removal of, 167

Enforcement power, WTO, 104. *See also* Dispute settlement mechanism

Environment: and development, analysis of interface between, 146; vs. development, developing country position on, 159; experts on, expanding interaction with, 131–32; and